Witnessing the
Soviet Twilight

Witnessing the Soviet Twilight

Accounts of Americans in the U.S.S.R. on the Eve of Its Collapse

Edited by
DOROTHY S. MCCLELLAN

McFarland & Company, Inc., Publishers
Jefferson, North Carolina

Index prepared by Clive Pyne Book Indexing Services

LIBRARY OF CONGRESS CATALOGUING-IN-PUBLICATION DATA

Witnessing the Soviet twilight : accounts of Americans in the U.S.S.R. on the eve of its collapse / edited by Dorothy S. McClellan.
    p.   cm.
Includes bibliographical references and index.

ISBN 978-0-7864-7944-3 (softcover : acid free paper) ∞
ISBN 978-1-4766-1496-0 (ebook)

1. Soviet Union—History—1985–1991. 2. Americans—Soviet Union—Biography. 3. Soviet Union—History—1985–1991—Biography. 4. Soviet Union—Social conditions—1970–1991. 5. Social change—Soviet Union—History. I. McClellan, Dorothy S.
DK286.W58 2014
947.085'4—dc23   2014001982

BRITISH LIBRARY CATALOGUING DATA ARE AVAILABLE

© 2014 Dorothy S. McClellan. All rights reserved

No part of this book may be reproduced or transmitted in any form or by any means, electronic or mechanical, including photocopying or recording, or by any information storage and retrieval system, without permission in writing from the publisher.

Front cover image: the Soviet red flag towers above the Kremlin in Moscow, December 18, 1991 (Associated Press/Boris Yurchenko)

Manufactured in the United States of America

McFarland & Company, Inc., Publishers
Box 611, Jefferson, North Carolina 28640
www.mcfarlandpub.com

To Nikola Knez
With deep love and respect

Table of Contents

Introduction 1
    Dorothy S. McClellan

State of the Soviet Union: View from the Ivory Tower 11
    Dorothy S. McClellan *and* James E. McClellan, Jr.

Moral and Spiritual Changes 34
    Howard L. Parsons

Coaching Soviet Baseball: Excerpts from a Sociologist's Journal 62
    William J. Byrne III

Perestroika and Ideology 95
    John J. Neumaier

Russia Between the Union and the Commonwealth:
    New Carpetbaggers and Old Dreams 118
    Carla Lipsig-Mummé

Worker Self-Management in Soviet Theory and Practice 126
    Aaron Bindman

The Crisis of Soviet Legitimacy 137
    Herman Schwendinger *and* Julia Schwendinger

Moscow Memoir: On the Status of Women 155
    Freda Casner

Perestroika and the Internationalization of Russian Higher
    Education: The Summer of 1990 167
    Donald A. Biggs *with* Robert J. Colesante

Perestroika in Philosophy: Report from Moscow State University ... 187
    Dorothy S. McClellan *and* James E. McClellan, Jr.

Why, When and How We Lost Russia 203
 JAMES E. MCCLELLAN, JR.

The Universality of Liberal Capitalism and the Possibility
 of Renewed Socialism: Reflections on the Soviet Coup of
 August 1991 215
 JAMES LAWLER

About the Contributors 233

Index 237

Introduction

Dorothy S. McClellan

More than twenty years have passed since the fall of the Soviet empire, an historic event the effects of which can, metaphorically speaking, be best described as having shifted Earth's axis. Organized in 1922 as a constitutionally socialist state with 15 republics, the political system of the world's largest country—covering 8,649,500 square miles, stretching across 11 time zones and 5 climate zones, with 248,709,873 inhabitants representing 100 nationalities—collapsed. On December 19, 1991, the U.S.S.R. was declared dissolved. By 1992 the Kremlin had lost direct governmental control over one-third of Soviet territory and almost one half of its population. The U.S.S.R. ceased to exist.

This book provides an intimate look at how Americans resident in the Soviet Union in its final days saw this unprecedented moment in human history. North American scholars from the disciplines of philosophy, sociology, psychology, women's studies, criminal justice, labor relations, religion, and education, we record here our insights into the dramatic events that marked the collapse of the Soviet Union and the transition to the Commonwealth of Independent States.

This collection of essays, prepared twenty years ago, was set aside to be opened in the year 2012, the ninetieth anniversary of the founding of the Soviet Union. Read today, the collection serves as a veritable time capsule that preserves eyewitness accounts of this dramatic episode of Russian history. We were, to a person, conscious of the enormous global significance of the historically momentous events we were witnessing. As academics it was natural for us to write about our experiences both from the perspective of our disciplines and in personal terms. Privately and collectively we wondered how our impressions would hold up over time. Many of the scholarly and journalistic accounts in the literature of the period seemed ideologically heavy-handed, overconfident in the correctness of their analyses, even arrogant in their certainty about the reasons for the collapse of the Soviet Union, its apparent inevitability, and their predictions for the future path of the country. I came upon the idea of collecting impressions from a group of colleagues whose opinions and scholarly insights I deeply valued, whose professional credentials and humility were palpable. They entrusted me with their manuscripts. The time has come to share them. It is for you to judge their value in understanding the past, present and future.

During the last years of the Soviet Union, most of us were exchange scholars at Moscow State University, the preeminent institution of higher learning in the U.S.S.R., often referred to as the Harvard of the Soviet Union. We lived for many months in the student/faculty dormitories and university apartments. We conducted research, lectured in our disciplines, participated in academic conferences and coached sports teams. The experience offered us the opportunity to participate in Soviet life—at the university, in homes and dormitories, shops, on the streets, in lecture halls, at cultural and political events, in churches, sports, aboard public transport and the Trans-Siberian Railway. Many of us were already well acquainted with Soviet life and thought, having studied, lectured and traveled widely in Russia, as well as the many republics of the U.S.S.R. over the course of our American academic careers—in the Caucasus, Kazakhstan, Moldavia, Siberia, Ukraine, Georgia, Uzbekistan, Belarus—as early as the 1950s.

We enjoyed close professional and personal relationships with Soviet colleagues, students and their families. We were privileged to have friends speak openly with us about their hopes, expectations and fears. As glasnost and perestroika emerged and developed, many people grew increasingly critical of traditional beliefs and confused about their identity and role in society. As Marxism-Leninism slipped away, still others lamented the passing of a system rich in social protection and opportunities for education and professional advancement. Some sought new identities in ethnic roots, some became enamored of Western capitalism, all sought to protect themselves in this crisis, a few retained loyalty to the ideas of socialism. The breakdown of a centralized command economy and loosening of political authority produced widespread anxiety in the present and uncertainty about the future. Together many of us wondered whether Russia could wrest itself from the old forces of Stalinist evil and the new forces of capitalist greed that struggled to determine the country's destiny.

In this crisis thoughtful people shared with the contributors assessments of their national history, its successes and failures, its victories, crimes and brutalities. In the essays included here, we examine personal struggles and triumphs in families and relationships, labor unions, factories, universities, and political life, distilling people's experiences in those unique times. Accounts range from concrete and intimate portrayals of individuals to theoretical discussions of ideology, economy, gender equality, capitalism and socialism, producing a multi-faceted portrait of this extraordinary period in world history. Each essay is preceded by a brief introduction written from today's perspective, usually by the original author of the essay.

The result is a set of observations on the transformation occurring during the time of perestroika and beyond. While we bring to our subject expertise from a variety of disciplines and represent different political views, certain common strands run through our observations and reflections. Our deliberations inevitably range over the history of the peoples and social system of Russia and the Soviet Union, and from time to time we speculate on the possible course of events since perestroika and the abandonment of socialism. We do not, however, leave the description of the New Soviet Man, the creation of which was the stated goal of the Russian Revolution, to those who parody it as *Homo Sovieticus,* "the species whose most highly developed skills involved the hunting and gathering of scarce goods in an urban environment" (Fitzpatrick 1999, p. 225).

To avoid being accused of attacking a straw man, we recognize that there *were* those who envisioned the new socialist person as the perfection of human being in whom the fullest, harmonious development of the physical, intellectual, emotional, and spiritual are combined and refined. There *were* truly committed individuals who believed that private ownership of the means of production was not the final and highest stage of history. We begin, therefore, with the assumption that a nation of ingenious, inventive, deeply spiritual people might have embarked on the difficult, thorny path of revolution and socialist construction for good, not for evil. For so many to have risked so much for an idea, one might assume there was *something* noble, grand, and forward thinking in their vision. Their argument for choosing such a course rested on the belief that on the economic base of capitalism one cannot build the material conditions for progress without war and imperialism, while socialism does not require those twin evils.

We fast forward to the 1980s. Three hours after the death of Konstantin Chernenko on March 11, 1985, Mikhail Gorbachev was elected general secretary of the Communist Party by the Politburo. He quickly took steps to address the problems of a stagnant economy, the legacy of the Brezhnev years. Gorbachev recognized that social and political restructuring were a prerequisite for addressing the economic issues. Glasnost and perestroika came to the university before they did to the streets. After all, Mikhail Gorbachev was the first head of the Communist Party since Lenin to be university educated, having received his law degree from Moscow State University. His wife, Raisa, held a doctorate from the Faculty of Philosophy where most of us carried out our scholarly work. Our Russian academic colleagues generally welcomed the principles of glasnost and perestroika both in theory and practice. They took pride in the fact that the Gorbachevs were alumnae; a university education had no doubt contributed to their broader worldview and democratic imagination.

The political climate in the first years of perestroika and glasnost was exhilarating, albeit highly unpredictable. The latter no doubt contributed to the former. Spontaneous demonstrations sprang up all over Moscow. Hundreds of publications appeared in the capital alone, thousands across the U.S.S.R., each calling for a distinctive approach to restructuring, each representing the interests of a particular group—the voices of a hitherto repressed minority or majority. Accounts of Stalinist horrors, victims and heroes filled their pages. Social transformation was shockingly swift. Political and social movements emerged initially as cathartic expressions of long repressed concerns. As this empire struggled to transform itself, economic conditions were harsh and challenging. Restructuring led inevitably to power vacuums, corruption, loss of social services, epidemics, food shortages, and impoverished people selling their humble possessions on street corners. In that vacuum unsavory elements proliferated, the Mafia prospered, and, as Durkheim predicted, crime and suicide rates skyrocketed. We watched, we listened, we talked, and we recorded our thoughts, feelings and impressions.

The coups of August 1991 and September to October 1993 clinched it. In the first, Gorbachev was held at his dacha in the Crimea by hardline members of the government who hoped to persuade him to declare a state of emergency or resign before a New Union Treaty could be signed that would reform the Soviet Union into a federation of independent republics. The hardliners attempted to take control of the government and planned an attack on the Russian parliament building, the White House. The failed *coup d'état* catapulted RSFSR president Boris Yeltsin to power for standing up to the tanks poised to attack the parliament. Gorbachev, perceived as inadequate in the face of the coup, was forced to resign.

Under Yeltsin's rule the Russian people saw their country and its resources put up on the auction block, the door opened wide to international corporations that scrambled to gain access to the country's resources. Russians watched vast amounts of wealth fraudulently sucked out of the country, the creation of ghost corporations and other grand corporate schemes to avoid taxation and funnel once public wealth into the private pockets of the few.

By 1993, with depression deepening, Yeltsin became embroiled in a struggle with the parliament over his harsh economic measures that included heavy taxes, skyrocketing prices, and a credit crunch that crippled industries. In the ensuing constitutional crisis, Yeltsin tried to dissolve parliament. When this failed, he ordered the storming of the White House by the military that resulted in the wounding and killing of hundreds of people (some reports say two thousand). Although Yeltsin was impeached by the parliament, he managed to consolidate and increase his presidential power.

As Hegel and Marx have told us, history always repeats itself, first as tragedy and then as farce. But in this succession of coups the usual order was reversed: history came first as farce and then as tragedy, a tragedy the climax to which is still unfolding. As Russians watched the parliament building, known as the White House, engulfed in flames, the result of army shelling, voices calling for reason and careful reflection rose. People who had longed for dramatic transformation, now called for calm and a return to some semblance of the predictability and stability of life as they had known it for seven decades.

By 1994 there was growing internal resistance to change. The Great Mob Wars raged, unrelenting dark skies hung over Moscow. Russians became disillusioned with the new path of glasnost and perestroika when these movements for openness and social restructuring failed to meet people's rising expectations for an open economy, an improved standard of living, participation in world trade and democracy—in short, for Russians to become full members of the global community. In August to September 1998 in the depths of economic crisis, "Russia's gross domestic product was half of what it had been in the early 1990s" (Kaplan, October 8, 2000). Yeltsin served as president until 1999 when he resigned suddenly and turned the presidency over to his chosen successor, Prime Minister Vladimir Putin.

The essays that comprise this collection capture the mood of the country on the eve of the collapse of the U.S.S.R. We begin with "State of the Soviet Union: View from the Ivory Tower," written by me and James E. McClellan, Jr., my late husband. It describes the dramatic changes occurring in the last days of the Soviet Union as experienced by Russian friends and colleagues, seen through our eyes, the eyes of two American academics who were returning to Moscow in 1989 and 1990 after lengthy previous stays. The essay shifts from a personal tone to a philosophical and political analysis of the remarkable events taking place.

"Moral and Spiritual Changes," a penetrating essay written by professor of philosophy and religion Howard L. Parsons after a lengthy stay in Moscow in the 1990s, gives voice to many of the Russian colleagues and students with whom Parsons worked on his numerous scholarly visits to the U.S.S.R.

In "Coaching Soviet Baseball: Excerpts from a Sociologist's Journal," William J. Byrne III takes us on the road with Russian sportsmen as they work to master the game that was then becoming an Olympic sport. His experiences over five months with the university-sponsored team competing in the top level league of the U.S.S.R. are particularly amusing, touching and revealing in the context of the period of perestroika and glasnost. Byrne arrived in

Moscow in 1990 on the eve of the 28th Communist Party Congress, the last congress of the Party before it was dissolved.

John J. Neumaier served as president of the State University of New York at New Paltz and professor at Empire College of the State University of New York. He and his wife and colleague, Sara F. Luther, spent two semesters at Moscow State University, first in the mid–1980s shortly after Gorbachev became general secretary of the Communist Party, and then in the winter of 1991 as the struggles between Gorbachev and Yeltsin intensified. His "Perestroika and Ideology" is a compilation of newspaper columns, prepared for publication in 1991, that capture the flood of ideological crosscurrents in the period of perestroika through descriptions of daily life and conversations with Russian colleagues.

Shifting ideological currents had dramatic concomitant effects on the social relations of production in the U.S.S.R. Carla Lipsig-Mummé's "Russia Between the Union and the Commonwealth: New Carpetbaggers and Old Dreams" helps us to understand how workers and trade unions responded to these changes. Lipsig-Mummé, a renowned professor of work and labor studies, shares her experiences in the early 1990s assisting trade unions in their "difficult transformation to democratic and independent workers' organizations." At the First International Conference of Trade Unionism and Self-Management held just outside Moscow in 1991, "as the Commonwealth was crystalizing and the Union dying," she met with sixty Russians and Byelorussians, as well as colleagues from more than a dozen countries, to discuss economic restructuring and seek critical alternatives to Yeltsin's "wild west marketization." One of the favored options considered at the conference was worker self-management.

Aaron Bindman had come to Moscow a few years earlier, in 1986, invited to carry out research on labor relations and worker self-management. His essay, "Worker Self-Management in Soviet Theory and Practice," provides us with a clear picture of how bureaucratic, centralized control of industry interfered with worker self-management and with individuals who wished to peer inside industrial facilities to get a closer look at the production process and at labor relations. Having carried out research in Yugoslavia on this subject, Bindman was prepared to do a comparative study but encountered resistance from Soviet authorities. His experiences help us to understand the barriers to democratic participation in economic restructuring.

In the same critical vein Herman and Julia Schwendinger, scholars in the field of criminal justice, trace the crisis of Soviet legitimacy from the 1920s to the 1990s. In "The Crisis of Soviet Legitimacy," they emphasize the contradictions between theory and practice in the Soviet model of socialism and "the complex tangle of socialist and anti-socialist relations" that led inevitably to the crisis of legitimacy in the 1980s which "swept away the smoke, mirrors and Potemkin villages that kept many from seeing the anti-socialist facets of Soviet life."

No examination of the collapse of the U.S.S.R. would be complete without discussion of women. Freda Casner's "Moscow Memoir: On the Status of Women" examines the changes and challenges that women in the Soviet Union faced as the country entered the uncharted waters of glasnost and perestroika. Having served as a faculty exchange scholar in 1983 and in 1988, Casner had a baseline from which to measure the effect of these political events on women. She presents Russian feminist responses to Gorbachev's reform and wonders what might have been had Gorbachev's plans not been halted by his fall and Yeltsin's subsequent rise to political power. While the devastating economic effects of "shock therapy" on women and families are enumerated, the dramatic changes in women's perspectives brought about by the Russian women's movement are seen as permanent.

The period of glasnost and perestroika had dramatic effects on higher education. As Gorbachev called for openness and restructuring, he encouraged contact with the West through academic exchange programs. Donald A. Biggs, with Robert J. Colesante, in "Perestroika and the Internationalization of Russian Higher Education: The Summer of 1990," summarizes ten years of experience, beginning in 1990, coordinating diplomatic visits of faculty, serving as a visiting professor in the U.S.S.R., and carrying out extensive research on the views of faculty and students concerning international exchange programs. Biggs' broad involvement and travel in the Soviet Union informs his writing, providing keen and honest insights into the culture and politics of the period and people. The study examines perceptions of students and faculty from Moscow State University, Leningrad University and the University of Kiev on the effect of foreign exchange programs on individuals and society. Biggs also examines the issues of brain drain and cross-cultural understanding, as well as the pessimism of Soviet university students and faculty about the future.

In "Perestroika in Philosophy: Report from Moscow State University," James and I share excerpts of a 1990 interview with the dean of philosophy at Moscow State University, elected by the faculty of 130 philosophers in 1987 to lead them through the restructuring of this largest faculty of philosophy in the world. In this penetrating, candid conversation, we have an opportunity to hear about the changes he carried out, his democratic worldview, and the importance of philosophy as an academic discipline. The piece provides a look at how perestroika disrupted the connection between Marxist-Leninist philosophy and political power.

"Why, When and How We Lost Russia" is the deeply personal and penetrating attempt of a committed progressive academic to explain the collapse of the U.S.S.R. James first visited the U.S.S.R. in 1958 and 1959 as a young professor at Columbia University who led study tours of college presidents and correspondents. His experiences there led him to believe that the U.S.S.R. "embodied, in the persons of its best and brightest youth, the promise of creating a socialist society and eventually a socialist world." In search of explanation for its failure, he comes to recognize that it was an experiment doomed to fail already in 1948 with the defeat of the Progressive Party in the U.S. presidential election. The Progressive Party's defeat ensured that Cold War politics would thrive and that the U.S.-initiated arms race would contribute to the Communist Party's maintaining hegemonic power in the U.S.S.R. for decades.

The final essay, "The Universality of Liberal Capitalism and the Possibility of Renewed Socialism: Reflections on the Soviet Coup of August 1991," is a defense of Gorbachev's policies of perestroika. James Lawler, who was a visiting scholar in Moscow in 1978, 1984–1985 and 1992, posits that Gorbachev hoped to navigate a complex course between the rigidities of old world communism and unregulated capitalism. Lawler argues that the path of market-oriented socialism promoted worker self-management and "undermined the powers and privileges of the old management class." Paradoxically, in order to maintain their privileged position they embraced capitalism. Thus, the main beneficiaries of the shift to capitalism were former Communist Party elites who replaced worship of the state with worship of the markets. Lawler maintains that the ability of the Russian people to prevent the attempted *coup d'état* in August 1991 was a direct result of the success of Gorbachev's democratization of the country through his policies of glasnost and perestroika. The Russian people rose up and refused to hand power back to the old guard. They took to the streets and the army refused the command to fire on fellow countrymen.

Many writers have engaged in tireless efforts probing the horrors and excesses of the Soviet era, enumerating the litany of failure, as well as vilifying Vladimir Putin as the embodiment of Russian authoritarianism. While Putin may be portrayed and perceived as an autocratic leader by the West, sufficient numbers to elect him president in 2012 viewed him as a protector of Russian national interests and resources, someone who restored national pride and was working to ensure national prosperity. In 2012, after 18 years of negotiation, Russia joined the World Trade Organization, where hopes are that Russia is being transformed into a modern, techno-managerial economic system. Today, the Russian government has effectively eliminated the old ideological terms—socialist, communist, capitalist—from its description of itself and other nations.

Whatever the case, few people who study Russia come away unmoved by the qualities of the Russian soul. The experiences, feelings, and opinions recorded here of an enormous social experiment that ended with the collapse of the U.S.S.R. are deeper and more profound when seen in light of the courage, endurance, intelligence, and nobility of the Russian people. Russia will never cease to fascinate, confuse, terrify, intimidate and beguile the West.

So, what is the destiny of the Russian people on our one and only planet Earth? While the final moves in this economic, geopolitical endgame have yet to be made, one thing is certain: Russia's key role in international politics and economics is assured by its vast holdings of natural resources, intellectual and military capital, and its strategic geopolitical position. The essays included in this collection will, we hope, offer valuable insights to a broad audience for years to come.

Our essays end with the recognition that as we look at Earth from space we don't see the boundaries that separate, we see the oceans and lands that unite us. As astronaut Sultan Bin Salman al–Saud of the Kingdom of Saudi Arabia put it:

> The first day or so we all pointed to our countries. The third or fourth day we were pointing to our continents. By the fifth day we were aware of only one Earth [Kelley, 1988, p. 81].

References

Fitzpatrick, S. (1999). *Everyday Stalinism: Ordinary life in extraordinary times.* New York: Oxford University Press.
Kaplan, R. D. (2000, October 8). Who lost Russia? *The New York Times.*
Kelley, K.W. (1988). *The home planet.* Moscow: Mir.

State of the Soviet Union: View from the Ivory Tower

Dorothy S. McClellan *and* James E. McClellan, Jr.

 This essay is written in two distinct styles and sections by two academics who spent a good deal of time at Moscow State University prior to and during the period of perestroika and glasnost. The first section is a most personal description of how quickly and dramatically Moscow and the university had changed by the winter of 1990 as the U.S.S.R. collapsed, told through the lives of colleagues and students whom we befriended. (They are given pseudonyms.) This section today reads as clearly as when it was written.

 The second section is a political analysis of these remarkable events and some predictions of the future. Looking back at the analysis and predictions, we might find reason to agree, disagree or revise them. Hindsight is always 20/20. But retaining them as they were written captures the authenticity of that historical moment, the confusion, the attempts of well meaning intellectuals to seek answers to unfolding events, a mixture of concern, regret, loss, hope.

 The windows in our suite are tall and wide. When the satin curtains that hold the Russian winter at bay pull loose from their hooks, as they do about twice a week, we stand on the wide marble sill to refasten them. We pause to look northeast toward the Moscow River, past Moscow State University's massive front entrance, its victory columns, the conifer-lined boulevard bordered on either side by the snow-covered forest of the Lenin Hills. Most days thick layers of clouds envelop all but the nearest objects, and we feel besieged by perpetual night.

 On the rare days when the clouds part, the sky turns shockingly blue and we can see the distant golden domes of the Kremlin. And for a grand, long moment we recall all this world capital has been and has seen. That perspective is what we are here for, a long, clear view. Even at its best, however, a view from this vantage point is limited; a window in this tower, once ivory, now grey, offers but a narrow perspective. A palpable dialectic pervades our physical and intellectual life here in Moscow; on this trip more than any other, we are conscious of how intimately we are involved in Soviet life and how narrow is the slice we know so well.

We have been guests of the Soviet Union on numerous occasions, lecturing, consulting, and conducting research, residents at Moscow State University for semesters on end. At our institutions in New York and Texas we have served as hosts and advisors to dozens of our Soviet colleagues in natural sciences, social sciences and humanities. Over the course of the past decade, we have been fortunate to establish uniquely Russian friendships with a number of these outstanding intellectuals. Such relationships do not come easily nor are they broken easily. Our friends have taken on the task of helping us to mold the current history of their great land into concrete images of color and vitality. Late into the evening, around our table or theirs, we eat, drink, laugh, cry, analyze, preach, plead and pray; shared life is a constant flow of thoughts in English and Russian, occasionally relieved by guitar and dance. What we wish to share with you are the thoughts of these intellectuals as they endure crisis in the U.S.S.R. today. And our perceptions, limited though they be, of what they have tried to impart to us.

Homecoming: Introduction to the Battlezone

This past December (1990) we were met at the airport by our oldest friends, the Suvorins, a marvelously handsome couple in their mid-forties, both teaching at the university. They had commandeered a ten-year-old Zhiguli to haul us and our four large suitcases filled with salami, cheese, books, paraphernalia of all sorts, all passed through customs with a wave after a glance at our "scientific exchange" visas. The bags stuffed in, Dorothy perched on Elena's lap, we took our first look at Moscow in six months. The view from the window was bleaker than ever before, an old black and white newsreel of the war years. Unrelenting grey skies, buildings, slush. Misha and Elena tried to prepare us for the worsened situation. We were upbeat, little concerned for our personal discomfort, inwardly torn between feeling like voyeurs and premature guests at a wake. For what real help could we offer? Our privilege, wealth, prosperity had set us further apart than ever before from these dear friends and longtime colleagues; we sensed for the first time that they had lost confidence in the future.

As we pulled into our "zona" for this December-January sojourn at

Moscow State, we felt the relief of the familiar in a foreign land. This time the huge building which had been our home for fourteen months over the last decade looked tired and old, rather than grand and imposing. What does one say when one sees a dear friend after some time and finds her aged, weary, humbled? Ten years ago the Roman letters VD, representing the third and fifth of the Cyrillic alphabet, announced for foreign guests the entrance to these two sectors of the Stalin Gothic structure; today the letters have been reversed. Everyone is learning English these days.

We were recognized and greeted by the men at the desk controlling entrance to the dormitory. We always joked that retired KGB officers are sent here to live out their final days supervising the younger generation. But they no longer asked for our *propusks* (id's), nor did they take note, as they did in the past, of every new face, quick to inquire about your intentions and destination. Using the single elevator still working in the bank of four, we transported our gear to the seventh floor to discover with delight that we would be housed in a "Fulbright suite," usually reserved for those prestigious guests. But the "administrator" who has the key had decided to go home for a long late lunch; we had no choice but to stack the bags and wait at the reception area on our floor, where the single surviving stuffed chair is now torn and lopsided. The telephone connections at the receptionist's desk have been torn from their housing, the surface looks cannibalized. During the long wait for our keys, we could find no focus for our eyes that did not reveal decay, neglect. Over the coming weeks we were to see drunken students vomiting in the hallways, breaking out windows, dumping their garbage on dark landings, screaming above the alienated chords of rock music. Each morning the tiny figure of an old woman in dark dress and scarf could be made out at the end of the corridor silently, stoically clearing away what she could from the damage of the night before. How different from all other visits when the best and the brightest of the U.S.S.R. visited our rooms each evening to practice English, talk about jazz, politics, the black market, drink tea and eat pastries.

Our lectures, consultations, and research were to come off in good form, but it was in those two hours that Misha and Elena introduced us to the real subject of our study, what life is like these days for our friends. It was like a flashback from a battle scene in a war movie when Misha and Elena recalled their undergraduate days here, twenty-five years ago. Graduate students were then given the "Fulbright suites" with telephones and beautiful views of the city. The parquet floors were waxed and polished. A *dezhurnaya* manned the desk at all times, receiving incoming calls for undergraduate students and keeping track of coeds' whereabouts after 11 p.m. The cafeterias served excellent meals on good china, white linens and fresh flowers adorned the tables. Paper napkins, all you needed, jutted from cut-glass containers. An honor and privilege then it was to be alive; to attend the Harvard of the Soviet Union was very heaven.

For the very first time Elena openly shared her hurt and indignation. On a recent trip to England, her first excursion to the West, she faced the vast difference between the quality of her life and that of her Western contemporaries and counterparts. "We are as bright, competent, hardworking as these British friends. Why must we live this way? What have we to show for our years of commitment and self-sacrifice?" In 1957 she and Misha were shining stars in the Russian firmament—when Moscow hosted the World Youth Festival, the strains of "Moscow Nights" filled the parks and squares, a Soviet satellite circled the skies. These postwar children were symbols of hope and the future. They joined the Communist Party, felt honor and pride in their membership. They believed in the selfless ideals to which their lives were dedicated. These are not intellectuals who for long years harbored secret bitterness toward their government. They suffered discomfort without complaint, participated willingly in the enormous social experiment of building socialism. They did it with flair, with innocence, perhaps, but never obeisance or passivity.

The first time Misha appeared on our campus in New York, everyone was startled. Expecting an awkward, shy, young Soviet scientist, undergraduate girls and faculty wives alike stared shamelessly at this Russian Marcello Mastriani. Elena, whom we met two years later in Moscow, is the embodiment of Pasternak's Tonya Zhivago, refined and urbane, tender and accepting. Their students saw them enveloped in the sophistication and urbanity of the West, but carved from the solid rock of Mother Russia. With no hint of the clumsiness and heavy-handedness we associate with old party stalwarts, they taught a new generation of Soviet youth and raised a lovely cosmopolitan daughter. Their tiny flat became a rendezvous for students and faculty alike, the phone rings incessantly, the huge dog barks, food and drink are always forthcoming, always delicious. On Elena's forty-fourth birthday in June their apartment resembled a flower shop, literally scores of friends crowded in to celebrate the remarkable gift of her life.

One weekday afternoon later in the month, Elena's weakened voice pled through the telephone, "Dorothy, I can't come today. I'm ill again." When she appeared on schedule the following day, insisting, "I'm better, really I am," the strain of the times showed in heavy lines on her face; her eyes were swollen and distant. We worked on our article; she pushed through the pain. Like many, Elena today feels betrayed, and perhaps more painful still, humiliated and violated, publicly and privately. Her anguish is expressed in headaches which aspirin, unavailable anyway, will not relieve. She seeks solutions in religion. A cross now hangs awkwardly from their bedroom door, on weekends we were ceremoniously hauled to exhibitions of icons, to newly restored monasteries and churches, we were presented a triptych to protect us on our journey, and prayers were offered for our safety and success. But Elena's headaches persist.

So Painful to Remember, So Hard to Forget

Foreigners familiar with the U.S.S.R. often used to remark that it was comfortable to return because everything stayed the same from trip to trip. Shops and cafes were always where you left them. Prices never varied, neither from year to year, nor shop to shop. The items were the same familiar patterns and styles—the tea set with orange polka dots, or Catherine the Great's exquisite gold and cobalt "blue net" pattern. Oh, how beautiful was the full set of dishes with life size pale pink roses sold at the House of China on Leninskii Prospekt. Always shortly upon arrival in Moscow, our custom was to go there to choose a new tea set to use while in Moscow and to serve as a gift to friends back home. These could be purchased for anywhere from 12 to 60 rubles. Each cup, plate and glass in the shop was painstakingly examined for chips or cracks as it was packaged with brusk efficiency. The saleswomen tapped their pencils against each object, filling the shop with wonderful pinging and panging. Such a flurry of activity as women consulted with one another about this or that pattern or piece, peering over the crowded counters, pushing to get a spot at the front.

As I (Dorothy) headed toward Red Square on our second day in town, I tried to note the store's location for my return trip home that afternoon. I scraped the frost from the window of the bus with my glove. Ah yes, there's the building. But the windows were gray with dust, the store deserted. "Is the House of China closed?" I inquired of the well-dressed woman sitting next to me. "Da," she responded, with bitterness and resignation, "like everything else." Not a glass or plate was to be purchased for rubles in Moscow.

Certainly there had always been shortages—toilet paper and vegetables in the early and mid-eighties, teakettles, cheese, chocolate, and soap in the summer of '90. A standard Soviet joke: What is socialism? It's when store shelves are empty and home refrigerators are full. With all the complaints about shortages, hostesses had piled their tables high with delicacies for guests. But now the shelves *were* empty, and an eerie silence hung over lines for the basics—milk and bread. In these difficult times one wouldn't think of coming to a friend's at mealtime without foodstuffs. And no one balks at the offerings, as they often had in the past. When inviting guests, Soviets joke, the polite host asks whether they prefer that he use his single ration coupon for sugar or toilet paper.

Nostalgia

On cold, bleak evenings when we found ourselves wondering aloud why we had traveled halfway across the Earth to come to Moscow again, we would conjure up images of the old Moscow, the city that had fueled our imagination for so much of our lives. On the eve of the celebration of the October Revolution, a small group of visiting scholars gathered in the mirrored dining room of the grand old Hotel National, across from Red Square and the Kremlin. Snow fell softly on the turrets and spires, St. Basil's beckoned, as we gazed outward from our table by the huge elegantly draped windows. We sipped Russian champagne, ate caviar and blini, then Chicken Kiev stuffed with fresh country butter and herbs. We danced with strangers, as is the gracious custom in the U.S.S.R., to beautiful Russian melodies of the string orchestra. And we toasted more than once a new beginning for this weary "superpower."

That was November of 1984; "perestroika" and "glasnost" were fresh ideas, sprinkled through every conversation, even on an evening of pure celebration. We left the dinner table shortly before midnight; snow caressed our cheeks and blurred our vision as we made our way across Prospekt Marx to join the crowd of young people converging after theater or dinner to witness the changing of the guards at Lenin's Tomb. The vastness of the square, cold and windless, the beauty of the conifers topped with snow, the storybook quality of St. Basil's colored wooden domes, the impenetrability and grandeur of the Kremlin walls and towers, the precise, compelling gait of the guards marching majestically across the expanse to the mausoleum, the clock chiming twelve, Americans reminding one another that it was from this very spot that the Soviet armies marched off to the front in 1941, our gallant allies... we savor in retrospect every detail of that romantic evening.

Perhaps it is *that* Russia we seek to recapture with each return, a romantic vision that bears little resemblance to the reality of any period of the nation's history. Though, truth be told, we do harbor a small hope that what is best and most beautiful in this vast, eternal empire can be preserved, its essence captured and distilled to inspire a new generation who may move this country into the twenty-first century with new dreams and visions, wrest it from the old forces of Stalinist evil and the new forces of capitalist greed that today struggle to determine its destiny. Hope is foolish, or so it would seem. But the current economic and political situation is harsh and ugly; the only foreigners who seem to notice are the vultures at the International Trade Center angling to grab a piece of the carcass. We, like our Soviet friends, thus face the choice between foolish hope and hopeless despair.

It Was Catastrophe from Beginning to End

Such is the constant refrain in Professor Aleksandr Tsipko's evaluation of the October Revolution and all its consequences. Tsipko is overweight, florid, compelling on the podium. It is said that he comes from the upper ranks of the former aristocracy in the Ukraine. His face and views are familiar fare on Soviet TV; his columns appear in both old and new journals, but he does not propose to his Russian audiences the outright support of monarchism he suggested to Americans during his visit here last fall. From a scientific, historical point of view, his vision of a "normal society" as the goal of Soviet political change is absurd nonsense. The religiously devout, class divided but culturally integrated social structure he pictures never was nor will be. Today, however, even scholars who should know better will insist: "Underneath, Tsipko is a deeply concerned person who's in tune with the inner realities of the Russian soul. There's a lot in what he says."

Is there nothing of the enormous human and material investment of the past seventy years worth retrieving? Often over the past six months taxi drivers and university professors alike would remark, "We don't know how to work, don't want to work, don't have a 'culture of work.'" The self-deprecating remarks are reflected in the attitudes of outsiders. Foreign investors are hesitant to venture the capital, technology or managerial skill required to make Soviet steel, coal, electricity, timber, paper production and so on competitive in a world market. The present managers and planners of the Soviet economy are more than willing to lend themselves to the creation of joint ventures, but there is considerable doubt, both in the U.S.S.R. and in the West, that the skills and habits developed as managers and planners of a command system are those required for success as capitalist entrepreneurs, doubt also that Soviet workers could or would accept the challenges and demands of speeded-up production and high technology.

Ivan Kuzmich came to visit us on Christmas morning, bringing a box of delicious Soviet chocolates and homemade preserves from wild berries his lovely wife had picked in the countryside around their dacha. He has been a Party activist his entire adult life. His father was killed in the war; he and his mother made it alone in the Ukraine in the difficult years that followed. Even as a child, the Party was his family. It helped him to receive his first-rate education at Moscow State. By dint of hard work, hard even by standards of often overworked Soviet scholars, devotion to Party duties, and considerable talent as theorist, he eventually rose to become chief of a department that has gained respect throughout the university. He has earned honestly the prestige and perks of his position. But this morning he is both exhausted and agitated. "I'm making myself physically ill over the problems in my country," he declares.

"Where are we going? What will become of us? All we had hoped to achieve.... We have torn away at our own self-respect. We have denied the good in anything Russian. Where can all this lead? We must build on our strengths, find what is worth saving, worth valuing. This negativism is destroying us."

These words were not new to our ears. Natasha, who translated our lectures into Russian, shared with us her mother's reflections on a lifetime of service to socialist ideals, teaching dialectical materialism at a technical institute, performing her Party duties, not just perfunctorily but with honest devotion. Her present feelings? "I am a foot soldier in a defeated army."

Every Russian a Character in a Russian Novel

It was Slava who made us see that Russians tend to think of themselves as characters in their classical literature—Turgenev, Pushkin, Chekhov, Dostoyevski, Tolstoy. Dramatic, tragic, ill-fated individuals, the strong and reckless, the weak and acted upon, all at the mercy of the tyrant or the single-minded, myopic bureaucrat. But are these the people who built the trans–Siberian railroad in an incredibly short seven years? Or those who dammed the Dneiper, engineered and created the channel between the Moscow and Volga Rivers? Or those who halted the German army 18 miles from Moscow? Certainly, history and experience point to a multi-faceted national character. Neither in classical Russian literature, however, nor in the imagination of Soviet citizens today does one see the strength, competence, confidence, forward looking revolutionary character of the ordinary Russian individual. Perhaps the rejection of this aspect of the Soviet personality comes as a response to its overemphasis in the art and literature of Soviet realism. As a viewer will seek subtlety and nuance in a caricature, as adolescents will cringe at overhearing themselves appraised by doting parents, so the Soviets are looking at seventy years of state-sponsored self-portraits with embarrassment, denial, and rebellion.

The omnipresent denial of diligence and skill is more than adolescent reaction, of course; it evinces centuries of ultimately unrecompensed bloodshed, oppression, heroism and endurance. Out for a rambling walk on New Year's Day with Alexei, a longstanding, respected member of the Party and faculty, a scholar's scholar, we wound up at the *Rechnoi Vokzal*, the grand River Station at the confluence of the Moscow and Volga Rivers. Except for an old woman in felt boots and kerchief sipping tea at her desk in the lobby, it was deserted on this cold winter afternoon. Sitting elegantly but sturdily above the frozen, snow-covered river, the station's long covered arches provide shade to summer travelers, now furnished us welcome protection from snow and wind. To be there was magnificent, uplifting. When we tried to share our appreciation of the place, Alexei remarked with embarrassment and awkwardness that this feat was accomplished in the days of Stalin's terror—1936—as if that fact rendered the accomplishment worthless. All things associated with Stalin are tarnished beyond redemption, symbols of shame and submission. The Stalinesque structures dotting the Moscow skyline are mocked and denigrated, and with them the toil and skills of Soviet workers—free and slave—which went into building them. "You see," a cab driver argued, "it takes the whip, the gulag, to harness the labor of Soviet citizens. Without that nothing would have been accomplished in the past nor will be in the future."

At the university, several friends reminded us that the various sectors of the huge structure are still referred to as "zones," the terminology of the gulag; for slave labor built much of the university. We remind them that slave labor was also indispensable to the construction of the Parthenon, but we do not, for that reason, hold fifth century BC Athenians incapable of work or creativity. Here, however, the legacy of horror persists in people's consciousness, making them spectators rather than participants in the great drama of life. Perhaps one scholar was right when he said, "Our people only read about life. Yours live it."

The New Iskra (Spark) Extinguished

There was a period, more than a year, less than three, when glasnost and perestroika rekindled optimism. Leonid is a senior international scholar, author of many books, visiting lecturer at universities across this country and in England. He once wrote with pride and euphoria, "Tamara and I, like everyone else in this country, sit glued to our TV sets day and night, listening to the voices of democracy. That this is happening here, that I have lived to see it, I would never have believed...." That was the fall of 1988, when the democratically elected Congress of Peoples' Deputies was convened, and the Soviet Union began collectively to debate its future. For a few moments people lived again in the present.

But one evening a year and a half later, our conversation with Leonid in his book-lined study turned back to 1930. While a student at Moscow State University, he worked at a nearby machine tool factory. Shortly after he began there, he watched his supervisor certify that skilled workers at the plant had fulfilled their production plan on schedule, when in fact they had not done so. Leonid, unwilling to keep silent about the obvious falsification of records, spoke to the supervisor. "Why are you doing this?" he asked. Reply: "If I don't, the workers won't get enough pay to survive." "Well, why haven't they fulfilled the plan on time?" Leonid pursued. "The necessary materials haven't arrived. The tools they need to complete the tasks are in disrepair. And the workers have to take time off to smoke," said the supervisor. "What else could I do?"

On to 1991. Each Saturday afternoon, Tamara's family arrives by train from a small city about two hours from Moscow. Dasha, Tamara's niece, her husband Dimitri and their two children, little Tamara, a blond Russian beauty of three, and her older brother Igor, thirteen, come for the weekend. They crowd into this two-room apartment, cooking meals together, sharing tales of the week's adventures. Construction workers by trade, Dasha and Dimitri abandoned their 40,000 ruble home in Tashkent, fearing for their lives as ethnic hostilities target Russians. Promised an apartment in return for assisting in the construction of a large apartment complex, they have been working for two years on the building that will be their home. Just this month, the supervisor of the project falsified the records and certified that the project was complete, although only the shell of the building and internal walls are in place. The flooring, plumbing, electrical work, kitchen cabinets, painting remain to be done. Dasha and Dimitri, living with their children in a dormitory room while construction continues, are emotionally drained. Exasperated with the inefficiency and fecklessness of supervisors and fellow workers, this ambitious, hardworking couple built their Tashkent home with their own hands; they hunger for opportunities to use their skills and harness their energy here in Moscow.

Had the supervisor failed to certify completion of the project, Leonid explains, no new contracts would have been forthcoming. Yet due to black marketeering in construction materials and equipment, inefficiency and ineptitude of workers, the terrible state of disrepair of construction equipment, the building is months behind schedule. "What will happen?" we ask. "Where will the materials come from to complete the building? When will your family be able to move in?" Leonid continues, calmly, "Many who want apartments badly enough will do the work themselves, use their own funds to buy the necessary materials on the black market, or simply make do until they have the funds to finish the work. The construction brigade may be able to use some of the funds allocated for the next project to complete certain features of this one. This is not the exception," Leonid adds. "This is how things are done. This is our tradition."

A Child Is Expected

Apartments are tiny by any standards, east or west. Elaborate formulas have been devised to determine entitlement to space. Additional allotments go to individuals with children, Ph.D.'s, grandparents, battlefield experience, etc. Both Semyon and Lara do research in "hard" science. Recently married, they expect a child in April and now live with Lara's parents in an apartment that measures forty-four square meters, 475 square feet, something less than our neighbor's 22' × 22' living room. All of them are scientists, three hold doctorates. They have carefully calculated their housing allowance, but no arrangement of the figures entitles them to more than 44m^2 of space for five persons; they cannot even enter their names on the many-years waiting list for their own apartment.

How do they take this? As Russians appear to take everything. With cynical humor, resignation, style and class. Both blond and strikingly beautiful, Semyon and Lara are what socialism was supposed to produce. Yes, socialism *has* created beauty. Born during the Khrushchev boom, they were raised on old socialist principles and country butter, milk, eggs, meat, borscht and wild berries. Naturally bright and healthy, they entered school and worked hard, absorbed all one could absorb. They advanced rapidly in science and mathematics, they learned English, they harvested crops and worked on construction brigades in the countryside, they hiked through Siberian wilderness. Blessed with natural grace and athletic ability, she won numerous tennis championships. Musically gifted, he qualified for special instruction in piano at a music institute. Neither chose those areas for future employment, nor was it ever expected that they should.

The "socialist person" was conceived as an individual in whom the spirit, the sensibilities, the body, the intellect, were in harmony. To sit across from them sipping tea today is to be convinced that they are the embodiment of that principle. When it comes off, it's mind boggling. Political sophistication, critical scientific understanding, humor, nuance, physical beauty, all with massive doses of personal modesty. Their initial reticence, which could easily be mistaken for unwillingness to disclose, one discovers to be simple delicacy of spirit and refinement. And, perhaps more than anything, kindness at not overwhelming us with all they are. For they are truly a marvel.

What will become of them? They'll soldier on, ever more looking westward in search of an outlet for the creative energy and talent so poorly utilized in their inefficient, undercapitalized laboratories. Their country is now too preoccupied with its very survival to make use of this national treasure, one created as a by-product of a process few understood, supported, sincerely believed or engaged in. Will their child ever know the opportunities for self-development Semyon and Lara have enjoyed? Impossible. They emerged from a window in history that opened briefly and has now been shut, in all probability, forever.

Doomed to Succeed

Walking back to the campus from an exciting circus performance on a cold winter night with Tanya and her sixteen-year-old daughter Dalya: arm-in-arm we braced ourselves against a strong, snow-laden wind. Enveloped in a new Persian lamb coat and black fox hat, Tanya was oblivious to the weather. She recalled, in a dreamy voice, another era, and Dalya hung on every word. She was born in 1944, and her earliest memories are of hunger and deprivation. Her parents did what they could to shield her, but she recalls their faces seamed with emotional scars of war and loss. When she reached Dalya's age, she was accepted to Moscow State University, there to join a generation of young people sharing the glorious life of college students—a wonderful new university, fine professional prospects, a world to build. Stipends were small, but sharing a bottle of champagne and making a meal of free samples at the peasant market made life worthwhile. She and Boris, a huge, sweet, bear of a man, were students together, married, lived in a small dormitory room even after Dalya was born. Both have succeeded professionally: She now teaches social work at the university; he heads up a computer laboratory serving numerous joint ventures, governmental agencies and banks.

Their talents and enterprise have paid off handsomely. Their apartment, like everyone else's, is small, but it is beautifully furnished and now under renovation. Her jewelry is rose gold and elegant. She comes to visit laden with gifts that are not only expensive but hard to find—damask, traditional Russian crafts, exquisite porcelain. *Perestroika* and *glasnost* were, for Tanya and Boris, the culmination of a shared dream, developments their generation of university students, unlike Leonid's, had confidently expected to occur in the natural course of things.

They had also expected that economic advances would soon match those now established in the political and social realms. But the latter expectations have now been shattered, and on the eve of the new year, Tanya experienced wrenching distress over the grim prospects for her country. Her own future holds no fears. Dalya is a dismayingly serious young woman; she has devoted herself to her studies and faces no hazards with the rigorous examinations for admission to Moscow State. Boris' increasingly valuable skills provide entré to numerous joint ventures and bring ample supplies of hard currency. Her own teaching position at the university is secure, for she is the sole expert in an expanding discipline. Perhaps it is the legacy of socialism that economic success and personal security are little solace when dealing with grief for the fate of her country. For Tanya, it is literally shameful to thrive while others must suffer. She tries to reconcile herself to living in a third world country. "How can we enjoy having so much when others around us have so little?" she asks. How long has it been since we heard such a sentiment from the more affluent academics we know in the U.S.A.?

Suicide Is the Only Honorable Act

For the first time in seventy years, Christmas was declared a national holiday. Atheist and Christian alike greeted the official celebration with pride, a symbol that Soviet citizens were no longer forced to deny an existential reality. We were invited to share the celebration with Leonid and Tamara; our fellow guests would be Leonid's long time friend, Georgi, and Tamara's closest colleague, Marina. In joyful anarchy we all joined in arranging a boxful of exotic ornaments and lights on the two Yule trees former students had delivered for Leonid. The aroma of *plov,* a delicious Uzbeki meat, carrot, and rice dish, blended with the fragrant fir and fresh tangerines Tamara found at the people's market. So familiar and comforting. After dinner Tamara turned up the music, a collection of contemporary Italian and French rock, classical American jazz and blues. All formality and pretense were set aside. The staid, frail Georgi who sat across from us at dinner, politely asked if he might remove his jacket. Doing so revealed a blue shirt with starched detachable white collar, an elegant pair of white suspenders and a figure reminiscent of Fred Astaire. When the music began, he bowed elegantly to Marina, an auburn haired regal lady just taller than he, and the two of them proceeded to glide and pirouette the length of the apartment. His grace and playfulness charmed and astonished us. From time to time we would rest, collapse in exhaustion actually, while Georgi regaled us with stories of his efforts to become a people's deputy.

With the skill of an accomplished raconteur, he evoked the euphoria of those early days of democratic experimentation and participation. Eleven candidates were certified for the initial election; he came in a strong second in the run off. He told of standing on soap boxes in parks and at construction sights, taking on and being taken on by fellow candidates. He spoke of horror and humiliation the day his chief opponent, a bitter rival, distributed a thousand copies of an excerpt from one of Georgi's many books to indicate the latter's unworthiness for high office. Lines reciting worn Communist clichés, reeking of obeisance and bad faith, were read to the crowd. In telling the story on Christmas evening, Georgi made his efforts to dodge that mud sound hilarious.

There were other evenings with Georgi, times when a guest's duty to be amusing did not interfere with the expression of true feelings. Amidst a group of young scholars, all perfect strangers, Georgi confessed, "I have written twelve books, and I am ashamed of every one of them. If I could destroy every copy of every one of them and start afresh, I could live with myself. But that is impossible. If I had any courage, I would leave here right now and go shoot myself." There were several of us to assure Georgi that he is not the only one who must look back on a career filled with self-serving toadying, bending the knee to fashion and authority, ignoring the truth one could see but had not the courage to say. Georgi, unlike some of us, had an excuse. At eight years of age, he had seen his father seized by the secret police, returned to his home a year later, declared innocent but broken physically and mentally, doomed to die a short time later.

This conversation, we could tell, did little to salve Georgi's distress, though it may have strengthened the backbone of some younger persons present. What it indicates, however, goes beyond these individuals: public acknowledgment of guilt, of cowardly silence in the face of the manifold abuses of the Brezhnevian stagnation, is widespread among Soviet intellectuals. Such a declaration is directed not only toward the sins of one's past, it can also serve as substitute for action to prevent such abuses from occurring in the future. It is catharsis but in itself not progressive politics. The candidate who defeated Georgi proved to be a total waste as a peoples' deputy, but Georgi is not prepared to challenge him next year when the present term expires.

Changing Colors

We came to know Slava many years ago when he visited our university as a graduate student. He has continued to grow both intellectually and corporeally, achieving truly grand proportions in both directions. Unique in our experience is his capacity for identifying political forces and evaluating their relative strengths and interactions. Trained as an historian, he notices the finest detail but never loses sight of its connection to the broader picture. After one puzzling interview with a renowned scholar, we asked Slava, "How is it possible that when we spoke with this man five years ago, he assured us of the success and power of socialist principles and educational practices, while today he continues to hold the same position of influence and power at his institute while rejecting the same principles he earlier espoused? He now condemns socialism, the Party, the bureaucracy. He has taken his seat as a democratic deputy."

"Many with power and influence in the new institutions—the congress of deputies, cooperatives, commercial banks—also wielded power in the past—in the Party, the bureaucracy, at institutes and even in the university. They have simply reversed their positions, from plus 2 to minus 2. They are chameleons on a Scottish kilt," declared Slava.

Our notes, our tapes, our memories are filled with dozens of additional faces, voices, scenes, unique insights—all crying to be shared with an apparently uncaring outside world. But we are programmed to think like scientists, to seek an overview from which all these different perspectives can be seen to focus on the same objective reality. And so, calling on all we have read (most particularly the book given us by Slava, *Posle Kommunisma* [After Communism] by the pseudonymous "S. Platonov") and all that our friends, a few of whom were introduced here, have tried to teach us, we venture the outline of an analysis, one which seeks to accommodate the facts so far encountered and project rational expectations for the next phase. Here goes.

Perestroika: Background Arguments

Without a thorough overhaul, the Soviet economic system cannot provide the basic necessities of life to the Soviet people, much less raise the standard of living and satisfy the demands of the intelligentsia. A thorough overhaul of the Soviet economy requires massive input of capital, including advanced technology. No Soviet political regime can long survive if it does not provide the basic necessities and satisfy the demands of the intelligentsia. No Soviet political regime can generate massive inputs of capital and advanced technology from inside the country. Therefore, any political regime with hopes of long tenure must seek and secure capital and technology from the capitalist world.

That argument can be proved valid with the simplest elements of the sentential calculus. And you may be sure that all Soviet political thinkers are acutely aware of the truth of every premise in it. Outside observers, however, both those conditioned to see the Soviet Union as an ever-menacing threat to American survival and those who view it as mankind's best hope for a just world, may be less assured of the truth of the claims just made. Why cannot the Soviet economy provide the basic goods of life to the Soviet people without massive inputs of capital? If capital is needed to effect modernization, why cannot it be generated from within the country, particularly by devoting the Soviet "peace dividend" to domestic production? Those are good questions which we will try to answer below, but let us reiterate: For the past six years or more, trained Soviet observers of their own system have taken all the premises above as simple givens for the next argument.

Any political regime that seeks continued tenure in office must establish those conditions of economic and political stability that will make the Soviet Union appear a profitable opportunity for capitalist investment. But no regime which claims to uphold the revolutionary traditions of Marx and Lenin, bases its power in tightly controlled unions of industrial workers, and encourages national liberation struggles throughout the world can gain the trust and confidence of international capital. The pre–Gorbachev Communist Party of the Soviet Union was exactly such a regime. Therefore, the pre–G CPSU could not hope for long tenure in office. Hence Gorbachev: "If not now, Comrades, when? If not us, who?"

Thus, perestroika. Let us recall, as if from the mists of time, the original goals of "socialist restructuring." Economic development was to shift from extensive to intensive, seeking to enhance the efficiency (in various senses) of existing productive facilities rather than building more new ones. Material incentives for both workers and managers were to be rationally organized, acting on the basic socialist principle: from each according to his ability, to each according to his work! Participation by workers in the management of facilities was sought because desirable in its own right, the very essence of socialist democracy, and also because recognized as essential to increasing productivity. Ending the arms race and reducing world tensions became the primary goal of Soviet foreign policy; success would make it possible to transfer the most advanced sector of Soviet technology, now devoted to military research and production, to domestic uses. While holding fast to basic socialist principles, the Soviet regime could thus conserve currency reserves for the purchase of capital goods and, where necessary, negotiate for foreign loans without jeopardizing sustained development of the economy.

Those were the goals. What have been the results of perestroika? A scientifically responsible answer would require a breakdown by sector and industry, down to individual institution, plant, shop, farm, school. But overall, the results are all too clear: a profound disruption of productive life and severe hardships not known since the end of World War II. Why did, does this occur? No law of politics or economics dictates that a socialist regime cannot invite investment by foreign capital and establish conditions under which that investment would be both prudent and profitable; indeed since the days of Lenin such arrangements have been concluded with mutual benefit to capitalists and Communists. Why did the well-laid plans contrived by Mikhail Sergeyevich and his gifted co-workers "gang sae agley"? To answer that we have to look at glasnost, which was the first and (perhaps overly) successful side of Gorbachev's reforms.

The Darker Side of History

Openness, i.e., absence of political control over human discourse, had become the rule (sometimes honored in the breach) in university and academic life long before it became general policy in Soviet society. In the natural sciences, the case of Lysenko[1] was invoked whenever academic freedom was threatened. Andrei Sakharov could be exiled and placed under house arrest, but the Academy of Science, despite Brezhnev's direct order, refused to expel him. (When the Academy met to vote the expulsion, one member rose to inquire whether there was any precedent for such a move. The president replied that exhaustive research had been conducted on just that question, and only one precedent had been discovered: on Hitler's order, Einstein had been expelled from the German Academy of Science. Even so, the vote against expulsion was not unanimous.)

Gorbachev was the first university-trained executive holding supreme Soviet power since Lenin. Glasnost was intended to bring to all levels and forms of social discourse the principles of academic scholarship: freedom and creativity for the individual thinker, discipline and responsibility in the collective search for truth. Things did not work out that way, of course. It was, as Vadim Medvedev recognized, "impossible to break the iron vice of the administer-and-command system, which impedes economic progress, without political reform" (*Perestroika Annual,* Vol. II, p. 29). But political reform— ending the Party's constitutionally protected dominance, together with glasnost and democracy—did not break but only loosened the "iron vice" and further impeded production and distribution. The reforms did, however, break habits of silence and resignation that for generations had held in check the widespread hostility of many Soviet citizens toward the Communist Party and everything, good and bad, the Party had stood for. Only a minority in either the proletariat or the intelligentsia openly expressed any real hatred of the Party when glasnost first began to spread from major centers to the rest of the Soviet subcontinent. But that hatred fed upon itself as new revelations of corruption, brutality, and inefficiency were eagerly reported by newly freed popular media; anti–Party feeling grew stronger as it brought to life and merged with long submerged class, ethnic, racial, national, and gender antagonisms and aspirations. In sum, with glasnost the "subjective factor" in history reasserted itself, with consequences disastrous for those who sought, in perestroika, a rational route to *socialist* economic development.

"It might have been otherwise" is the constant refrain in this tragedy. There were those in 1985 who advised Gorbachev to make good his use of "revolution" applied to perestroika: unleash the masses, flood the streets with workers, pull every bureaucrat out of every office, put shovels in their lily-white hands, make *them* take on the physical rehabilitation of the country. Cultural revolution equals catastrophe, as we all know. But had the country taken at once the full brunt of a quarter century of stagnation, it might by now be well into the process of recovery, whereas today the political landscape contains *no* coherent vision of a satisfactory resolution of this concatenation of crises.

A Three-Fold Foul-Up

Aye, the crises are multiple. Start with the Soviet Constitution, which is a muddle of parliamentary democracy, presidential democracy, and Soviet democracy. Powers of various branches, of various levels of government (all-Union, republic, local), are ill defined; there is nothing like a Supreme Court to reconcile statutes, administrative decrees, and judicial actions with constitutional requirements. The fundamental issue of the right to secede from the Union, one we settled in 1861–65, is still hanging fire. And yet: if the economy and social structure were functioning with reasonable efficiency, the complex constitutional crisis confronting the country could and would be resolved by processes of compromise and conciliation—satisfying no one, bearable to all. But the economy and social structure are not working well enough to provide the stability required for constitutional compromise. And in the absence of a strong, effective political system, there is no way to bring the economy and social structure back into effective performance. (By "social structure" here, we refer to mechanisms of social reproduction, education, communication, religion, professional organizations, etc., which form coherent patterns of belief and desire in individuals and stable patterns of expected behavior in society at large.)

Nothing need be added to all that has been written about the sad state of the Soviet economy. It is an axiom of contemporary philosophy of science that events are over-determined: there is always more than one cause capable of bringing about whatever actually occurs. The truth of that two-pronged axiom becomes clear when one seeks to explain why the Soviet economy is as it is. We could begin with what is called, perhaps euphemistically, the STR, scientific-technological revolution. Soviet economists and political scientists have developed beautiful models which demonstrate that the traditional Soviet planning system, *Gosplan*, is radically deficient as a mechanism for allocating goods and services in a complex, research-driven economy; its failure is predictable by pure theory: it's almost as if every telephone call in the U.S.A. had to be handled through a single switchboard in Kansas City. The continuing influence of *Gosplan* in key sectors alone is enough to create economic dysfunction.

Or take the case last June when every newspaper was quoting the report that there were *many* more rubles floating in the market than goods to purchase with them: at just that point, then-premier N.I. Ryzhkov announced that six months hence the prices of all goods would be doubled or quadrupled. Those with rubles immediately bought and hoarded everything they could store; producers warehoused everything that would not rot; everything, including matches, soap, aspirin, toilet paper, even salt, disappeared from the shops and has been scarce since. A remotely comparable boo-boo would be an announcement by the Federal Reserve Board that some dark night about six months hence the money supply would be doubled or quadrupled. That would throw even our resilient system into chaos.

Or take the growing influence of those elements in the Soviet economy known as the "Mafia." Those Soviet citizens and foreign investors who would utilize the many opportunities for private enterprise opened by recent legislation find it necessary to buy costly "protection" for their physical equipment and the continuing health of their personnel. Even more discouraging, they find that goods and services needed to conduct their operations are controlled by hidden cartels who will bleed off any profits those operations might generate. It will take years of trial and error to develop a system of commercial, financial legislation and regulations clearly marking what is legal and what illegal in these many new forms of economic activity. (Look what happened in the U.S.A. when we made relatively small changes in the regulation of savings and loan banks!) In the meantime, the KGB has been given emergency powers to seize records and impound merchandise in their campaign against "economic crimes." For obvious reasons, those moves are far more likely to frighten than reassure potential "honest" entrepreneurs.

We could go on adding factors, any one of which would have been enough to throw the precariously managed Soviet economy into a tailspin. What they add up to is this: stripped of rhetoric and ideology, perestroika equals changing the ownership of capital. These changes were expected to generate increased production, particularly in agriculture and consumer goods, thus yielding savings in hard currency (e.g., that spent for foreign grain) that could be invested in both consumer and capital goods. Not only were these expectations not fulfilled, production has actually declined in a number of key areas. What all this does for the political and social structure of the country, for the hopes and aspirations of concerned individuals, can be seen in every day's reports of further breakdown of the Soviet system as a whole.

It would take far more space than allowed here to examine the changes occurring in Soviet education, religion, home and family life, professional associations, criminal justice, and so on as a result of perestroika. Let it be noted in brief: in every aspect of life, the absence of stable expectations for the future means anxiety in the present. The psychological malaise that such a state would engender in Americans is there tempered by traditional Russian black humor, by a cynical, fatalistic acceptance of unknowable reality.

What Does the Future Hold?

It is somewhat like predicting the weather. Very general long-range forecasts are fairly accurate but of limited utility, likewise forecasts for the next few hours. Not accurate enough to be of much use are just those middle range predictions we would like most to count on, details of the weather next season. Similarly, the long range political outlook for the U.S.S.R. is exactly what some foresaw and refused to be a part of: the restoration of *diktatura* (dictatorship, a word destined, like perestroika, for international currency). The short run will inevitably show continuation of the trends noted in the previous year: concentration of legal power in the hands of the executive, tightening the screws on democracy and dissent. (How thoroughly those two concepts are intertwined in Russian history!) Needed but impossible to produce are trustworthy answers to: What kind of *diktatura*? By whom, how and when will it be set in place? With what consequences for the economy and other aspects of Soviet life? With what consequences for the place of the Soviet Union in international relations?

What do Russian scholars and intellectuals foresee for themselves in the next phase of their nation's history? It is here that the tendentious distinction between authoritarian and totalitarian forms of dictatorship becomes a source of comfort. An authoritarian dictatorship is one in which individuals are left (mostly) free to pursue their own affairs so long as they do not meddle in politics or higher-level economic activities, while totalitarian dictators seek to control every aspect of human life, usually in service to some ideal transcending the immediate interests of the society—eternal salvation, the will of Allah, international communism, the thousand-year Reich....

The coming *diktatura* will be of the authoritarian variety. Direct political intervention into scholarly life will be limited to those occasions when universities or other intellectual organizations and publications become foci for resistance to political authority. This past December democrats in the Supreme Soviet granted autonomy to Moscow State University; no dictator is likely to find it worth the struggle to reverse that action. The days when unbelieving philosophers were forced to teach dogmas of Marxism-Leninism to equally unbelieving students will not return. By fairly unobtrusive methods, discourse among intellectuals can be screened from the media of the masses and left alone. The ideological content of primary and secondary education can be controlled, as in the U.S.A., without imposing onerous restrictions on scholarship in "humanistic studies," i.e., philosophy, literature, history, psychology, sociology, or political science. In short, a barebones outline of academic and intellectual freedom seems likely to survive from the heady days of glasnost and democracy.

So prospects are not entirely dismaying for intellectuals holding secure positions in the academies, universities, institutes, and literary establishments. But here's the rub: few positions in any such institutions can be considered secure, *very* few in the humanities. The case can be made that subsidies for the intelligentsia were, along with defense expenditures and grants to third world client states, a major drain on the Soviet economy, a contributing factor to its present malfunction. Expansion of higher education was built into *Gosplan* at rates reflecting political goals rather than actual needs for college graduates in production. In both the natural and social sciences, research institutes were established more with an eye to absorbing graduates than to provide data needed for economic development. Given a Marxist view of the purpose of social power—to establish the material conditions for the fullest and most harmonious development of individual talents and capacities—expanded opportunities for higher education and intellectual employment for graduates are goals worth pursuing in their own right. But there were also self-seeking motives for such a policy by the Party: industrial workers are less restive if their children seem destined for white collar jobs, while unemployed members of the intelligentsia have traditionally formed the core of radical movements of both left- and right-wing revolutionary tendencies.

The question has to be asked: What is going to happen to the (tens, hundreds?) of thousands of individuals employed in intellectual work which cannot be justified on the grounds of economic profit and efficiency? When the Ministry of Higher Education assumed control of East German universities, *all* the faculties of humanistic studies were summarily dismissed. Such instruction in those subjects as is deemed necessary will, in the future, be provided by Western trained scholars. Unemployment benefits provided by the Federal Republic will there keep those dismissed from starvation. There is no comparable system of social benefits available in the U.S.S.R. Whatever happens on the political front, a tragic brain drain is inevitable.

Which returns us to the hard syllogisms with which we began. The present legal democracy cannot establish the conditions required to attract foreign capital. The difference between large and small scale investments is key to understanding the difference between the economic goals of perestroika and the coming *diktatura*. The democratic movement tried to make potential profits appear so large that entrepreneurs would ignore otherwise unacceptable risks. On that basis, small investors will import popcorn machines, perhaps, but Siemens will not be tempted to imitate McDonald's in establishing an integrated system of chemical production, nor Toyota to take over the manufacture of Volgas. (The poverty of American banks puts us out of the running for those prizes.) If Soviet plants are to acquire the machinery and markets necessary to compete internationally, speaking bluntly, the coming *diktatura* will have to put the country as a whole on the auction block.

What regime could survive while selling off the national treasury, the land's resources and the labor power of that intensely patriotic people? Here we cannot pretend to encapsulate the ideas of others. Every Soviet intellectual can project a plausible, usually deplorable, scenario. Here is ours. Begin with the *nomenklatura*, those holding positions requiring approval at the highest level, formerly by the tsar, then by the Central Committee of the Party, today by the president and Council of Ministers. (Thus the *nomenklatura* is a group remotely like those whose appointments require Senate confirmation in our system.) Some faction within that group will establish dependable ties to the KGB and army, two institutions retaining (relatively stable) internal cohesion, the latter immensely strengthened by the recent display of American violence in Iraq. The re-emerging industrial unions and disaffected intelligentsia will be enlisted in an all-out campaign against the dominant faction's rivals, a campaign directed both ostensibly and actually against the still-surviving corruption, inefficiency, and brutality of those in power. When credible opposition has been crushed, the army and KGB, even the local police, will be turned against workers and intelligentsia to insure that a cheap and reliable labor force will be available to potential investors.

Elimination of political democracy should prove relatively simple: Soviet citizens have grown disgusted with the endless debates in the Congress of Peoples' Deputies; beautiful speeches have not produced effective action to solve life's immediate problems. At the same time, this campaign of repression must leave legal and financial scholars freedom to work out flexible, sensible codes and procedures which will make the U.S.S.R. an attractive place to do business. Artists and cultural figures must have leeway to create an environment that, to the managerial elite, makes Soviet cities attractive places to live. Educational excellence must be maintained for the now-smaller proportion of youth pursuing academic and technical studies. With or, preferably, without military and political control, constituent republics will be bound to the (however renamed) U.S.S.R. by trade and culture; national elites will submerge antagonisms, as all respond to the unprecedented economic opportunities opened by full capitalist penetration of the socialist homeland. The dominant faction itself will emerge as partial owners of immense wealth, leapfrogging their counterparts in Deng Xiaoping's clique in China. The proletariat and lower-level intelligentsia will suffer what they must, while producing the surplus value required for sustained profits. Moscow State University will be completely refurbished, possibly using labor power not unlike the slave gangs who built those stately buildings under Stalin's personal supervision.

Even as that scene develops to its climax, does one not hear strains of "The Internationale" beginning to swell in the wings? Listen harder.

Note

1. T.D. Lysenko, agronomist, virtual czar of Soviet biology under Stalin. His extravagant theories severely retarded genetic studies in the U.S.S.R. into the 1960s.

Moral and Spiritual Changes

Howard L. Parsons

Swiftly moving economic and political transformations in the Soviet Union culminated in late 1991 in the dissolution of the U.S.S.R. At the same time have come moral and spiritual changes—demanding these transformations, stimulating them, and driven by them. By "moral and spiritual" I mean people's basic beliefs about the distinctively human (or "higher") values, about the direction, end, and significance of human living—and the readiness to commit oneself in practice to such values. Belief in these values normally imports a framework or system of thought—a philosophy that is personal or social, secular or religious.

The essay that follows, written in 1990, is a record of a society in transition. My study of subsequent changes and my month-long visit to Moscow in the fall of 1991 confirmed the continuance and even the acceleration of the transition found in 1990. While I have tried to report faithfully the events and statements limited to my field of observation, the observations and reportage have not been free of my own sympathetic view of the general notion of socialism. I must confess that this viewpoint colors and shapes the meaning and moral significance of the observations—just as any viewpoint would; and no reporter, despite disclaimers of "neutrality," can be free of some such viewpoint.

On September 1, 1990, I arrived at Moscow State University to begin a series of lectures on "Marxism and Christianity." Soon thereafter, I met a journalist of longtime acquaintance. In half-jest he remarked, "You must be the only Marxist in Moscow." Although I had known that the ideological landscape in the U.S.S.R. had been shifting for some time, I was unprepared for this hyperbole, even in jest. But during the days and weeks of my three-month stay, the truth of my friend's remark became increasingly clear.

The chair of my department, the Department of the Theory and History of Religion and Scientific Atheism—its name recently changed from the Theory and History of Scientific Atheism—had warned me: "Keep in mind in your lectures that our students are against Marxism." Then, at my first lecture, the students protested, almost in a chorus: "We don't want to hear about Marxism." Faculty members verified this hostility among the students, saying that very few students now have elected to do major study in the theory, history, political economy, and other aspects of Marxism-Leninism. When I asked a faculty member why the students rejected Marxism, he replied that they had to do so, that it had been "imposed" on them, that "they did not choose it." Someone said that the students' animus against Marxism had been particularly acute in the scientific and technical institutes—believable news, considering that many United States' students in the hard sciences have little interest in the humanities and social studies whatever their content.

One day in November 1990, as I walked through the halls of Moscow State University, four program advertisements on one bulletin board caught my eye: guru Maharaja, astrologist Sergei Bronski, pastor Vladimir Kulikov of the Evangelical-Christian Baptists, and Grigorii Yatsutovsko, practitioner of mysticism (magician). I could hardly believe my eyes. In 1980, ten years previously, when I was also on a lecture assignment in the Faculty of Philosophy of the University, such advertisements would have been unthinkable. University authorities strictly limited or forbade the on-campus presence of religious leaders, "idealists," and foreign academics and ideologists. Now, after more than five years of perestroika and glasnost, all bans were off. The borders were permeable. During my three-month period of lectures at the University several fundamentalist preachers from the United States addressed student audiences, urging them to accept Christ and to contribute money for study materials. Representatives of Sun Myung Moon's Unification Church had recently been on campus conducting a contest to award scholarships for students to attend a conference in the United States. Russian Orthodox priests and Baptist preachers gave lectures on the campus. When I asked some professors if they saw any danger in this sudden opening to ideas that sharply collided with the doctrines of Marxism-Leninism, they replied that democracy requires such freedom.

This widening of the accessibility of religious ideas parallels changes of attitudes in philosophy. Among teachers and students there is a rising interest in existentialism. A conference on its Danish founder, Soren Kierkegaard, was held in the fall. Phenomenology, the inquiry into the content of personal awareness and being, was growing. For the first time since before the 1917 revolution, several editions of Friedreich Nietzsche's works were being published. In 1990 a major publishing house, Progress, brought out the selected works of Alfred North Whitehead, a major Anglo-American philosopher whose work in philosophy of religion has had a special impact on U.S. philosophers. During the recent period of perestroika, the proliferation of private publishers, sometimes engaged in joint ventures with Western firms, has facilitated such printing, though the houses still under state auspices, like Progress, are competing for the new market.

This dissemination of new ideas—emerging from within the Soviet Union and from foreign sources—is not only a phenomenon of perestroika and glasnost. It is a manifestation of the sea-changes occurring in the outlook of people generally. The stagnation and decline of the economy, inflation, scarce foodstuffs and other consumer goods, deteriorating public services such as medical care and transport, the manipulations of the mafia, widespread corruption among the *nomenklatura* and party leadership, ineffective parliament, the fluctuations of the Gorbachev, administration—all have led many to doubt the value and relevance of socialism in the solution of their problems. Many students, especially the younger ones, were given to describe this situation with extravagance: "Socialism is a total failure." "We have lost seventy years." "Marxism is a crime." Even those who still believe in the theory and value of socialism hold that it was incompletely put into practice. What existed is variously described as "administrative socialism," "state socialism," "petty bourgeois socialism," "utopian socialism," and the like. When I asked one student "What is socialism?" she replied, "That's an untasty question." Many students now are averse to thinking about their socialist history, viewing it as an unqualified failure. But it was evident to me that many had not carefully studied the theory of socialism.

Among thoughtful students the universal mood is one of self-criticism and soul searching, a process both personal and social, contemporary and historical, national and international—international in the sense that the U.S.S.R. is a union of different republics with their own nationalities. Where and how did we go wrong? What did the Bolsheviks say and do? (There is a common confusion of Bolshevism with socialism.) Is there a class struggle? Does it conflict with humanism? What is socialism's philosophy of the human being, society, human nature, and universal human values? Did the Bolsheviks understand it and apply it? What are the alternative philosophies? What ought I commit myself to? Do I have a fulfilling future to believe in, to hope for, to work toward? Nearly all of the students with whom I talked were negative in their estimate of socialism, their country's history, and their personal futures. The prevailing feeling toward the past, present, and future is one of disillusionment and betrayal. Students tend to be absolutist in their judgments. The Bolsheviks, it seems, did everything wrong and nothing right while the prerevolutionary period of Russian history takes on the rosy glow of a golden age. Though people differ on what changes must be made, all agree that the existing system cannot continue unaltered. But I looked in vain to find a broad consensus on the needed direction.

The breakdown in the economy—and the uncertainties in social and political life—have brought with them a grave moral and spiritual crisis. Beyond the everyday questions of where and how to get food, how to stretch a shrinking ruble, how to earn more money (buying Western goods and selling them for profit), how to find medicine and buy and get reliable health care— there remains the residue of inescapable questions of human living. Are human beings basically selfish or altruistic? Does their social system (socialist or capitalist or another) make an essential difference to their natures? Will the values of a free market be canceled by selfishness and exploitation? Can I trust people? Can we achieve progress, both material and spiritual? Is there an objective and absolute ground for moral values? Is it found only in religion? What does religion have to offer that Marxism does not? What ought I to do? What can I have faith in? What can I hope for?

The roots of these philosophical doubts and searchings lie in fact as much in cultural changes as in economic ones—cultural changes that appear to have parallels in certain developed societies in the world quite independently of their particular economic and political systems. The "counter cultural revolution" and its conservative reaction that shook the society of the United States in the 1960s seems to have commenced in the U.S.S.R. a generation later, in the 1980s, though moving more slowly. These cultural changes are interconnected with a complex of changes—the growth of large, impersonal economic structures, science and technology, economic and political bureaucracies, mobility of population, and urbanization, mass education, rising expectations among people, the increase of armaments, the nuclear and ecological threats, and foreign invasions and wars. Such changes include a disturbed family life and decline in the influence of "soft structures"—family, school, religious institutions—and the weakening in the transmission of basic personal values from one generation to another. Private and public morality have been separated. The old values of patriotism, loyalty to tradition, hard work, planning, sacrifice for the future, and close family ties have been eroded by the new values of individual choice, self-realization, consumerism, and immediate gratification. Among the youth the resulting confusion and uncertainty about personal values, personal identity, a place in the scheme of things, and the meaning of life have issued in a search for commitment and the entertainment in thought and practice of various paths of life. Over against these new experiments a conservative cultural movement has emerged, and so the battle has been joined.

For some years this critical soul-searching in the U.S.S.R. has expressed itself on a large scale as a shift of interest—as a matter of emphasis, not as a complete shift—from established state socialism toward a new system, from monism toward pluralism, from the social toward the individual, from the objective toward the subjective, from the material toward the spiritual, from a centrally planned society toward distribution of power, from the future toward the concrete and historical, and from enthusiastic idealism toward pragmatic realism.

(1) *From the established social system toward a new system.* For most of its seventy-three-year history, Soviet socialism offered a world outlook that gave cohesion and guidance to social life and that inspired individual effort and devotion through the famine and civil war, the five-year plans for the construction of a new economy (with even the oppression and mass deaths under Stalinism), the Great Patriotic War, and the postwar reconstruction. And since the early 1970s the economy has stagnated and failed, people increasingly have lost faith in the system and its ideology. Perestroika, commencing 1985, legitimized social criticism and the deepening crisis in the economy. It offered a compelling material reason for questioning if not rejecting socialism. Bread speaks louder than doctrines. A common complaint now is that the ideology of socialism was forced on people, denying them the right to criticize it and the exercise of even a minimum of freedom toward the system. One philosopher has argued that Marxism-Leninism had a trickle-down theory that viewed its success to be dependent on the Central Committee of the CPSU as its source. But the consciousness of many people was crushed under the "megatonnage of dogmatisms."

Among students the charitable view of Marxism as a theory is that it is a dream, an idealistic abstraction, an ideology, a utopia—not a science for the direction of social action. Some repeated the views of their professors that it is a "religion," "an ideology, not a science," and a "foolish doctrine." Many of those who once freely accepted the teachings and directions of the Party, it was said, finally became disaffected by the discrepancy between the professed ideals of their leaders and their real practice. One middle-aged Communist told me: "In the 1950s and 1960s we young people went off with great enthusiasm to work on the Trans-Siberian Railway—sacrificing, disciplining ourselves, suffering, sheltered and very poorly fed, sharing the slogans of the leaders. But later it turned out that they were wasting millions of rubles on the project and building plush houses for themselves and securing other privileges." Some students feel that the people have lost touch with the vital values of their cultural tradition because communism rashly and swiftly displaced them with other values. "The class struggle has falsified values here, misrepresenting what are true values." "Before the revolution of 1917, our people had respect for the value of personality. But since then we have struggled to achieve only class values. The end of communism will mean the return of personality." Some scholars attribute this crisis in human values in part to the isolation of the U.S.S.R. from the international community. Those who have traveled to the developed industrial societies of the West are impressed by their high standard of living in the material domain and by the level of economic, social, and political life—the enterprise, productivity, freedom of expression and variety of opinions and lifestyles, media, and democratic institutions such as parliamentary forms and voluntary civic associations (of which the U.S.A. has two million). Of course one must question whether all such values are or ought to be "universal human values." In any case, students feel alienated from their own needs and longings and self-actualization. They are searching for a new social system in which they would achieve personal fulfillment.

Not everyone has thrown away the concept of socialism. "Nobody knows what socialism is," said an avowed socialist. "We have never had socialism. We are an artificial, wounded, sick society, a concentration camp society. Your society of the U.S.A. is sick from riches, while we are sick from misery. Yet we love the socialist idea." It was his belief that socialism has to be build "from the inside" and not (as in Soviet history) "from the top down" by centralized authoritarian power and abstract slogans. For him, as for other intellectuals, private property is the key to diversity, independence, and individuality of thought and action, opening up the opportunity for democratic decision-making and the creation of a genuine socialist order. Moreover, large numbers of working people still adhere to socialism and will be found in the parties and groups that uphold it.

A sociologist defended the theory of socialism.

> People judge capitalism by looking at the stocked shops in capitalist societies. So they are nihilistic toward socialism. But I hope that conservatism in the best sense of that position will not allow society to fragment under the impact of nude nihilism. Socialist ideas are not utopian. The numbers of intellectuals in the countries of the world are growing. The nature of intellectual work and the character of labor generally demand democratization, collective principles, humanism, and respect for personality in all countries. A basic principle created by socialism is that the quantity and quality of one's labor ought to determine one's income. While this is a trivial truth, it was not applied in our society. We had the principle of a "limited fund of wages." Each enterprise was allotted a definite sum for its wages. More than one generation grew up under this principle. So people learned to limit their own work because if they worked more and better, the administration made the price of work (wages) less. So work was cheapened because of the limited fund of wages. Yet the principle has worked—until today. When Gorbachev visited Sverdlovsk last year a worker asked him, "Will you tell us when an uncle at the top will decide that I can work outside the limited fund of wages?" Gorbachev answered only in generalities. Thus, such a simple idea can't penetrate to our top leadership.

No one seems prepared to predict precisely the shape of things to come in world outlook and social system. But many concur that the extremes of anarchy and authoritarianism, of chaos and repression, loom as dreaded alternatives. They justify this fear with the observation that throughout their history the Russian people have tended to swing to violent extremes. A student cited the abrupt movement after 1917 from the religious faith in Christ to the secular faith in Marx. "The Russian soul has only polarities without any mediating link between extremes." For some the search for a method of moderation must look away from both the free market in the Western mode and the old style of centralized control to what Gorbachev has called "socialism with private interests." To achieve a dynamic balance in the economy it would be necessary to avoid (a) "Marxist capitalism," which would be "very primitive," lacking in the restraints on the market gradually developed in the West over a long period of time, and (b) a reversion to military-bureaucratic-party repression which some right-wing groups are trying to provoke.

The argument for extensive but limited private property is both political and economic. (Some believe that the radical proposal from the Yeltsin team of economists, taken right out of Milton Friedman, would "legalize the shadow economy" and aims at giving amnesty to the mafia.) The argument is that a stable and creative society requires a variety of perspectives freely developing, interacting, checking, modifying, and improving one another. Said one, "The English, French, and German souls have had oppositions—empiricism and objective idealism and rationality and mysticism"—while the Russians have had only isolated extremes. Private property among citizens—in "a civil society"—would give the material basis for private, independent opinions which, constructively interacting, would generate the political dynamic for stability and advance. As someone put it, "Democracy works only if people are economically independent—i.e., in business for themselves, or selling their own labor in the market." State socialism, by guaranteeing people security, has robbed them of the conditions of independence.

Another, extending the argument, asserted that Marxist socialism has not worked in Russia because classes and class struggle in the sense that Marx understood them did not exist and still do not exist there. Citing Willie Brandt, who said that the working class in Germany lacked the specialized education, knowledge, and skills to make good use of its rights and possessions and therefore it was not ready to assume control of the economy, he said that the key to the new stage of development of humanity are the scientific and technological strata.

Most appear to agree that now the principal economic and political factions contending for power are the right wing, the center, and the left wing. On the right wing are groups advocating a strengthening of national tradition and strong state power: monarchists, neo–Stalinists, the old-line Marxist-Leninists of the CPSU, some leaders and laity of the Russian Orthodox Church, the bureaucrats in the state apparatus and elsewhere, the nationalists such as the neo–Slavophiles, the KGB, the military, and the mafia who stand to lose by either a reformist conservatism or the genuine competition of a free market. On the left wing are the forces calling (with various emphases) for faster movement toward private property, free enterprise, parliamentary democracy, human rights, a law-governed state, and "civil society." Some forty parties have been created, many of them small. According to a poll of the Post-factum Information Service in the spring of 1990, the most popular political group is the Democratic Platform. Its outlook is similar to that of the Social-Democratic Party of Russia patterned on the European model. This party now has the strongest representation in the Supreme Soviets of the U.S.S.R. and the Russian Federation. The centrists around Gorbachev are pursuing a course between (a) the "steadfast communists," among them the Communist Party of the Russian Federation, along with other groups on the right, and (b) the leftward pull of the social-democratic forces.

Intellectuals who gravitate to the "free market" model of Western capitalism are lured by illusions about both its promises and its perils for people. In their disillusionment with state socialism, they have embraced an illusion of the opposite kind. After Margaret Thatcher's resignation as premier of Great Britain, a writer in the *Moscow News* (issue of December 9–16, 1990) praised her "dignity," "charm," "straightforwardness and inner conviction, still rare qualities in Soviet politicians." Her work in the second half of the 1980s, he said, "could easily be called perestroika." Her aim was "consistent privatization of state property, renunciation of state interference in business, transition to the market regulated by itself only"; and she did "a great deal to carry it out." But the writer, Sergei Volvets, is blind to the effects of Thatcherism on the people as a whole: The tripling of unemployment to more than two million, the creation of a mass of fifteen million living in poverty, the deterioration and destruction of national health service, the decline of educational opportunities for working class children, the hobbling of trade unions by anti-labor laws, and subservience to United States policy of escalating armaments and attacks on national liberation movements. Like this writer, many intellectuals are naive about the fact that unregulated free enterprise will bring exploitation of workers and bitter class conflict between workers and owners. Perhaps this is the necessary baptism of suffering that some Soviet people must undergo in order to grasp the realities of the capitalist system.

(2) *From monism toward pluralism*. Several thinkers, including longtime Marxist-Leninists, commented on the oppressive monism of Russian ideology,

both in the Russian Orthodox Church and in Marxism-Leninism since 1917. The students with whom I talked were hungry for plurality and variety in every domain of life—in lifestyles, art, literature, ideas, philosophy, religion, politics, economy. At the same time they were oblivious to the hazards of plurality—the dispersion of attention, the quick but shallow satiety, and, in the marketplace, the brutal competition, the stress, the dehumanization, and "the war of each against all." But the reason for this turn toward variety is the experience of excessive security, a monotony installed by a pervasive state organization, and an uncritical equalization of people in the workplace. "In our state socialism," said a professor, "we homogenized everything. We are spoiled and too monistic. We treat all people equally." This equalization leads to the discouragement of good work when good workers realize they are not proportionately rewarded and are maneuvering for privileges. Inequalities become unfair and undeserved. Thus, while some professors share the same housing and cafeteria lines with students, others connected with the bureaucracy enjoy superior accommodations.

Variety of thought and outlook develops of course when people are free and ready, willing, and able to interact with persons of conflicting views and to learn to live with variety, to give and take in creative and constructive ways, to express themselves honestly and to listen appreciatively, and to grow in the process. Not a few students I met showed the results of isolation from knowledge of any serious encounter with sharply opposite points of view. In a classroom discussion when I suggested variation in the roles of women and men, one student declared with certainty that the traditional gender roles are "deeply tied to biology." For some, the issue of homosexuality was met with silence or humor, and one student seemed to equate homosexuality with lust. A philosopher engaged in some of the first research in the U.S.S.R. on feminism told me that conditions have not been ripe for a strong feminist movement in this patriarchal society—"patriarchy" meaning a cultural mode of domination. Another observed that while some women are ready for their own liberation, they have produced no theoretical works, lag behind Western women in this regard, and "invent" their works because they do not have enough "theoretical experience." But old stereotypes are tenacious: a Soviet man, once married to an American woman, was convinced that "all American women are feminists—and that is a problem for American men."

Likewise in religion, concepts have been limited and tolerance retarded by the narrow range of religious practice in society. The culture has not produced the variety of faiths that have proliferated throughout United States history. As we discussed Protestantism, some students who were Orthodox believers did not see this faith as having equal status with their own. One said it is "not a real religion" because it is secular and identifies religion with changes in the world; another, that liberal Protestants, tolerant of the permissive morality of the 1960s in the United States, are not religious. These views of the students, while Orthodox, did not go as far as the All-Russian Conference of Orthodox-Patriotic Forces, meeting in Moscow in October 1990, which went on record against pornography, all Jews, "those who side with the Jews," those who pray together with "heretics" (Catholics, Protestants, etc.), and the media's insults of the Russian nation, Orthodoxy, and the monarchy—which is to be restored.

In this setting I understood with new clarity the historic role played by Western Protestantism, together with capitalism, in spreading the doctrines and practices of individualism with voluntary association in communities. A Russian historian, not religious, put the comparison in this way. The Protestants of the West, he said, in their struggle against the medieval order strove for their freedom of faith and for the democratic state. "They believed in putting garments on Christ." But our people of Russia, never having experienced their Middle Ages or the Reformation, are now, in a secular age, faced with "a naked God."

(3) *From the social toward the individual.* I was describing to a professor the unrelieved mess made in the communal kitchen on the floor of our graduate student dormitory. "We are not diversified, developed, differentiated," he explained, "not concrete and careful about individual tasks and conditions and details." Many believe this lack of initiative—surely not universal, else the society would not function—must be remedied under a new economic system when the rewards of work of able-bodied adults will be directly tied to their individual performances. "We had no Renaissance or Reformation," repeated another, "no emphasis on the individual. We had a very strong collective feeling throughout our Russian history, and it was intensified during the Stalin period. But the new Soviet person is very one-sided and primitive like the peasants of the past, with a social feeling of *Gemeinschaft* [community of interest] rather than *Gesellschaft* [intimate fellowship]." Still another said, "We were utopian. We did not understand that when Marx said that 'man is the ensemble of his social relations,' he meant not just economic relations but human and personal relations." And a sociologist compared the Soviet Union as a "conglomerate" of nationalities, religions, and other elements to the "community" of the United States.

In reaction against this "homogenization," students are attracted to and take up a variety of systems of thought, ranging from Hari Krishna, Russian Orthodoxy, and monarchy, to anarchism. One of the student leaders in the Confederation of Anarchisto-Syndicalists told me it has about one-thousand members, no bureaucratic structure, and no dues, publishing a journal,

Obshchina (Community) in 40,000 copies, at one ruble per copy. The highest value for these anarchists is freedom—"not as Marx conceived it but as freedom of choice and policy," which is impeded by centralism and political parties.

To illustrate the growing individualism and chaos in the country let loose by perestroika, a sociologist referred to the unending and seemingly unproductive marathon of talk in the parliament. The two primary words there now, he said, are *Doloi!* ("Go away!") and *Dai!* ("Give me!"). Moreover, the emergent individualism is often materialistic. A political scientist who represented the Social-Democratic Platform and participated in the first congress of the Communist Party of the Russian Federation, speaking against the majority, said that in a discussion someone had risen to say, "Perestroika is bad—before it, we had sausage, and now we don't." The scientist answered: "But look, now we have more freedom and can speak about everything. Freedom is more important than sausages." Yet during this period of shortages, a sizeable portion of the people side with the Sausage Platform.

Students, however, as might be expected, are concerned about the political and personal rights of the individual and the higher needs beyond the economic ones. They agreed that their society should not copy the United States, but they asked me what their society might learn from ours. I redirected the question to them, and they answered: "Initiative in many areas, starting with the economy, civil rights, equality, freedom of speech, political organization and action, freedom of conscience, conviction in politics."

For these university students, many of whom have lost their belief in socialism as theory and as social system, existentialism holds an interest because freedom is central for this philosophy. An undergraduate student said of his fellow students, "Each one of us has his or her own philosophy of the individual. It is not Marxism or religion. Many of my friends believe life is absurd—as for Camus and Heidegger." After some of us attended a performance of Leonid Andreev's play *Thou Shalt Not Kill*, which dramatized the question of freedom and destiny, a student remarked that it was existential, situating the human problem of faith like Karl Jaspers "at the boundary of life and death."

But the movement from socio-centric attitudes and values toward an egocentric world view worries many, especially those of the older generations. "We are losing our unique spirit of collectivity, grabbing or seeking immediate material goods," said a graduate student devoted to the Slavophiles. "People are like naive children believing that if we go to the market economy, we will be rich like the West." She noted that in Holland and England, for example, capitalism developed gradually from the 1600s over a long period and that in the beginning people were religious, honest, trusting, and thrifty, not greedy and selfish. "But if we go to the free market, we'll be selfish and competitive and materialistic, and the result will be chaos."

In the nineteenth century, the Slavophiles, in opposition to the Westernizers, put forward the central concept of *sobornost,* which Sergei Bulgakov defined as "the liberty in love which united believers" and which was said to distinguish the Russians and the Orthodox Church from the institutional authoritarianism of the Roman Catholics and the divisive individualism of the Protestants. Some Marxists I talked with believe that this accent on collectivity is basic to the character of the Russian culture, though distorted now by the theory and practice of socialism. "It is necessary to create a modern collectivity," said one, "developing individuality, responsibility, and decision-making. We cannot save the personal self in *sobornost;* salvation must come through a unity out of responsible individual behavior in everyday life and socialist collectivism."

Perhaps the Anarcho-Syndicalists manifest this movement from the social to the individual most sharply. An editor of *Obshchina* has said that his party does not want to eliminate state power but to redistribute it, with power residing at the bottom and not the top. Ministries would be abolished and self-financing economic centers set up in various regions. The state must give up all control over the means of production, turning it over to the individual working people at the grassroots.

In response to new conditions, scholars are now paying attention to the role of the individual in history, a problem about which Marxists have long argued. Assessing the place of Gorbachev in Soviet society, a veteran scholar at the University said,

> Eventually we would have had a change in our economy, but Gorbachev's election hastened it. It is this particularity of history, this personal factor, that our laws and predictions can't take account of—and never will. This state of affairs is like the three-body problem that Newton proved can't be solved. We might say Gorbachev was a miracle sent by God. Our leadership said and believed consistently that in the event of a war with the United States, we would win. But Gorbachev was the first among our leaders to say that no one would win and all would lose. So if he had not appeared, we might have had a war. And that would have been the end of everything.

(4) *From the objective toward the subjective.* Some traditional philosophy has asserted the reality and value of the human subject and human thinking, regarding the environing world of society and nature as secondary or even illusory. Over against this view, Marxism staked out the claim of objectivism—contending in the spirit of science that the material world is prior to our arrival on the scene and that the objective powers and laws of nature strongly determine our life and consciousness and must be understood if we are to survive and freely create our lives in accordance with our needs.

Today, with the erosion of belief in socialism and Marxism, many people question the objectivism of Marxism and have turned to the subjective and human factor in personal and social life. Perestroika, in fact, makes the human factor basic to the creation of a new society; and glasnost has sanctioned the right of people to explore and express the feelings, ideas, ideals, and symbols of their subjective worlds. Hence the efflorescence of the arts and a new interest in the questions and values of religion as ways of meeting the demands of our private and personal lives.

So I asked my students why their fellow students at the university turned out in such large audiences to hear evangelists from the United States like John Maizel and Josh MacDowell—Protestant fundamentalists who preached on the campus when I was there.

The students, they answered, are curious to see and hear typical Americans, for they seldom have the opportunity; they are attracted by "the exotic" and "the forbidden"; they want a cheap copy of the Bible, which ordinarily costs one hundred rubles or more here; and some of them are in search of a faith.

Religious faith as traditionally understood and carried out in Russian history is a polar opposite Marxism. It is the cultivation of subjective feelings and images, centered on a state of mind rather than on the outside world. As one Orthodox student said, it is "concerned with salvation of the person and forgiveness of sins." When another declared, "We shouldn't speak about God; God is not an object outside of us," and another interpreted religion to be "a search for a personal God," for a divine being continuous with one's individual personality. My mind flashed back to my classroom at home where I was hearing the same chorus of religious subjectivism from my students.

In matters philosophical, these young people seem to have been starved for the nutrition of the imagination, for the "adventures of ideas," for the freedom to climb the mountains of various "world hypotheses," for the liberation of spirit that comes with firm comprehensive beliefs about the self, others, society, history, and nature, and one's place, duty, and destiny in the scheme of things—national, international, planetary, and cosmic. Marxism has had positions on such questions. But in this society, for various reasons, the institutions have not developed to nurture these needs. The people of the U.S.S.R. have borne the unrelenting burdens of the years—civil war, massive sacrificial labor, totalitarian terror and death, the toll of the Nazi invasion, the deprivations and stresses of the Cold War, the economic crisis of the last twenty years. Through such history Marxists have concentrated on making the command economy work and, in social and political affairs, on austere adherence to the historical doctrines of Marx, Engels, and Lenin. The result, in intellectual inquiry and institutional life, has been a neglect of the needs and interests of the unique individual personality. (The problem of the lonely and alienated personality amidst large impersonal structures seems to be common to all developed industrial societies.)

Into this equation of change, of retreat from the objective world of social construction to the private world of feeling and meaning, must be figured the factor of fatigue. Many people are tired of struggling with food shortages, long lines, the scarcity and poor quality of consumer goods, cramped housing, crowded buses, worsening public services, limited opportunities for leisure, and the almost impenetrable and parasitic bureaucracy. So they seek relief in the inner world of the soul—in the arts, in religion, in new ideas, in substance abuse and crime (both rapidly increasing), in dreams of emigration and a new start in life. In the past, people dreamed of emigration to the land of paradise in the afterworld; today, the dream is directed to a paradise (imagined) on Earth—the United States, Canada, Australia, New Zealand, Western Europe, Israel.

Yet while people are tired physically and spiritually and there is a malaise of spirit among youth, most carry on, sustained by a toughness that through history has inured them to hard knocks and neediness. A professor of philosophy pointed out to me that in spite of the heavy load of incompetent and lazy bureaucrats that the society must bear—there are eighteen million of them, plus their families—"many people still work hard and will always work hard according to their natures. They are our saviors—they work like Sisyphus." He was teaching a voluntary course for students at the Moscow Conservatory. "The students here," he said, "are highly specialized, hardworking, disciplined, and sacrificial. To enter for study, they must survive severe competition. For my class at 2:00 p.m. they come tired, having risen early and worked through the day. The paradox is that to enrich others with their art, they make themselves poor, deprived of a well-rounded life for themselves." I think we can take this as a parable whose point applies generally to the people of the U.S.S.R. throughout their history. People have sacrificed themselves on the altar of hard work for others.

At the same time the sense of individuality has suffered. The self of sensuous enjoyment and abandonment, of meditation and self-awareness; the self that savors the simple pleasures of food, clothes, and a comfortable dwelling; the self of inner images, subtle feelings, ideals, contemplation, memory, imagination, and reverie—these have not been particularly favored in social arrangements. The independent self of initiative, self-sufficiency, and autonomy in action, for which perestroika is calling, is sometimes like a fledgling yet to take wings, confined within the cozy collective nest of the central command economy.

"Our most serious crisis," said one observer, "is the destruction of the ideological or spiritual influence—because we have had no development of personal consciousness." This of course is an exaggeration—for he, like others, speaks out of a developed consciousness. Self-awareness, he meant, is better developed in the West. He had been impressed by an eleven-year-old American girl who, when I asked her what her self is, had replied, "My body, my mind, and my soul." Such a level of self-awareness, he believed, would be rare in the Soviet Union. But what he and his fellow intellectuals do not recognize is that the stamp that acquisitive, capitalist society puts on the self is one of "possessive individualism," narcissism, and consumerism; in an intensely competitive world, people must awake to themselves and that world and live by their wits if they are to survive and enjoy the amenities of "the good life" promised them by the sexy sirens of advertising.

Today with the country's borders open to all foreigners and the internal barriers to ideas down, educated people are rushing toward ideas and practices that give hope of filling their psychological needs. Members of the Central Committee of the CPSU engage psychologists as consultants. American psychologists conduct seminars. Werner Erhard of EST fame and wealth has led several classes in Moscow—at his usual high prices. Dale Carnegie's bestseller of the 1930s, *How to Win Friends and Influence People,* is available; I found a student reading it. The newly printed books in philosophy that are popular are those directed to the very concrete, individual, and personal. And of course the evangelical religion of the Protestant West and the mysticism of the East appeal to persons in need of security, love, and peace.

(5) *From the material toward the spiritual.* The society of the U.S.S.R. is in the throes of a double crisis: the crisis of an economy that does not adequately provide the material and cultural necessities of the populace and a moral and spiritual crisis. It is true that, as one scholar said, "Survival is the number one problem. Most people are not interested in socialism. They are concerned about everyday problems like buying enough food to put on the table." But lurking behind the anxious and unending search for food and clothing are the haunting questions about the future of socialism, the hazards of a market economy, the uncertainties of the future for self and family and society, and the meaning of life. Both the grandparents and older parents, who built the industrial and agricultural base of the socialist order, sacrificed everything to defend it against the devastating Nazi invasion, and gave up the best years of their lives to reconstruct the country after the war, are now moved to ask: "Is this the promised end?" Likewise the youth in the university and the young parents brought up to expect that the material and cultural goals of socialism would be consummated for them in their own time, now find themselves nearly empty-handed, facing a bleak future. A young parent said to me: "For nearly a century we couldn't carry out the most simple tasks, such as providing bread

and butter for each person. So the students are right when they tell you, 'Don't tell us about Marxism. Give us bread.' Young people feel deceived. 'You promised us,' they say, 'but you didn't deliver.'" This sense of betrayal cuts deeply into the believing spirit of the youth.

This is a crisis of belief, of conviction, of trust. The irony of the social system is that it is now the victim of its own success. The Brezhnev period of the 1960s was one of relative recovery and prosperity. But in the early 1970s signs of economic stagnation appeared—a widening gap between the world's advanced nations and the Soviet economy—in income growth rate, efficiency of production, quantity and quality of products, scientific and technological development, and advanced technology, all connected with overemphasis on gross output at the expense of capital construction and quality, and excessive expenditures on the production of raw materials and energy and on bureaucracy, fraternal assistance to other countries, and the military.

So there is a common tendency to blame socialism for all the ills of society and to repudiate it out of hand. But people confuse a certain Soviet deviant version of socialism with what the classics of socialist thought actually stated. To explain the fact that for so long many people, sincere believers and faithful followers of the leadership, were idealistic and abstract in their conception of socialism, people frequently used the term "utopian" to describe Marxism-Leninism. Some claimed that the Russian character for centuries prior to the Bolshevik revolution was religiously idealistic, deeply in need of a belief in an ultimate meaning for history, a salvific vision. "The essential Russian consciousness is eschatological, so that the world will be changed for the people from beyond by a savior." Thus the people looked to the Communist Party, to Stalin, and to Gorbachev. While some of my informants did not accept the proposition of popular messianism (attributing it to intellectuals), it seems clear that for a long time most people believed in socialism and the Party as its standard bearer, relying on them to bring them a progressively better life. Inherent in this faith was an element of dependency and passivity, which for some analysts was a major cause of stagnation since the 1970s and which lingers on as "the stagnation of perestroika." The passivity has been reinforced by the disillusionment with a very ambitious vision—with some considerable achievement—of what life might be. Although Marx and Engels wrote against the "utopian socialists," faulting them for not starting from the material world in their theory and practice, they took over their optimism, the belief in unending progress, and the utopianism of the Enlightenment—the dream of "the heavenly city of the 18th century philosophers." But that dream has crashed against the brutal realities of poverty, backwardness, war, Cold War, and a Draconian political system. Yet it has not been destroyed; the framework of the dream remains.

To explain this fall, this fading of hope, people go back in history to 1917 and before. Among some there is now a spontaneous sympathy for the tsar and his family and a condemnation of their cruel treatment by the revolutionaries. There is a lot of Bolshevik bashing; the Bolsheviks are now reappraised by some as barbarians, destroyers of culture. A philosopher mentioned a recently published letter of Bukharin, written in 1924, showing him to be "an utter cynic," an intellectual who called Russia "the Big Mud" and who hated the villages and countryside. But in the opinion of some sociologists with whom I talked, the media, especially journals like *Moscow News*, have carried the process of iconoclasm to an extreme. One of them compared the Soviet press to the press during the Chinese Cultural Revolution, when it incited the Red Guards to violent attacks on authority and tradition.

Many critics lament the abrupt break with all Russian tradition after the Bolsheviks took power. As they interpret history, all institutions of the past that defined and gave coherence to Russian history and culture were to be superseded sooner or later by the culture and morality of the working class. Family, school, neighborhood, relations at the workplace and on the farm, politics, the arts, religion—all would be created anew by a proletarian culture. But, according to critical theory, such creation was impossible. For centuries the Russians had found guidance and coherence in living by means of their religious tradition and culture. Shaped by this undeveloped, pre-capitalist culture, they knew nothing of clear class differentiations, specialized labor, personal autonomy, state law for the regulation of interpersonal transactions, political democracy, and moral norms that cut across class lines. So when in 1917–1918 religious hegemony collapsed after the Bolsheviks assumed the reins of government, people did not know how to behave. Their God became "naked," and "the naked God led to nihilism." Communist morality moved into the vacuum, but it did not take hold because it was abstract and idealistic and not grounded in the everyday habits and customs and traditions of the people. A philosopher summarized the situation in this way:

> The root of our trouble is our lack of spirituality *(dukhovnost)*. The "new man" in the Soviet Union was superficial, with no roots in tradition and history, lacking in spirit and unconnected with eternal values, lacking in conscience *(sovest)*. After the revolution of 1917 the ground was clear and the working class became the bearer of the new morality. But it had no historical roots, no deep foundation. Morality became stupid and criminal. People believed that we are what our immediate relations make us. The result was vulgar Marxism. As a political theory Marxism became simple and vulgar: first, meet the material needs of the people with food, etc., and then add culture for the soul. But the CPSU was concerned not with meeting the people's needs but with ideological cleanness and the struggle against the doubters of ideology.

Another philosopher gave a similar but somewhat different account of the origins of Soviet socialism. In 1917, he said, socialism started from "the deep inherited psychological set of the Russians, exemplified in the Russian Orthodox Church, the conservatives, and the mentality of the peasants." He believed that Lenin recognized this fact but did not analyze it or weigh it heavily. "He and the other Bolsheviks tended to be too theoretical and not concrete and historical. But the mentality of the people remained backward—authoritarian, obedient, ruthless, subjective."

"So," he continued, "between the high, abstract theory of socialism and the everyday habits of people a state system of administrative command grew up to govern social life." His conclusion was that "socialism as a theoretical system and an ideal came too soon to Russia because the deep and needed psychological state of attitudes, values, beliefs, habits, and customs were not in place to enable it to succeed."

Those who still adhere to Marxism and socialism and want to make them apply to present circumstances argue either (a) that the theory was misconstrued in the U.S.S.R. or (b) that Marx's work was a critique of Western European capitalism describing the sources of the self-negation of private property within well-developed capitalist society—and that in Russia in 1900, 80 percent of the peasants had no private property (except a poor hut and cow)—and that therefore the theory even when correctly understood could not be applied.

(6) *From a centrally planned society to a distribution of power.* This means a shift from a central administrative control of economy to local autonomy, from central economic dictation to a free market, whether, unregulated or regulated, from the monopoly of one party in politics to a multiparty system, from autocracy to parliamentary democracy, from purely theoretical science and technology to their productive application in industry, commerce, and agriculture, from stagnation in the differentiation of work skills to highly developed professionals, from the absence of firm and enforced laws to the establishment of a strict legal system that protects human rights and adjudicates in accordance with justice the conflicting relations between individuals.

To describe their ideal society, many intellectuals commonly use the term "civil society," particularly those who have been in the West and can compare the standard of living and culture with their own. There is a certain sense of inferiority and envy toward the West, a distress that they have fallen behind, and a resolve to change things. One of them said to me, "We are outsiders, not members of civilization."

While most people support most of the shifts now in process, many are apprehensive about the egoism and chaos that a free market would bring—

though at the same time they are fearful of an authoritarian tendency from the right evident in the monarchists, conservative Orthodox believers, neo-Stalinists, militarists, extreme nationalists like members of *Pamyat,* and others. The Yeltsin team wants an economy that, in the words of a centrist, "would lead to a seventeenth and eighteenth century capitalism of robbery"—privatizing property and legalizing the extensive shadow economy already in place and giving amnesty to the mafia, said to control fifteen to twenty percent of the economy. Some of the extremists on the left consider the Communists to be criminals and want them brought to court for trial.

A proponent of the "mediate, creative way" told me: "We can't copy the West. We must find our own way by the historical creativity of the people themselves. There is no *a priori* model." Another said, "To follow the model of the West is not for us—never. If we follow it we will get class war. There are no prospects for capitalism here. The free market will be a disaster. It is necessary to renew the socialist concept, but it must be a universal model for the decisions of all. Yet the working class does not have the education for holding power. The Western way will disintegrate Russia. We will get thirty-three independent small republics fighting for many decades. The present governments of Europe and the U.S.A. understand this. They need Russia as a great power. But our democrats don't understand it. Therefore, we need now an ideology in the traditional national style. The state needs it. It is our only link between people." He envisages a new form of socialism growing out of Russian customs and values.

Likewise, somewhere between the liberal centrists who favor a regulated free market and the extreme right-wing authoritarians stand the members of the Communist Party of the Russian Federation, described as the left-wing of the CPSU. Formed in June 1990 they number two million in a CPSU of almost nineteen million and have held three congresses. They want to transform socialism, eliminating the bureaucratic system and creating a democratic party. They would develop an economy of, by, and for the workers, not for the *nomenklatura,* maintaining the workers' social security and reviving the soviets (councils) as organs of the working people. Elections in the Party and government would be carried out by delegates from the unions, collectives, plants, and farms, the organizations at the lower levels electing delegates to the higher levels.

As for the whole CPSU, its strength and continuance are problematic. One estimate is that 75–80 percent of its members are ready to leave it, and a longtime member of the Party described the present membership as "social-democratic."

(7) *From the future toward the concrete and historical.* A commonly voiced criticism of the Communist Party and its leaders for more than seventy years

is that it was abstractly oriented to the future, not fully aware of the concrete problems of the present, and arbitrarily cut off from the past. Several of my friends excoriated the Bolsheviks, not excluding Lenin, for a naive, blind, and total rejection of Russian history and the illusory dream that a viable society could be built from scratch. "In 1917 and thereafter we made the mistake of destroying all our past and starting afresh."

Marxism was founded on an unswerving faith in progress—its heritage from the Enlightenment. At the same time, as someone pointed out, the Orthodox Church promised an ideal society in the future. "But," he said, "now we have a crisis in ideology, for we crushed the ideology of Stalin and what ideology can we believe?" The promised future has not arrived. One of the students said to me, "We are opposed to the teaching of a belief in progress. Most of our generation do not believe in it."

In this mood of disappointed hope, many have turned to their past—Russian history before 1917—for stability, guidance, and solace. They have reexamined and reappraised the Russian Orthodox tradition, the Slavophiles (Kireyevsky, Khomyakov, Samarin, Aksakov), Dostoevsky, Soloviev, Berdyaev, Frank, and, among others, Bakunin and Shestov. For some, this turn backward engenders nostalgia toward a time when things were orderly and secure—the period of Stalin, the period of the tsars, the period of Peter the Great, the period when Orthodoxy was in its power and glory. In philosophical inquiry also, nostalgia has revived questions that transcend particular times and are of permanent concern to people—questions that Marxists often considered meaningless or irrelevant or did not, in the critical view, adequately address—grave personal decisions, anxiety, loss, and grief, the feeling of alienation and meaninglessness, human destiny, the spiritual dimension of history, beyond the economic and political, the person in the ecological order, death, deity.

Many, especially those of the generation who came to maturity at the time of Khrushchev (they are now middle-aged) as well as the young adults in their twenties and thirties, feel that they have waited too long for "the future." During a seminar on love, a woman professor who had served in the Great Patriotic War told the students, among other things, that one's love should be devoted to future generations. At this point my interpreter, a young woman professor, perhaps thirty years old, could not resist turning to me and commenting, "Too many people here have sacrificed to the future under an illusion, and now they have nothing. Life ought to have its meaning here and now."

There is another reason why people do not want to orient themselves to the future. The future is uncertain, and they are afraid of it. Some believe it will be torn by strife, as society lurches from one extreme to another, unable to find a middle way of stability. Said one person, "All efforts and claims of civilian peace and consensus in order to preserve the wholeness of the state are like cries in the desert."

(8) *From enthusiastic idealism toward pragmatic realism.* "The Russian mentality is total; the Western mentality is partial, pragmatic, and concrete." So said a scholar of Russian history. It was his view that the break in continuity with past Russian history at the time of the 1917 revolution holds an important lesson for understanding the strayed course of socialism and for grasping what needs to be done now to correct that course. His idea was that Marx's theory of historical evolution and the emergence of socialism presupposes an economy of capitalism that is highly developed economically, politically, and culturally. In the early hours of the October revolution, it seems, the Bolsheviks had an opportunity to work with the Mensheviks, but some of them fell to quarreling with them, and the opportunity was lost. (It is known that throughout his life Lenin harbored a deep distrust for the liberals.) Thus, the possibility of a gradual development of socialism out of the foundations of a rapidly growing private economy, political liberalism, and an advancing culture was passed by. Large numbers of intellectuals were exiled and liquidated, and the new socialist system was deprived of their skills and experience. Still, after the NEP started, the scholar observed, Lenin realized the need to change, and early in 1923 he expressed his views in his last three articles—"On Cooperation," "Our Revolution," and "Better Less, But Better."

According to this assessment, the policy of the Bolsheviks was impossibly idealistic. It was not rooted in the existing economy or in the concrete needs, habits, and values of the great masses. It succeeded only at enormous material and human cost. Fervor for motherland and socialism carried the society through the Five Year Plans, the forced collectivization, the persecution, the Great Patriotic War, and the postwar reconstruction. But in the early 1970s leaders became increasingly aware of a crisis in the economy, and some of the dissidents warned that society had lost its way.

Belief in the future, whether the future is seen as secular or otherworldly, whether to be realized gradually or abruptly, is sustained by an ongoing tide of enthusiasm and optimism. Russian religion and philosophy have been permeated by romanticism and idealism. True, the Westernizers took up the materialist viewpoint, but they too believed in the future, as did the Slavophiles and Marxists. And this meant a comprehensive, unified point of view that in principle solved everything—or most things—without recourse to the indignity of dealing with the conditions of everyday life. This tradition has been sharply different from that of the West, which has been more pluralistic, empirical, and utilitarian—characteristics associated with the long development of science and capitalism. When Marxism merged with this tradition, the result was a mixture that neither Russians nor Marxists would have wished or foreseen.

In a peculiarly rich and not always consistent way, Marx had combined the organicism of the tradition of Rousseau and Hegel with the individualism and mechanism of the British tradition of Bacon and Adam Smith. He brought together the dramatic, historic idealism of Hegel with the practical observation and generalization of empirical science. Like Plato, he was convinced that the world of nature, society, and history is governed by form and law, but he also adopted the Aristotelian view that particular things develop toward their natural ends, Marx believed in what George Catlin has called an "ideal, voluntary community," a Platonic and Hegelian model for political society. But at the same time he shared the eighteenth-century democratic faith in individuals, their cooperation, and their common decision-making whose coercive state would guarantee the liberties of one and all but would not impose its ideal on any. He mixed the communitarian and libertarian models, idealism and realism, voluntarism and consensual state coercion.

In the tradition of Russian idealism, Lenin responded positively to both the idealism of Hegel and the attempt by Marx to transform the idealistic dynamism of Hegel onto a materialist base. He wrote that it is impossible to understand Marx's *Capital* completely without understanding the whole of Hegel's *Logic*. But while Lenin grasped the imperative need for the creation of democracy among individual workers in the new state, he did not live long enough to lead in the securing of democratic practices on a firm and widespread foundation. The result was that, under conditions of economic and cultural backwardness, the demand for massive and rapid development of industry and agriculture, and later the threat of invasion, a highly abstract and static Hegelianism came to dominate Marxism among many leaders who had inherited a monistic view of history and who, unlike Marx, had little knowledge or appreciation of democracy.

Thus the assertion that "the Russian mentality is total; Western mentality is partial, pragmatic, and concrete," while in need of qualification, points to a significant difference in the two traditions. The forward-looking Russians now want to change that.

But they realize that they cannot easily change long established cultural habits. For example, Moscow State University in the near future will probably become autonomous, cut off from all or much of its subsidies from the state. How will its administrators, faculty, and other staff cope with the problems of drawing up a budget, raising revenues, fixing expenditures, employing faculty and other personnel, establishing working conditions and salaries, and the many other tasks for making this huge institution viable? Realism, good judgment, efficient organization, and creative, flexible managerial skills are needed. But these qualities have not been adequately developed under the old hierarchical, bureaucratic system.

The attraction of Marx's thought was and still is its economic explanation of social inequality, namely, the extraction of surplus value by the capitalists from the workers, and the revolutionary proposition that if the workers seize control of the instruments of production this source of inequality can be abolished and social justice can prevail. A high ranking Communist, now chastened and critical, explained: "Looking at Marx's theory of surplus value, we Communists proceeded to organize production and distribution without any notion that our plans were not to be found in the works of Marx. We thought that simply by doing away with the capitalist management of production, we would do away with exploitation. But we didn't succeed. And when at last we looked into Marx's works, it was clear that he had offered no concrete observations on how to run a socialist society. But Marx and Engels did not see the state as a possible exploiter. Why? Because the workers would be the statesmen, and because the administration of the state would be impersonal."

This distance between humanistic theory and all-too-human practice has deformed both the material and psychological sides of economic relations. One faculty member who is a new chair of his department has found it very hard to introduce changes because his colleagues have grown content to do a minimum of work and to draw their salaries. Their jobs are guaranteed by the system. As an interviewee said,

> We have many administrative workers like secretaries, but they don't want to work and don't know how. But why should they? A secretary is paid only 100 rubles a month. The gasoline for my car costs more than that. So we need material incentives, making for competition. It's not a matter of equipment but of bureaucratic mentality that pervades all spheres of our life—passivity and the expectation that the state will take care of people's security in their jobs. Moreover, because of the absence of objective laws to regulate personal behavior in economic relations, the bureaucratic system fills the vacuum and runs the economy and social relations. The individual person is thus at the mercy of the bureaucratic system. To survive the person must find a place in it. Many people are superbly clever at finding ways of not working. But I think that some people are working and producing foodstuffs and other commodities now as they did before the shortages. Anything can be bought here—it only takes time, chance, and money. For example, one can speed up the granting of a visa to Germany by paying 100 to 200 rubles. The result is that our society is reduced to an exchange economy—but not of the capitalist kind. But even the bureaucrats are not clear on what must be done to change this.

People obtain goods by bribes, barter, exchanges with relatives and friends, state-granted privileges (as given by law to war veterans, for example), contacts with the southeastern republics where produce is grown, and foreign currency shops (if they have been able to wangle the currency).

In the present situation it is no longer an academic question of choosing between idealism and practicality. Except for a small though growing privileged class of conspicuously wealthy—there are said to be now 140,000 millionaires—circumstances are compelling people to scramble to get food and other necessities for life. The average housekeeper spends perhaps two hours a day in lines at shops—unless she has the connections and money to get the goods in expensive shops or through the network of the shadow economy. A housewife in Zagorsk, who works full-time and whose family monthly income is about 800 rubles, told me she does not have the time to stand in line to buy inferior food, so she spends half the family income on food of high quality. At university cafeterias and restaurants, one can buy a full dinner for one to one and a half rubles. But fifty-five million retired persons are said to have fixed incomes of only 60–130 rubles per month. It comes as a surprise to see professors also hustling to earn money—foreign currency especially—in order to supplement a precarious income, to fight inflation, to provide education and housing for their older children, and to make provision for their own and their family's future. Engagement in a joint enterprise with a foreign firm, though risky and hedged about with restrictive laws from the bureaucracy, is one way to do this. One professor, fired for his proposal to introduce new readings (such as Marcuse, Sartre, and feminism) into a curriculum on Marxism, was doing this.

Economic strain stirs emotions of anxiety, anger, hatred, resentment, and scapegoating. Thus the strife of nationalities with one another is both effect and cause of the general economic and ideological turmoil. Antagonisms between different nations are longstanding. They are rooted in the historic relation of Russian imperialism to the smaller, dominated nationalities and in traditional religious animosities—as the Azerbaijan Muslims against the Russian Orthodox. These antagonisms have been revived in the current economic crisis. An historian told me that the nationalistic revolts today are in reality revolts against the rich by people suffering from economic inequities. He maintained that in national policy the Russian people are not to blame. For the Russian republic, thirty percent of industrial profit goes to the Union government, while for the other republics only ten percent of their trade income is paid. In the export of fruit to the Russian, Ukrainian, and Byelorussian republics, the southern republics, holding a complete monopoly against foreign competition, are able to charge such high prices that they cost the individual consumer fifty rubles per month. The Union price of potatoes, grown in Russia, is ten *kopeks* per kilo, while in the north the price for oranges grown in the south is two rubles (twenty times the price of potatoes). So people blame the

Jews for this problem. Again, Uzbekistan sells melons to Russia at two to three rubles per kilo and buys oil from Russia at twenty-four rubles per ton, about one-tenth the world market price. As a result of favorable quotas for the admission of non–Russians to Russian universities, the percentage of Russians with a higher education is now in fact very low compared with that of the other nationalities. Old nationalistic prejudices have surfaced in response to these conflicts.

Every informed person I talked with believed that the republics should become sovereign if they so choose, though people agreed that all are and will be closely interdependent economically. No less significant is the fact that twenty percent of all marriages in the Union are between persons of different nationalities, and sixty million persons (in a population of about 290 million) live outside their own national borders. So to be realistic, any national policy if it is to succeed must take account of the economic and cultural internationalism that is already embedded in and between geographic regions.

Conclusion

Far-reaching changes in the moral and spiritual outlook of the Soviet people have occurred in the last decade. When I was teaching at Moscow State University in the fall of 1980, I found the students to be respectful toward authority, idealistic, optimistic, and, while critical, relatively well satisfied with their society, their personal lot in life, and their future. Few expressed the desire to emigrate. They were fearful of a nuclear holocaust and hopeful about the prospects of peaceful coexistence. Today these qualities have greatly diminished, and some seem to have turned into their opposites. Some students are skeptical toward all authorities, and all are skeptical toward some authorities— political, religious, economic, academic, etc. It is open season on "ruling circles" and the received opinion from Marxism and socialism. Anger and scorn toward Soviet history have exploded. While pessimistic would be too strong a description of all students, I discovered none who would be called optimistic in the 1980 sense of that term—and none who was fully satisfied with his or her conditions and prospects. Many entertained the fantasy of emigration—an unthinkable possibility in 1980. No student mentioned the danger of nuclear holocaust and the need for peaceful coexistence. Students feel either that, given the U.S.A.-U.S.S.R. detente and disarmament policy, the threat of holocaust has disappeared, or—more probable, I think—that the threat is insignificant relative to other issues. Socialism in theory and practice, more or less accepted in 1980, is now a target under passionate attack by many and is openly criticized by most of those still committed to it. Such criticisms, however, especially by the youth, do not always sort out the achievements from the failures; and the "social guarantees" of education, medical care, vocational preparation, employment, accessible culture, and the rest are mutely taken for granted.

Some attitudes, beliefs, and values of the students have not changed. Students are still curious about foreigners and foreign countries, with a special friendliness toward Americans. They are eager to travel abroad and relatively tolerant of bureaucracy (though now much more critical). They are commencing to reflect on the issues of human rights, democracy, sexuality, and gender roles.

What of the future? If the course of history outside the U.S.S.R. does not suffer any catastrophic changes, the people of the U.S.S.R. have a chance to avoid the Scylla and Charybdis of chaos and repression and to find their own creative way to reconstitute a seriously disturbed and disordered society. The preeminent question is: Can the people make socialism work? Can they mobilize their collective will and create the democratic machinery in political and economic life needed to construct a cooperative commonwealth with liberty and justice for all?

What is being tested now is both the theory of socialism and its application in everyday life. In its most general and human form, the theory is that the altruistic impulses and actions of people can subordinate the selfish ones. Some critics of socialism—who adopt the theory of psychological and ethical egoism—believe that the failures of Soviet socialism are proof once again that socialism is founded on a false view of human nature. They believe people are and ought to be selfish rather than altruistic. The idealistic dream of socialism, they contend, has failed repeatedly in the past and is destined to fail in the future. The conflict now raging in the souls of thoughtful persons in the Soviet Union is this one between the two doctrines: individual impulses versus social ones, privatization of property versus public ownership, egoism versus altruism. At the moment, many are leaning away from public ownership because they have concluded it has failed and is unworkable.

This same conflict has persisted throughout Western history since the first-century Christians "had all things in common" (Acts 2:44) and set themselves apart from the self-centered secularism of the Roman Empire. Later, monks like the Benedictines formed communities with shared property and goods. From the eleventh century onward the rise of new cloth industries, commerce, and cities brought a challenge to the agricultural economy of feudalism with the Church as the chief landowner. Caught between these two conflicting systems of exploitation, the unemployed and the working poor in city and countryside turned to ideologies that promised freedom from sufferings—to the Waldenses, Cathari and Albigenses, Beghards, Lollards, and others. The great ideal of these religious revolutionaries was a version of the biblical dream of one single society of equals, united by the principles of justice, fraternity, and freedom, a society free of domination and exploitation by individuals and classes. The economic base for this was to be communal property.

Unable to tolerate the threat of the new industrial and commercial classes and the popular movements allied with them, the Church declared these ideologies to be heresies. In southern France it wiped out the Albigenses in a bloody crusade. But so powerful was the pull of the idea of communal property that even groups within the Church like the Franciscan Spirituals took it up. In 1323 Pope John XXII found it necessary to condemn "the stark ideal of a propertyless perfection" (as R. W. Southern has called it) and to declare "the doctrine of complete poverty of Christ and his disciples heretical." The Church had put its stamp of approval on private ownership, the foundation of the post-feudal system that in time would grow into capitalism and dominate the modern world. Church hierarchy thus rejected the cornerstone of the early Christian community—common property. Yet the struggle for common property continued among the people and expanded throughout the Protestant Reformation—in the Taborites, Anabaptists, Diggers, Levellers—and down through the utopian communities of the eighteenth and nineteenth centuries and into the socialist revolutions of the twentieth century.

According to my Moscow sources, the Bolsheviks held this stark ideal of a propertyless perfection. Perhaps so. But perfection did not materialize. The state property, the fruit of the total appropriation of the old private property—in land, industry—was not turned over to the people for possession, control, and management. It fell into the hands of a political party that in turn appropriated it for their own private use. Even so, people created a system that secured the needs of survival and development for large masses: food, clothing, housing, health care, education, jobs, culture, equal opportunity, recreation, and pension.

The present social situation is fraught with danger and opportunity. A January 1991 letter from a scholar in Moscow, still a socialist, summarizes it in this way:

> Morally and physically life in Moscow is getting to be more difficult and uncertain. Leadership is shifting to the right. Privatization of the party and the state looks like a long-range process. Partocrats are going to be capitalists but for them it is harder than for feudalists to be businessmen. Gorbachev's transformation of the party-state apparatus into something capitalist has slowed down. It's really a hard job for him. "Ruling circles" do not feel any need to change their position in policy, economy, and so I am afraid that three major forces—the people (consumers), the hardline bureaucracy (plus generals and the military-industrial complex), and the mafia (real underground and semi-legal business) will not wait. They are trying to undertake steps which will lead to

rebellion and finally to the new dictatorship with overwhelming elements of national–Bolshevism and small elements of authoritarianism. But now the general feeling is one of fear, expectation, apathy and black humor. And in spite of all this I believe that we will overcome this critical situation. I believe in common sense and the market economy. The last is not a solution, but people have to have bread and butter, and they have to learn how to work well.

Today on the stage of Russian-Soviet history the people in their various factions and parts are enacting a Shakespearean drama. Folly and violence have torn society out of its natural and healthy order of life. Day by day disorder deepens. The mass of people are baffled and seek only the security of daily bread. The forces of individual freedom, in economy and political life, are driving in the direction of chaos and civil strife. The forces of social authority are driving in the other direction toward brutal recrudescent repression. Both, unconsciously or not, are bidding to restore the disrupted social order with fresh blood and violence. The better part of wisdom is to find a sane and nonviolent course toward order and creative stability. But the actors to play this role of reconciliation and peace have yet to appear on the scene.

Coaching Soviet Baseball: Excerpts from a Sociologist's Journal

William J. Byrne III

Over two decades have gone by since I wrote the following account of my five-month experience coaching baseball at Moscow State University (MGU) in the former Soviet Union in 1990. When the International Olympic Committee announced in 1986 that baseball would become a gold medal sport starting in 1992, the Soviets decided that they would try to introduce and develop a baseball program. In the first couple of years of their uncertain efforts to learn the game, coaches from Cuba and Nicaragua had given them some early assistance, and I then tried to expand their knowledge and skills somewhat further, while at the same time studying their larger efforts to develop the new sport.

In the weeks just prior to my leaving for the U.S.S.R. in 1990 the American media showed considerable interest in what I was planning on doing. They portrayed it as a somewhat unlikely project and had a lot of fun writing about it. The *New York Post* carried a story under the headline "Yankee Set to Teach Reds About Baseball," and they wrote that my inability to speak Russian meant that I could not say "Play ball!" or "Strike three!" but that I did have cue cards that in Russian said "Keep the curve ball low" and "Get ahead of the hitters." I was also interviewed on one of the popular New York City morning radio shows. In the Hudson Valley the Middletown *Times Herald Record* and *Poughkeepsie Journal,* as well as other regional papers, carried stories and some of this coverage was picked up by the wire services. The *Times Herald Record,* which was a tabloid, put a large full-color photo of me on the front page, wearing a red and gold lettered CCCP baseball cap, standing in front of a large red Soviet flag, while tossing a baseball in the air and holding a bat, glove and Russian language skills book in my other hand. Inside accompanying the story they had a mock baseball card with my photo on it and a caption reading, "Perestroika All-Star, William Byrne, Position—Pitcher, Professor—Throws right, Thinks left."

Over the next two decades the Russian Federation National team would eventually compete in the European baseball championships and World Cup but never qualify for the Olympic Games. A Russian little league team did make it to the Little League Championship Series in Williamsport, Pennsylvania, in 2002, and 13 Russian baseball players have signed minor league professional contracts in the United States since 1990. Also in 1992 the *Wall Street Journal* published a feature story about a Russian baseball team coached by my friend Valeri Varinsky, who had been an assistant coach at MGU during my time in Moscow. The collapse of the Soviet Union in December 1991 reduced government financial support for the fledging baseball program and slowed its development. Then, in 2005, when the Olympic Committee announced that baseball would no longer be a gold medal sport, the Russian government withdrew financial support for baseball and the future of the game in Russia was evidently threatened.

During my five-month stay in the U.S.S.R. in 1990 I wrote a series of newspaper articles and each time I had to stand in line for over two hours at the telegraph office on Gorky Street in Moscow to use the one fax machine to get my handwritten stories back to America. Now of course it would have simply been done via the Internet.

Communication technology, however, is not all that has changed since my 1990 experience. As it turned out I was an eyewitness to many of the evolving and extraordinary social, economic and political changes that culminated in one of the most momentous historical events of the twentieth century. In order to give the reader a better and more intimate understanding of the social ferment that was occurring at the time of my 1990 experiences, I will describe it through the eyes of a Soviet friend I first met in 1985 and then saw again in 1988 and 1990.

On July 8, 1990, Sasha came to my dorm room at MGU and we talked about the frustrations and fears of the people and the rapidly changing events that were shaking the foundations of the Soviet system. He described his efforts, along with three other workers, to build a house in the country.

> When you have nails you have no hammer, and when you have a hammer you have no nails. When you need a crane the procedure is so complicated you just go to the road and put out your hand like for a taxi and stop a man with a crane. He comes and it is twenty rubles to pick something up and twenty rubles to put it down. When you need materials you go to the materials place and there are none, so you go to the other place and the man will sell you what you need without any thought about the owners, whether state owned or a cooperative, and

you put it in your car. But the militia will stop your car and ask for papers of sale, and you have none so when you give them your passport you tuck in 50 rubles, and they say "Hmm, OK, no problem," and they put the 50 rubles in their pocket and hand you back the passport and you are on your way. It's very hard to build the house. My friends and I figured out the cost and found that the payoffs amounted to more than the materials.

During the ten years of Soviet involvement in the war in Afghanistan Sasha had been called back to active military service at least twice. Even though the last Soviet troops had left Afghanistan over a year before, he still used strong body language as he talked about the personal pain he suffered from "the terrible mistake of Afghanistan by Brezhnev." Although better now, he said that he had stomach, gum and teeth problems for years after his return because of the terrible water and tropical disease, and that even the medical institutes could not diagnosis it. "Many of our guys did not die from bullets but from disease," he said. The military call-ups also had severe impact on his family life as well as his career at the institute where he had worked himself up to a department head, but while in Afghanistan his position had been taken by others. He said he did not think that the Institute of Marxism-Leninism would even survive because it had been traditionally paid for by the government but now the government was telling the Communist Party of the Soviet Union (CPSU) that they had to foot the bill. Already he said there had been layoffs and there will be more, and unemployment is a reality for the whole staff in the future.

He now had a job paying 400 rubles per month that he got because of old acquaintances and people who knew he was an expert on ethnic and republic nationalities. He was an advisor on these matters for a deputy in the Supreme Soviet but he said that this job would soon end because of ideological differences. He said it was "allowed now to have more than one job" and he actually had five or six part-time jobs. In addition to the one described above he also worked at the Institute of Marxism-Leninism; was teaching "political science," which used to be called "scientific Communism" at MGU and the Institute of Culture; and was trying to create an "initiative" involving a private publishing venture which meant that he was looking for people with money. He sighed and said that "one good job would be better than five or six because I am very tired." In addition he complained that banks may tell you that you can't have your money until next week, and that they are floating your pay check, and even though he had his directly deposited it was not available on pay day. He expressed concern for the masses saying that only 15 percent of Soviet families even have a bank account and that those with incomes of less than 350 rubles per month cannot survive in a free market economy. He added one more comment about banks: "There is a three-day line when you convert rubles to the maximum of $300 that is allowed for Western travel costs, unless of course you pay the militia 100 rubles which will then get you to the front of the line."

Shifting his comments to the economy, he said that economic "shock therapy" would not make good sense and soon lead to chaos. Already by 1991 he said there would be ten million people out of work and the government had no unemployment insurance plan in place. CPSU functionaries will be laid off by the hundreds of thousands and many delegates to the upcoming 28th CPSU Congress are functionaries and they will be making decisions that affect their own jobs. Inflation he said was already 10 percent and by next year it will be 20 percent. Addressing the currency issue he said that Western currency is already being used all over illegally and he suggested a dual system be created during the transition period. A system of "wooden rubles" along with ration cards could be used to get the necessities at state stores for the poor. At the same time "bonus-type rubles," perhaps backed by gold, could be used in free market stores by people who earn enough to afford them. He felt strongly that the coming autumn would be the critical period economically because of the increasing unemployment and rising prices.

Sasha made it clear that he did not like Boris Yeltsin because he was a "populist" with "mental roots into a strong authoritarian system." He could be "dangerous" as he could not abandon his authoritarian beliefs. Mikhail Gorbachev, on the other hand, "should not have given himself only two years as party head as it will not be enough time to produce results," Sasha claimed. He said he feared there would be civil war in many regions as it has already occurred in Armenia and Azerbaijan. He was of the opinion that in many republics they are trying to create "bourgeois independent states" and class divisions would surface and lead to more civil war. He ended his political comments by saying there are currently debates going on within the KGB, the army and virtually everywhere else.

Now in the late winter of 2012, as I re-read my notes of this twenty-two-year-old fascinating conversation with Sasha, I am amazed at how clearly he seemed to have his finger on the pulse of what was happening in the last months of the Soviet Union. His views of Boris Yeltsin were most insightful, as the world would soon discover in late September 1993, when Yeltsin defied the constitution by dissolving the Russian Parliament and ordering the military assault on the Parliament building in early October 1993. I hope this brief insight through the eyes of a "local" into the exciting events of those extraordinary days in 1990 will help the reader of the following article better appreciate the social, economic and political context that surrounded my five-month stint coaching baseball in the former U.S.S.R.

Arrival at Moscow State University, May Day, and Victory Day

It's the second week of May 1990, almost three weeks since my arrival in Moscow by train from Finland, and already my experiences tax my brain's capacity to remember. The MGU coach and a group of players presented me with a bouquet of red carnations at the Leningradski Train Station, and after a teeth-chattering wild dash across the washboard streets of Moscow by car, we arrived at the beautiful Japanese-built baseball stadium which lies in the late afternoon shadow of MGU's main building.

We practiced that afternoon and every day after that except for the May Day and Victory Day holidays. I was coaching the MGU sponsored team that competes in the top level U.S.S.R. league. I initially watched, then made limited suggestions, and then generally seemed to be regarded as the coach of authority, organizing practices and coaching not only the players, but also the coaches. We traveled to a variety of Soviet cities for tournaments. The day I arrived, the team had just returned from Vladivostok, which is almost as far from Moscow as New York.

This is one of the world's largest universities and truly international with several thousand students from foreign countries. Undergraduate and older graduate students, married students with children, and exchange faculty like me live together in these dorms along with more than an occasional cockroach. It was an opportunity to have unlimited daily interaction with the rest of the world. It might be baseball field talk with Cuban students about U.S. policy toward their country, or late evening talk with my Vietnamese friend about what it was like to be a teenage girl in Hanoi during the American bombing, Christmas week 1973, or perhaps elevator conversations with Africans or Russians about my old Brooklyn Dodger cap, Orange County Community College (OCCC) sweatsuit or my strange long, wooden, thin-barreled fungo bat used by coaches to easily hit towering flies to outfielders in practice. It's hard to remain inconspicuous in this get-up as I walk to the stadium. Even MGU security police never ask me for an ID when I return; it seems I am well known.

My arrival coincided with two of the most important Soviet holidays. May Day involved a long festive weekend of parades through Red Square (for the first time no military units) and fireworks. Then May 9 was truly one of the most exciting and simultaneously emotionally moving days of my life. It was Victory Day, the 45th anniversary of the defeat of German fascism in World War II or, as Russians say, the Great Patriotic War. Few Soviet families escaped personal loss, a total of 27 million deaths. In more personal terms, for the young girl from the Ural Mountains across the hall, it was both grandfathers, a grandmother and an uncle.

This was a day to honor the military and its millions of veterans, so it began with two huge military parades through Red Square and on to sunny but windswept Gorky Street to my vantage point. I quickly used up four rolls of film standing among the tens of thousands of people of all ages lining the street as hundreds of Soviet tanks, rocket launchers, armored personnel carriers and trucks loaded with soldiers sitting in neat rows rumbled past.

So here was the famous menacing Red Army that Americans speak of and portray in evil terms, with the tank commanders in their leather motorcycle helmets and jackets and mustaches seen only from the waist up protruding from the turrets. My military historian colleague at OCCC would have been in his glory as the fully decked out generals in jeeps with unit flags flying sped through the swirling exhaust and clattering roar of the tanks.

But a closer look revealed the young teenage faces of the thousands of soldiers from the many European and Asian Soviet Republics, with their shy smiles, wind tousled hair and festive unmilitary-looking waves to the crowds. Many carried colorful balloons and flowers and often daffodils protruded from gun barrels. It was reminiscent of American anti–Vietnam War demonstrations of the 1960s when I saw fellow protesters stuff flowers in National Guard gun barrels in Colorado. After the last tank passed, a large military band appeared and started marching down Gorky Street toward Red Square. At Pushkin Square, which is the location of McDonald's restaurant, they stopped and let more bands in native costumes of the Republics flow out of side streets into Gorky. Then to my surprise I heard a band playing "When the Saints Go Marching In," and out from under the trees hovering over the park came large American and Soviet flags each snapping side by side in the wind, and behind them a drum and bugle corps from an American Legion Post in Waltham, Massachusetts.

My memories rushed back to the winter of 1981–82 and my first visit to Moscow. It was a time of lunatic ranting about "evil empires" and the possibility of "winning a limited nuclear war," and I recalled the chill and depression I felt that bleak winter standing in Red Square. It was then that I became convinced that only people-to-people contact between the two nations could put an end to that type of mentality. Never in my wildest dreams did I think that only eight years later I would be in Moscow coaching baseball and witnessing such a scene unfold in front of a McDonald's in Pushkin Square.

The Russian military band broke ranks and rushed forward and gave a hearty shout of "har-rah-shoh" (very good) and the Waltham band continued down Gorky Street to the tune of "Yankee Doodle Dandy." The Russian band regrouped and marched behind and then the people flooded the street and we all marched down Gorky en masse spilling into the huge square below the Kremlin. The emotion was overwhelming and I felt tears streaming down my cheeks. For the first time in many years of Vietnam and Central American policies that I opposed, I could feel good about "Old Glory" because this day it represented the positive things the American people could produce when free of irrational fears. As the Waltham band disbanded in front of the Bolshoi Theater, they were engulfed in throngs of friendly and grateful Russians, and a number of the American band members were alternately consumed and embarrassed by their own tears.

The remainder of the day the streets and parks were awash with the living monuments of the Great Patriotic War. The veterans, now in the autumn of their lives, gathered everywhere into groups of 10 or 20, often holding aloft small red reunion signs with gold numbers and Cyrillic letters designating their military units. Their chests were covered with medals, some in old uniforms and others in sport coats. Women in their 70s wearing medals, most widows of soldiers, but many veterans of the Red Army themselves, dressed in World War II uniforms with knee-high boots and "overseas" caps straight out of the pages of Life magazine in the early 1940s. They embraced, wept, conversed, received flowers from children, posed for pictures, explained what their medals were for, and sang and danced in small clusters. Often teenage girls happily danced with the aging veterans. Over and over I felt the choking rush of emotion to my chest and throat as I moved from group to group throughout the day. At 10 p.m. all the church and tower bells in the Kremlin rang as they did in 1945, and this was followed by a 360-degree fireworks display around the city of Moscow. Even as midnight approached, hundreds of people still stood silently around the eternal flame and flower-heaped memorial to the Unknown Soldier at the foot of the Kremlin wall.

Baseball Road Trip to Rural Soviet Georgia

This is my 33rd day of coaching baseball in the Soviet Union, and I am beginning to feel the weariness that I see in so many Russians. Our MGU team just completed a ten-day road trip, and yesterday I spent all day hand washing clothes in a small dormitory sink and walking all over the concrete streets of Moscow trying to purchase life's necessities. As so many Soviet women know, these activities are a terrible drain on one's time and energy.

When this team goes on a road trip, it's something that you will find hard to imagine. Not only did we go back into the rural hills of Soviet Georgia, but our journey seemed to take us back in time a couple of centuries. A two-hour and fifteen-minute Aeroflot flight on the tail mounted three engine TU-154 jet liner deposited us near the city of Kutaisi which is about 160 miles west of Tbilisi. When we descended and depressurized as we approached the landing, my feet were suddenly surrounded by a puddle of water that seemed to be coming in through the seams of a nearby exit door. Also, our utility infielder Gleb, who spoke good English, had cautioned me to not let the stewardess see my camera as we made our approach, and that I would soon see why. It was clearly a joint military civilian airbase because out of my window I saw scores of Migs and SU 27s parked along the sides of the runway as we landed. We then took three bus rides southwestward in vehicles that I would have thought only existed as props for Hollywood movies about old Mexico or the Middle East.

At one two-hour layover the people were coming and going with large round loaves of bread, strings of flapping chickens bound for the chopping block, squealing baby pigs in large cloth shopping bags, pails of fruit and grain or large sacks over their shoulders. Many of the women had long black skirts with head wraps and a piece of cloth draped across the face just under the eyes. A group of droopy-eyed, dark-haired, sinister-looking men huddled around some type of gambling device while Middle Eastern–sounding music blared from a loudspeaker and stubby yellow battered buses splashed through the puddle-filled ruts of the bus lot. Standing in the middle of it all with their bats and baseball equipment, dressed in a variety of American or Japanese baseball hats and jackets, were the two other Russian coaches, thirteen MGU baseball players ranging from 20 to 34 years old, and me in my old Brooklyn Dodgers cap. Before boarding the next bus some of our guys bought round loaves of hard crusted bread and ripped them apart so we could all share. While wandering around the area I had come across an ancient looking machine that popped out donut like objects into a bin which they then dusted with powdered sugar. I had one and it was good so I bought a couple of paper bags full and we all shared them while we waited.

On each bus, all seats and standing room were taken by the locals and us, with our baseball equipment and suitcases piled to the right of the driver or on our laps. The pails, sacks and animals often accompanied us and at one time a woman stood squashed against my shoulder and seat carrying a white chicken dangling on a string tied to its legs, sometimes squawking, sometimes flapping its wings so that feathers floated toward the open window. We careened down a series of awful washboard roads, with our horn sometimes blaring to pass a truck or warn a cow, pig, or goat to get off the road. We sped past fields of grape vineyards, tea bushes and fruit trees, as well as many square metal roofed one or two story stone or brick houses all surrounded by grape vines and sturdy fences with big closed metal gates.

We finally arrived at the small town of Vani where the tournament was to be held. From there we headed six more miles up into the foothills of the Caucasus Mountains. The dirt road twisted its way up the sides of the mountain past cliff-like drops of 300 feet with no guard rails, and twice a day for ten days we would travel this route. The vegetation was exotic and subtropical and the snow-capped mountains towered overhead. We finally reached the "health" spa that we were to call home for ten days, a beautiful forested location which included a roaring stream.

Since we had not had a meal for 13 hours, the food that night did not seem so bad. Eight days later, however, it was "Thank God it's Friday," and only four more meals before we left. We got virtually the same meals every day. Chunks of fatty meat in rice or buck wheat covered with greasy gravy for breakfast, lunch, and supper. The bread was OK but the hot tea was full of sugar and you often you had to flick a floating ant or two off the surface because the tables were usually crawling with ants. The best thing was the kasha, a cream of wheat type of cereal that might occasionally appear at any of the day's meals. After about five days I pretty much just existed on bread and tea so I lost considerable additional weight.

There also was no hot water, no showers, no toilet seats and no toilet paper or towels until the eighth day. There were hot tubs for soaking in a detached community building and I sometimes saw our players washing in the ice cold stream. The days were usually sunny and pleasantly warm and the nights were crisp and a bit damp, but the stars seemed unusually close and bright.

We played seven games in eight days with the teams coming from Leningrad, Moscow, Georgia, Kiev, Habarovsk and Tashkent. In Moscow we played on a beautiful artificial turf stadium, the gift of a Japanese college president, and where ground balls took predictable hops. In Georgia the two fields were very rough and a mixture of soccer field and cow pasture. Cows and pigs roamed the sidelines and occasionally would cross the infield requiring the umpires to drive them away. Maybe 60 or 70 townspeople, mostly younger, would sit on the ancient bleachers and laugh and try to figure out what was going on.

All the teams have a sponsor, and all but the two Moscow teams pay their players about 200 rubles per month salary. In most cases that was their only job. That's about $34 per month, a lot less value than received by a United States college scholarship player, so be cautious about any charges of professionalism. The Kiev team was the best in the tournament and last year's (1989) runner-up for the national championship. Kiev would like an invitation to the U.S. and can fly Aeroflot for rubles. However, once in the U.S. they would have no Western currency and would have to be housed, fed, and transported by U.S. groups. I thought maybe my Hudson Valley community would like to do this next spring. They could play local college teams and maybe attend a big league game in New York.

While I had seen our MGU team make significant progress in the first month in response to some of my practice activity changes, this first tournament competition revealed just how much further they needed to improve as we lost our first six games. We were beaten by Georgia A 23 to 11, Leningrad 14 to 13, Georgia B 13 to 3, Kiev 18 to 10, Tashkent 15 to 12 and Habarovsk 6 to 3. Bone headed base running was a major factor in our losses to Leningrad and Habarovsk. The other problem was that while I had significantly improved our pitchers' mechanics, we simply did not have enough pitchers to play seven games in ten days. This meant that they routinely pitched with only one day's rest after throwing over 200 pitches in their previous start. Head coach Halid believed that players can only play the one position that he had assigned them which made it hard to create the versatility our small traveling squad needed. I did get our husky 34-year-old second string catcher, one of our best hitters, into the starting lineup in right field by hitting him about fifty fungo fly balls just prior to a game, and thus proved to Halid that the many repetitions quickly improved his fielding skills. I also worked one night after supper with a big strong-armed, left-handed outfielder who I thought could do some pitching. In half an hour I had him throwing some sliders to go along with his fast ball, but Halid was reluctant to use him in a game.

In the final game of the tournament we beat the Moscow Aviation team 28 to 6, but Halid and I had an ugly run-in near the end of the game. Since we were ahead by more than twenty runs I put a couple of substitutes including Gleb into the game. Halid had been sitting in the bleachers but he came running onto the field shouting, "Nyet" and some other things I couldn't understand. I yelled back, "If not now when do we give our subs a chance?" which he couldn't understand. I found out later that Halid was accusing me of trying to deliberately lose the game. The players and the assistant coach told me privately later that Halid was acting crazy, but from that moment on my role in coaching the team was significantly reduced.

When one of the Georgian teams lost in an upset a spectator threw a rock and hit the Moscow umpire on the head knocking him unconscious and putting him in a hospital. That evening I told the umpires they should refuse to take the field unless they were given protection, but the Russians said, "This is Georgia, nothing will be done." Yet the next day there was a militiaman standing behind the backstop throughout the game. Many Georgians wanted independence and there was tension in the air judging by the nervousness of the Russians concerning our location. While the Georgians gave two gallon plastic jugs of wine to the Georgian and other Republic teams, they didn't even want to sell wine to the two Moscow teams. The burly bus driver who drove us down the mountain each day for the games was a pretty crude guy. While he would sometimes stop and pick up friends and pretty girls, he also got pleasure out of swerving the bus at older women walking along the edge of the road and forcing them to leap and sometimes tumble into the ditch. One day on the way down he took a fancy to my old Brooklyn Dodger baseball cap and insisted that I let him try it on. He looked at himself in the rear view mirror and smiled from ear to ear. As we got closer to town Gleb whispered to me that he was going to keep the cap. I had gotten the same feeling so I figured that while he was still driving was the best time to make my move. I stood up and stepped alongside the driver with a friendly smile on my face and when he was going around a sharp turn I gently lifted the cap off his head and put it on mine. When I turned to step back to my seat the nearby MGU player's eyes were bulging and they seemed to be almost holding their breath.

Actually the Georgians treated me with great respect and curiosity. I found out from Gela Chihriadze, who was a very refined and nice man, and evidently the first Georgian baseball coach, that I was the first American that had ever been into those foothills. After one of our games an English-speaking woman journalist from Georgia sent a man for three round loaves of hot bread that she gave me and I shared them with the MGU team. The players were quite impressed and then the next afternoon the local Communist Party secretary and his sports director drove Gleb and me 50 miles back to Kutaisi for dinner in a restaurant with the TASS woman. The rutted roads resulted in two flat tires on the way, but the car trunk was full of extra tires. There were still statues of their favorite son, Joseph Stalin, in many villages. The Party secretary said that Stalin had won the Great Patriotic War and I replied that the sacrifice and bravery of the Soviet people had won the war despite Stalin. He said, "Nyet," even after I had given him a whole lecture on Stalin's bizarre behavior on the eve of the German attack on Leningrad in 1941, which Gleb confirmed by saying that his history professor had said the same thing. It was only when I said that the Soviets were wise not to trust the western allies, especially Winston Churchill, Harry Truman and General George Patton, that the Party secretary then said I might have been right about Stalin. After dinner when we were driving around Kutaisi I saw an ice cream kiosk on a street corner and said it looked good. He abruptly stopped the car and even though I said I only wanted one he bought a whole paper bag full of ice cream cones.

Another night the "resort" manager invited me, Gleb and the MGU head coach to dinner in his two-storied home. He had a shower, sauna, billiard table, and a dining room table full of fresh vegetables, chicken, nuts, wine, vodka and cognac. Around the table were three Soviet army officers including two majors, one in combat fatigues, and a lower ranking military neurological surgeon. Standing against the wall were the manager's wife and a jeep driver. With Gleb serving as translator there were many toasts to peace as well as some arm wrestling and the Georgian wine flowed like water. The hefty and gregarious major flattened Gleb immediately, but was very frustrated when he lost the first two matches to Halid. I think Halid let him win the third match on purpose because he realized that it would have gone on all night if the drunken red-faced major didn't eventually win.

Their tradition was to "bottoms up" each time, and the glasses were the size of coffee mugs. They questioned why I would only drink half a glass as they refilled each time, and I said it was an old American tradition. They said, "But this is Georgia," so I did a drum beat on the table with my silverware and said, "I march to my own drummer." They laughed and seemed to accept my pace. Yet even with this special dispensation, I was almost as pie-eyed as they were by midnight as we staggered out into the darkness and they left in their jeep.

We were in a frontier military zone 40 miles north of the Turkish border, 40 miles east of the Black Sea, 230 miles north of Iran and 390 miles north of Iraq. Two or three times each day we were shook by sonic booms of military jets patrolling the border. I recalled how just a few days before I had been on a Soviet airbase runway lined with scores of silver Migs and SU 27 fighter planes all underneath their own individual concrete sod-covered shelters. I also had recently read in a month-old *Herald Tribune* that American president George Bush had authorized the assignment of more than 500 new air-to-surface nuclear missiles to Turkey. The paper reported that they were capable of striking 600 miles deep into the U.S.S.R. How different you feel about this reality as you sit with your Soviet friends rather than on the banks of the Hudson River in Poughkeepsie, New York.

The day we flew back to Moscow it was raining, so to stay dry we had to stand under the fuselage of the jet while waiting to board the plane. The ground crew was working right next to us refueling the plane and despite the fact that there was a no smoking symbol right next to the fuel intake valve, all of the men were puffing on cigarettes. When I pointed to the symbol and looked at the supervisor he hesitated but then said something to the workers. They looked defiant but eventually took long slow last puffs before snuffing out their cigarettes. The plane was full of overweight Georgians, suitcases packed with bottles of wine, and our baseball bats and equipment lying loose on the floor of the aisle. There was no buckle on my safety belt so I had to just tie a knot in it. The MGU dorms back in Moscow looked like the Hilton Hotel compared to our quarters in rural Georgia.

In the two or three weeks after our return from Georgia, Halid took a much more active role in organizing and running our practice sessions. Much of what he chose to do was useless, and what he did not do was even more counterproductive, such as letting the pitchers go that entire time without facing hitters in a practice game situation, despite my pleas that they would become rusty and have trouble throwing strikes in the next tournament. He flitted around during the workouts giving advice to the players, much of which I could see, and assistant coach Valeri confirmed, was incorrect. Unlike Halid, Valeri is respected by the players, but he is dependent on Halid for his job, so he needs to tread softly. I tried to work individually with the players and help make Halid's practice routines as productive as possible, but it was frustrating because we were not working on things I knew we desperately needed to do.

Baseball in Central Asia and Problems of Perestroika

It was with considerable apprehension that we made the mid–June four-hour Aeroflot flight from Moscow to the central Asian city of Tashkent in the Soviet Union's Republic of Uzbekistan. This Aeroflot jet was much larger and more luxurious inside and the meal they served was pretty good. Our catcher Vova Tarasov had carried my forty-year-old brown suitcase with the Hobart College decal on it from my room at MGU to the family car for the ride to the Moscow airport. I sat in the backseat with his grandfather who had numerous Soviet campaign ribbons from the Great Patriotic War attached to his sport coat. Vova's other grandfather was actually a veteran of the German luftwaffe. He had flown Stuka dive-bombers in the Spanish Civil War and later piloted Junker 88 bombers based in Hungary in World War II. He married a Hungarian woman and was shot down and became a POW of the Russians. Since he was an engineer he was required to stay in the Soviet Union after the war and help construct housing destroyed by the Germans. His wife joined him in the U.S.S.R. and eventually Vova's mother was born who married a Russian man. Vova said that the grandfathers don't talk about the war and it was only since Gorbachev that the family has spoken about it openly.

All day long Radio Moscow had been carrying reports of ethnic violence in the neighboring Soviet Republic of Kirghizia, only 150 miles from Tashkent. The fighting between two Muslim groups would cost the lives of over 70 people during our ten-day baseball tournament, but fortunately as it turned out, we saw no evidence of any conflict in Tashkent.

Even at 1 a.m. as we stepped from the plane into the clear star-studded Asian night, waves of heat radiated from the airport runway. On the bus drive into the city I saw many people sleeping on the roofs of their one-story houses. Before getting to bed at 3 a.m. head coach Halid would only tell us to get up at 8 a.m. but nothing about breakfast or game time. This was typical of his tendency to seldom reveal more than we had to know, and as a result we were kept totally dependent and powerless to make any personal plans.

Five hours later we rolled out of bed and were told to dress immediately for an 11 a.m. game. We waited about one hour for a bus that took us directly to the dust bowl field, without any food or drink, to then play a game that was to last four and one-half hours in the blistering 95 plus degree dry desert heat. After the game as we gulped down a barely cool and weak mixture of syrup and water, I asked my two MGU baseball player companions, "How do you like being treated like cows?" "Well, not very much, I guess," one replied with a tone of resignation.

In defiance of the heat, our five foot seven inch starting pitcher Sergei had been all heart as he threw over 225 pitches in a complete game 11 to 9 victory over a team from Soviet Georgia. He also voluntarily served as bat boy and after the game ran two victory laps around the outer perimeter of the field. The next day Halid let him throw batting practice prior to a 22 to 10 loss to Leningrad, and on the third day he again started and pitched seven innings giving up twenty-four runs in a 30 to 20 loss to another Georgian team. It was only after I showed him my own elbow scar from bone chip surgery thirty-five years ago, that I was able to convince Sergei to remove himself from the game or risk serious arm injury.

With both team benches under makeshift open-sided tents made from hotel bed sheets, and with players and coaches taking to the field with hand towels tucked under their baseball caps and hanging down their necks, it looked like a scene from *Lawrence of Arabia*. On this day and throughout the tournament a number of fly balls were lost in the bright white sun, and even ground balls sometimes disappeared in a burst of exploding sand. Every ball or player's foot that hit the ground raised a lingering puff of dust, and there were many dusty tumbles that resulted in bleeding elbows and knees. There were a couple of very nice women dressed in nurse's type clothing at the games who provided first aid help and also wet towels that they placed on our necks and heads to combat the effects of the suffocating heat. By the end of this third game loss the MGU players and coach were in total disarray with the players exchanging sniping criticisms of each other and their coach.

While inept coaching does lead to a great deal of justifiable player criticism of coaches, I found that many Soviet players spend too much time bickering or blaming each other rather than accepting responsibility for their own obvious mistakes and errors. Many of the players are excellent athletes and have achieved some success in other sports. As a result, they are often difficult to convince that any improvement in their baseball performance levels beyond what their natural athletic ability is currently producing requires that they learn and use correct fundamental baseball skills.

One of the major problems of Soviet baseball is that they do not yet have a generation of coaches that have played the game themselves. Like many players and sponsors, the initial interest of many Soviet coaches in the foreign sport of baseball was motivated by the realization that their involvement could provide opportunities for both domestic and overseas travel. Some Soviet coaches have made maximum use of their contacts with Cuban, Nicaraguan, Japanese and American coaches and teams, and as a result do reasonably decent jobs of coaching given their limited experience with the game. Other Soviet coaches either have not had the opportunity for these overseas contacts, or do not have the interest, aptitude, or personality to take full advantage of foreign assistance. My own four-month experience working with the MGU baseball team had been a source of great satisfaction as well as frustration, but Halid's personality greatly complicated the problems.

MGU assistant coach Valeri Varinsky is a fifty-two-year-old Russian, a former rugby player, and a professionally trained coach who understands coaching psychology. He quickly absorbed and put to good use the specific baseball coaching techniques he saw me use during the first month when I served as the organizer and decision-making coach for both practice and games. He did not perceive me as a threat to his position and seemed as fond of me as I was of him, as he often affectionately referred to me as William Will-yam-ah-veech Byrne.

MGU head coach Halid is a thirty-something Tatar and a former boxing team member. He did not in my judgment seem very interested in the game of baseball or have much knowledge of it. However, he did obviously enjoy his position of authority as head coach and keeper of the key to our beautiful MGU owned $3.2 million artificial turf baseball stadium, which was probably the finest baseball facility in Europe. Unfortunately, unlike Valeri, I believe he did perceive my superior baseball knowledge as a threat to his authority, and as a result, after my very productive first month of coaching, he severely limited my role thereafter, much to the disappointment of most players. I learned of similar stories from a number of frustrated foreign businessmen and specialists who were in the Soviet Union to advise minimally competent Soviet managers, who desperately needed the Western expertise, but who were threatened by the superior knowledge of the visitors, and therefore made only minimum use of the assistance.

MGU staggered through two more losses to Kiev and Tashkent. In the 12 to 7 loss to Tashkent our pitcher Alex threw hard the whole game and gave up only one earned run in eight innings. Our team made six errors in the first three innings when Tashkent scored eleven runs, but Alex walked fifteen batters, which was what I expected after Halid had not had him pitch to batters in three weeks. After the first few games in Tashkent when I realized that Halid was determined to limit my coaching role in the tournament, I sometimes would leave the MGU bench and stand by the backstop to better watch the pitchers. On a couple of occasions pitchers from opposing teams came over and asked me to demonstrate the proper grip and finger placement for throwing a variety of pitches, and I obliged as Halid watched from the MGU bench. Finally before our game with Kiev my friend Oleg, who was their shortstop, approached me near home plate and inquired about why I wasn't coaching. As I was telling him Halid quickly walked over and shook my hand before ushering me to the MGU bench. Since he had left Gleb back in Moscow, who he clearly disliked, he then had English speaking Philip, a backup catcher to ask me what I thought about the previous day's game. After that he obviously made an attempt to involve me in the coaching during the remaining tournament games.

MGU upset Habarovsk 17–13 in our final game, and in so doing prevented the Far Eastern team from qualifying for next year's major league, and helped a Georgia team slide in the back door. MGU had already been eliminated from the next year's major league which would be reduced from 14 to 10 teams in 1991. During the last days of the tournament, rumors of money being offered to teams to "fix" games had circulated, and after our last game victory, several Habarovsk players and fans threatened the umpires and accused them of being paid off by the Georgians. Although I had observed that the Georgian baseball officials seemed to have and spend an excess of rubles, I had seen no suspicious umpiring calls during the game. When some people cornered plate umpire Arkady against the backstop, I quickly walked over to his side and glared at his antagonists. They seemed momentarily reluctant to lay hands on him and then the Tashkent officials ran down the embankment and escorted him out of the angry situation. Arkady wore a gold Star of David on a necklace and during the following weeks I came to know him as a gentle and sensitive friend.

After sleeping the first night with the team at the sports hotel, Halid had moved me across town to the first class Hotel Uzbekistan. He said that if I gave him $100 U.S. he could exchange it for many more rubles than the standard exchange rate. This would easily cover the 60 ruble per night cost of the hotel room and also give the MGU team the Western currency they needed to pay entry fees for future international tournaments, he explained. I knew it was a sleazy convoluted deal because he was very concerned that my friend on the Kiev team did not find out about it.

The only air conditioning was in the lobby and dining room of the hotel and my room was on the extra warm top floor. It was stifling hot even at night and you could see heat lightning in the distance but it never rained. I took lots of cool showers, even in the middle of the night sometimes, but my room's standard Soviet "bath towel" was more like the size of a thin western dish towel. As an experiment, when I went out one morning, on my bed I left a copy of the front page of the spring Middletown *Times Herald Record,* which featured the large color photo of me flipping a baseball in front of the Soviet flag. When I returned that evening there were three neatly-folded, large Western-sized bath towels on my bed. It seemed like the maid and floor lady decided that I was a VIP.

The city of Tashkent had a population of about 2.1 million and was less than 250 miles from China, Afghanistan, and Pakistan, and about 450 miles from India. About seventy percent of the republic's inhabitants were Uzbeks and eleven percent Russian. During World War II many people from the eastern Soviet Union, particularly orphaned children, were evacuated to Tashkent. It is a mainly modern city, as a result of being rebuilt after a 1966 earthquake, and is the center of a cotton, fruit, and vegetable industry that was entirely dependent on an extensive but wasteful flood-type irrigation system. On the flight out we had gone over the Aral Sea and you could see boats stranded miles from the waters edge of the contracting body of water. The changes brought about by glasnost and perestroika were reflected by the range of acquaintances I made during my ten-day hotel stay. There was an American attorney from Seattle negotiating the opening of two hard currency pizza restaurants; a German cotton buyer; a British trade company representative trying to buy Soviet scrap steel for European clients; a United Nations representative from Tanzania who was arranging a conference on caterpillars; a French businessman trying to sell computerized cloth cutting machines; two Israeli specialists who were advising the Soviets on how to build a more efficient drip-type irrigation system; a French journalist doing an article on Soviet women; three men from Burlington, Vermont, one a member of the state legislature, who were shocked to hear there was a baseball tournament in town, but who briefly attended one of our games before being driven to shelter by the intense midday heat; and four North Korean trade representatives and their Soviet host who were somewhat baffled when I presented them with a selection of baseball cards one night in the hotel restaurant. The American card companies Topps and Score had given me hundreds of baseball cards that I had handed out to opposing teams and spectators throughout my stay in the U.S.S.R.

Another person I met was a very bright 28-year-old English speaking Intourist woman whose fiancée had been killed during the war in Afghanistan. She was attractive, quite tall and had once been a basketball player. She was born in Tashkent but her parents were Russian. When talking about the issue of independence for Uzbekistan she said some Uzbeks wanted an Islamic republic, and already they dominated most of the top level positions in government and industry, so the minority population of Russians was worried about their future. She said that while there were a few Uzbek feminists, but not in the Western sense, there was little that they could do because their husbands would punish them and the police would be of little help. She continued by saying that Uzbek women have five or six children and many complain to her but they see no way of changing the situation. When Uzbek women marry they go to live with the husband's parents and the mother-in-law is the boss, so there is great resistance to modernization of dress, etc., in this situation.

She complained about her inability to get promoted to a policy making position despite the fact she knew more than any of her bosses. She spoke of the problems of dealing with Uzbek men at work where they tried to treat her like an Uzbek woman. She tells them, "I am not an Uzbek woman so don't treat me like one." She said she "knows these men well" and some you have to "sort of use camouflage and be soft, but careful, to get their co-operation," while with "others you have to be very strong when dealing with them." Even if she improved her skills, she said, "I will meet resistance and people will try to block me, or my manager will not promote me because he does not want to lose my services and skills." At the University she had majored in foreign languages with an emphasis on English and Persian and had once dreamed about becoming the Soviet ambassador to the United States. She is still very determined to rise in her chosen career but does not know if she can succeed. She said she wanted to get into the Diplomatic Academy in Moscow, which required exams, and even though she was confident of doing well on them, she still needed to find the right connections and get many recommendations. Her engineer father (who had died) once had those connections but now she had no access to them.

Although most of my non-baseball time was spent hanging around the hotel lobby, restaurant and bar, I did get around the city a bit either on the clean modern underground metro, the buses or on foot. The people in Tashkent were friendly, less hurried and not as tired-looking as people in Moscow, nor did I see any long lines of people waiting to buy things. There was also a huge outdoor market where, unlike in Moscow, there was an abundance of fresh vegetables and fruit being sold from kiosks. I was struck by how similar many of the people looked racially to Native Americans in Arizona and New Mexico. One night I went to the nearby Tashkent Opera House and saw *The Barber of Seville*. Halid continued his friendly gestures by inviting me to an Uzbek pre-wedding banquet in the Uzbek district of Tashkent. It was a fascinating evening held in an outdoor courtyard and there was lots of food including fruit, soup, shish kabob, cookies and champagne. Halid had told me that Uzbeks do not drink very much and I saw no one who was drunk. There was a lot of dancing and Middle Eastern–sounding music, but at about 11 p.m. all the females disappeared for the rest of the night. The dancing continued, however, and as it turned out Halid was a good native dancer. Men would tuck rubles into the belts of the dancers who would then give them to the band members.

On the last night of the tournament there was a spontaneous party at the Hotel Uzbekistan restaurant that attracted players and coaches from most of the teams. As usual there was lots of vodka, wine and mainly all-male native dances. There were many toasts and good-byes exchanged between myself and numerous coaches and players I had met from a variety of Soviet cities during the course of the season's competition. Some players and coaches from various teams thanked me for my help and a couple even said that they thought MGU had shown great improvement since my arrival. I also received a couple of exploratory job offers for the next season. Specifically I was told that Tiraspol down by the Black Sea would like me to come and coach in the fall or next spring and summer. They were one of the top six teams in the major league in 1990. They would put me up in an apartment or hotel and pay me all the rubles I needed. There was a very warm and sincere feeling of comradeship and they seemed quite fond of me.

The party went on until two hours after the restaurant was supposed to close, but the next morning I was up at 6 a.m. after just 4 hours of sleep and still feeling the effects of the vodka. The Tashkent coach drove two umpires, the "Queen Bee" blond woman who represented the Baseball Federation all week, and me to the airport. After an hour wait we took off for the return flight to Moscow at 9 a.m. in a wide-body jet with two engines on each wing. The thing I remember most clearly about my flights that summer was that we never seemed to circle the airports; we just seemed to go straight in for the landings.

Life in Moscow

I arrived back in Moscow just a day or two before my wife Sydna arrived from the United States for a month's visit. When I met her at the Leningradski Train Station with the traditional bouquet of red carnations, she was shocked at how gaunt I looked because I was seventeen pounds lighter than when she last saw me. While she had been to Moscow once before in the protected world of one of my college tours, she clung to my side like glue as we made our way through the confusing masses of people into the metro for the ride back to MGU. She immediately got a good taste of how difficult life was in Moscow when we learned that there would be no hot water at MGU for ten days. It was shut down for the annual spring maintenance procedure. We both initially had a feeling of disbelief, but after a few days of turning the hot water faucet on and finding there really was none, all we could do was laugh about how her last shower was in Poughkeepsie and mine was in Tashkent. She also soon found out why life here leaves you so weary as we figured out that on an average day we walked up and down between 400 and 600 steps, in addition to the numerous level miles we routinely walked.

It seemed like during Sydna's visit an inordinate amount of our time was spent trying to find a place to eat. While there by myself I had often just bought a loaf of good hard crusted bread for a few kopeks from the MGU bakery and chewed on that throughout the day. It wasn't that there was no food to eat, it was more a matter of finding something that you could identify its content, and that you had a desire to eat. The student cafeteria was very cheap but really totally unappetizing. My old standby for the midday meal was the MGU professor's dining room but it closed for the summer not too long after my wife arrived. Since I could not read the menu, I had to wander around the room until I found someone eating something that looked good, and then ask them to put their finger on the item on my paper menu. Almost every day I ate there I got a salad, soup, beef stroganoff, potatoes, ice cream, bread, diluted juice and tea. It cost me one ruble and 85 kopeks. It was not that easy for my wife because she was a vegetarian. The students could also eat there but you rarely saw them because it took them about a month to save enough money from their meager student subsidies to afford the cost.

The first-class Cosmos Hotel for tourists was the only place I found that served a buffet lunch that you could pay for with rubles, but it was a long series of metro rides to get there. There was also a distant store owned by a company from Finland called Stockman's where you could use a Western credit card. It carried Western foodstuffs but was frequently sold out of many things. I looked for peanut butter for four months but they never had any, then to my great glee it suddenly showed up about a week before I left in August. When Tatiana, the helpful SUNY coordinator who lived on the 23rd floor at MGU, gave me a small table refrigerator, I had a few more options. Also because of perestroika there was a new outdoor vegetable, fruit, meat and cheese market that I could get to by an above ground tram. Nothing however was refrigerated, even milk, and you had to haggle the price. While there was a community kitchen on my dorm floor, the boiled over food on the surface of the gas stoves meant that when you lit the burner multiple cockroaches would try to exit their havens under the burners before being incinerated.

I had only eaten in the new Canadian-owned first Soviet McDonald's down at Pushkin Square on Gorky Street about three times. It was a huge multi-level restaurant with perhaps twenty cash registers and crawling with an eager, well trained and hard working young Russian staff. The food was of the same quality as in North America and very popular with the Russians. An initial problem with Russian potatoes not making good French fries was solved by the importation of Canadian seed potatoes which were then used to create a local Russian supply source. The Canadian ownership was able to convert their ruble based profits into western currency by using the rubles to purchase Russian vodka and sell it in the West. My hamburger, French fries, soda, ice cream sundae and tea cost 4 rubles or 75 cents U.S. The reason I did not eat there more often was because the line stretched all the way around the football field–sized Pushkin Square, with the average wait time being about fifty minutes. One time I was in line for one hour and forty minutes with the shortest wait being ten minutes on a rainy night. Once my wife arrived the availability of a fish filet made McDonald's a very attractive option for her, and she probably ate more French fries in four weeks than she had in the previous twenty years or more.

Despite the relative hardships compared to home, it didn't take long after my arrival in the spring for MGU to feel somewhat like home, because it was a place to sleep and eat, create a circle of friends, and feel a sense of belonging and comfort. I lived on the 5th floor in two side-by-side fifteen-foot-long by eight wide rooms with a sink, small shower and toilet. Each room had a single bed, desk and bookcase. Normally these suites housed two undergraduate students. There were at least 23 floors in the building and a bank of four elevators; however only one elevator operated at a time because they used the others for spare parts I was told. I got my hair cut for 40 kopeks or 7 cents U.S. every couple of weeks by an attractive middle-aged woman in the basement near the bakery. My wife even got her hair cut for 2 rubles or 40 cents U.S. Every month I went to a nearby administrative building to stand in a short line with other employees to pick up my MGU stipend of 260 rubles. The financial people were quite efficient and serious, at least until the day I started following and showing an amused interest in a long strand of an indoor ivy plant that literally ran through three offices, at which point the ladies stopped working and showed me their other office plants. We had a friendly conversation, completely by hand gestures, about indoor plants at MGU and my home in America. After that when I picked up my monthly pay I was greeted by friendly smiles.

The maintenance staff at MGU also seemed quite responsive but had limited or outdated tools. The electricians who fixed the short in my wall light had no testing equipment but repaired it with pliers and a screwdriver despite the flying sparks. After the undergraduates went home for the summer the MGU Hygienic Patrol ladies in white aprons and masks came around to dust the rooms for cockroaches. I wouldn't let them in my room because I suspected that the white dust they were pumping in the rooms and hallways was probably DDT. After being careful to clean up crumbs, I had up to that point had only one or two cockroaches; however in the days following the spraying I had scores of them, as my room seemed to have become their bomb shelter.

My inability to speak Russian beyond a few key phrases was by far the most frustrating and limiting reality that I had to endure during my five-month stay. Knowing the Cyrillic alphabet, however, was very helpful. Just the shear energy that you had to expend trying to communicate the simplest things gradually wore you down physically and emotionally. Occasionally I went to the Hotel Cosmos or the Hotel Intourist on Gorky Street just to listen to tourists speak English. On one of those occasions I came across three American newspaper editors who were part of a tour of U.S. editors. They were startled to find out that I was an American coaching the MGU baseball team and they asked me questions about my experience for over an hour. They then asked me to come back the next morning and talk to their whole group.

The language barrier led to some amusing incidents. One day when I went to take the MGU elevator downstairs I noticed smoke coming out of an old leather couch near the elevator. I lifted the cushion and saw that there was extensive fire underneath from a dropped cigarette I assumed. The floor was wooden and I didn't think it was safe to try to beat it out, so I quickly took the elevator down to the main floor lobby where the elderly man and woman sat at the desk keeping an eye on who tried to enter the dormitory areas. I got their attention and then went to a nearby wall poster which had a flame and cigarette on it warning of the danger of fire. I tapped the fire image with my finger and then pointed upward while holding up the five fingers on my other hand. They just stared at me and the man waved his hand sort of in disgust. I repeated my gestures at the poster and then ran back to their desk and said "fire" over and over. The man just turned his back on me but the woman seemed interested. I pointed to her desk phone and she finally nodded and picked it up and made a call. In about five minutes I saw about six or eight men come around a corner at the far end of a long hallway and head in our direction. They walked rapidly and wore security type uniforms and carried buckets of sand. I led them to the elevator and up to the fifth floor. When we stepped out of the elevator the couch was still burning and they quickly tore it apart and poured the sand on the hottest spots. When we took the elevator back down the fire brigade leader shook my hand and patted me on the back while repeatedly saying "spa-see-ba" or thank you in Russian. The old woman smiled at me every time I passed from that day on.

Another day when I returned to my room there was a note in Russian on my door. I asked the girl across the hall what it said and she told me it was reminding me to vote that day in the election of the local Soviet. I decided to give it a try so I went down to the main lobby where there were a number of tables with people sitting behind them, some ballot boxes and a temporary red carpet. I walked up to a man and showed him my library card for the Library of Marxism and Leninism which had my name on it in Russian. He opened a large registration book and started looking through it while I said nothing. Finally he said something in Russian and as soon as I spoke in English he immediately stood up and said, "Nyet." I started laughing and then he did too. He showed me the ballot and indicated that you were supposed to cross out two of the three names that appeared on it.

The language problem really created an enormous mess when I had to deal with the MGU Militia. An increasing petty crime rate has been one of the disturbing outgrowths of perestroika and when I returned to Moscow from Tashkent I discovered that a thief had entered my dormitory room and stolen about twenty personal items. This then involved me in a very interesting and sometimes comical, but very lengthy process of reporting the theft to the local militia (police). It began with my original detailed letter (with Russian translation) reporting the theft and then progressed to interviews with investigators Sergey and Vladimir, in which they painstakingly, with the help of a translator, filled out a detailed handwritten militia report form. They then had me draw a picture of each of the stolen items and finally I had to write another letter to the chief of the 6th District of the Moscow Militia requesting that he take action. Investigator Sergey's sense of humor was apparent when I reported that one stolen article was an uninstalled brand new travel burglar alarm. After learning that many of my sociology students were Police Science majors, he plucked his Moscow Militia badge off his winter fur hat and presented it as a memento. Then, he, Vladimir, my wife, who had just arrived for a visit, and I posed for a series of photos.

While this theft report procedure was very cumbersome, the militia does have a very efficient method of dealing with speeding drivers. When stopped for speeding a driver has a choice of paying ten rubles on the spot to the militiaman, or going to court where if found guilty they face a fifteen-ruble fine. During the one evening I watched the militia operate a radar speed trap, all the drivers chose the ten-ruble settlement, including a wise-mouthed twenty-year-old who initially stalked back to check the radar reading for himself, then angrily paid the ten rubles and tossed the receipt defiantly over his shoulder. I might have been inclined to give him another ticket for littering, but throughout the spring the Moscow Militia seemed to be very patient. Even under very trying circumstances I found them to be very calm and almost passive and noticeably devoid of macho responses to occasional challenges to their authority.

The reaction of my closest Soviet friends to my theft was one of almost personal humiliation. While these intellectuals strongly supported perestroika, they also feared that in the headlong rush toward a market economy, profit-making, consumerism, and an emphasis on money, the Russian people were in danger of losing their dignity and their traditional caring values. Since I had spent the last 25 years of my professional life studying and teaching about American social problems, their observations found a very sympathetic ear.

I think that the better you were at being flexible and creative, the better you were in dealing with the daily frustrations. As an example I made friends with a Russian lady who worked at the Scandinavian Airlines Office (SAS) in Moscow. She agreed to give my letters to a flight crew member so that they could be mailed in Sweden. I had been trying to contact an American named Dave Clark whom I had met on my flight over in April. He was coaching baseball in Sweden and I wanted to alert him to the possibilities of coaching in the U.S.S.R. that I knew he was interested in doing. I also found that smiling got you a long way in the U.S.S.R. The one thing I never did adjust to was the constant presence of cigarette smoke that seemed to be everywhere.

When Tatiana went on vacation she got me the proper papers to allow me entry into the American embassy so that I could pick up the SUNY-related mail. The embassy had done away with most services for Americans in Moscow because it had become too much of a burden. There was always a long line of Russians outside the gate waiting to apply for visas, but with my SUNY papers and passport I was able to just go directly to the Marine guards and gain entry after some brief questioning and eyeballing. Each visit I had to sort through the stack of envelopes that were addressed to Americans in Moscow and pick out the two or three that might be for SUNY people, including myself. One day I met an African American who was in charge of cultural affairs. He showed me around the embassy grounds and pointed out the huge brand new brick building that had been built but could not be used because the masonry was full of electronic bugs. He also invited me to the cafeteria for lunch which was a real treat. One of the interesting things he said was that embassy personnel could not talk to Soviet citizens outside the embassy grounds unless they were accompanied by another embassy employee. One day during a practice at the MGU stadium I noticed a small group of men who were watching from the stands. They were drinking beer and making sandwiches from slices of bread in a Wonder Bread package. I went up and spoke to them and they were surprised that I was an American, and as I suspected they were electricians from the American embassy enjoying their day off at the ballpark.

I had a mixed bag of experiences meeting traveling Americans while in Moscow and it always gave me an odd feeling. They generally questioned me like I was almost a native of Moscow even though I had barely scratched the surface of understanding things, but yet I also felt a strong sense of identification with my new home which created some degree of social-psychological distance between me and my fellow countrymen. It certainly was not the case when it was people I already knew like the elderly Quaker couple from Poughkeepsie or the Port Jervis, New York, high school social studies teacher. In those cases they came to my room at MGU and I happily showed them around the city until they were exhausted. They actually enjoyed it so much that they temporarily left their tour groups to spend more time with me.

A few traveling baseball teams from the U.S.A. also showed up at the MGU stadium. Athletes in Action, an adult amateur team, played a game against us and after the game handed out bibles which some Russians happily took but many more rejected, and some later even privately criticized the proselytizing effort. There were also several traveling youth teams from Indiana, Oakland, California, and a pitching school from southern California that played a Moscow youth team that MGU assistant coach Valeri had developed. The parents of some of the southern California kids made the trip from the U.S. and a few actually embarrassed their fellow parents because of their arrogant know-it-all, superior attitudes and comments. One mother was especially obnoxious and said, "These people don't even know that the home team always sits in the third base dugout." I had been eaves dropping on the comments without saying anything so they assumed I was Russian, but at that point I said, "Nyet, it's not true." She haughtily said, "Yes, it is, and just how would you know?" obviously still confused about my nationality. I told her the Yankees, Mets and San Francisco Giants all use the first base dugouts at their home fields, and suggested that she look at a video of the earthquake at Candlestick Park and notice which dugout the Giant players exited. She then said that the Los Angeles Dodgers use the third base dugout, and I told her she was finally right about something. Then she angrily said I don't need this and stormed off.

The former major league all-star player Steve Garvey and his wife showed up at this youth game. He evidently was contemplating making a movie about Russian baseball. My wife and I talked to them for a while and later that evening while we were standing in the long McDonald's line at Pushkin Square, a couple of our MGU players showed up with Garvey and they pulled us out of the line and took us to the entry to McDonald's. They then convinced the manager that this was really Steve Garvey, who had once played for the San Diego Padres who were owned by McDonald's famous developer Ray Crock. This then got us the royal treatment and we were soon seated inside. Sydna whispered to me that if there really is a St. Peter at the gate this was going to be a black mark against us.

Another incident that happened also made me embarrassed by "my fellow Americans," as the politicians all say. I was in the usually quiet lobby of the Intourist Hotel one evening drinking a beer when I suddenly heard some very loud boisterous talking. It came from a group of what looked like young teenage boys dressed in gray sweat suits. I walked over near them to better hear what language they were speaking and just as I suspected they were Americans. At that point one kid pulled the sweat pants of another kid down to his ankles so that he was bare-assed in the hotel lobby. I asked them who they were and they said they were an all-star ice hockey team of sixteen-year-olds from the Boston area. They had been easily beaten that day by the Soviet All Union Team of sixteen-year-olds by more than ten goals. They said they had tried everything to slow the Soviet kids down including tripping, holding and punching them and even skating into their goalie but nothing worked. When they found out I was an American baseball coach, they asked me to come to the next day's scheduled game and root for them. They had no idea how to get to the game but said it was called the Spartak rink. I looked at some Moscow maps and located the rink, so the next day I took a series of metro and above-ground tram rides to what appeared to be a working-class area of Moscow that I had never been to before. I got off the last tram in the area where I thought the rink must be and started walking through some back yards of the large concrete apartment buildings. I stopped people and said Spartak and then made believe I was skating with a hockey stick. I attracted a lot of attention and eventually someone caught on and directed me right to the rink.

Once inside I saw some men I had seen at the MGU baseball games and they recognized me. It turned out they were youth hockey coaches and they invited me to sit on the end of the Soviet team bench. The father of one Soviet player sat next to me in the first spectator's seat. Again the Soviet sixteen-year-olds skated rings around the Americans and soon were ahead by many goals. Between periods I was invited into the Soviet locker room and it was interesting that it was very quiet as coaches went around to individual players and spoke softly to them. On the other hand out in the hall you could hear the American coaches in their locker room yelling at their players and trying to get them emotionally charged up. As the game progressed it got very ugly as the Americans virtually tried mugging the Soviet players when they could catch up to them. The Russian father to my right just shook his head in disgust and I felt considerable contempt and shame for what I was witnessing. All I could do was look at him and give a thumb down disproval sign for what my countrymen were doing. He gave me a faint smile and nodded his head in response.

At one of our late afternoon MGU practices I noticed about a half-dozen well dressed young men in coats and ties sitting in the stands and watching. At the end of our workout they came down to the field and they spoke Spanish and some broken English. It turned out they were from the Cuban embassy and they politely asked if they might use a bat and ball so they could play for a little while. I gave them what they wanted plus my glove and a couple other players' gloves. They pulled off their ties and coats and dashed out on the diamond and took turns hitting ground balls to the infielders and played sort of a fantasy game where they even added sounds effects by making a mock roar of the crowd noise deep in their throats just like I used to do as an eight-year-old kid in my backyard in Poughkeepsie. They dove in the dirt for ground balls even in their good suit pants and white dress shirts. After twenty minutes or so they were sweaty and dusty but full of joy. I gave them all my remaining baseball cards with Latino surnames and they eagerly examined them and commented among themselves in Spanish. They thanked me and wanted to know why an American was coaching baseball in Moscow but wasn't allowed by my government to go to Cuba. I told them it was really a stupid policy and of course they agreed. They invited me to come visit their embassy or in the future even come to Cuba by way of Canada or Mexico.

During the course of my five-month stay in Moscow I made a lot of acquaintances beyond the baseball community both at MGU and at other places in the city. I also had a handful of good interesting friends at MGU. The very attractive and bubbly undergraduate girl who invited me to her journalism class seemed to flit in and out of my life periodically perhaps because it gave her the opportunity to speak English. Irene, the wispy undergraduate girl from the Urals who lived across the hall from me, was a constant, everyday friend. She was my quickest go-to translator when there was a need, and for her I was someone she could endlessly practice her already excellent English with, and also an older and more worldly person she could discuss world affairs with as well as the future of her own country which she was very worried about. Within the first week of my arrival we had a standing room only three-hour discussion in her room as friends and other dorm residents gradually arrived and filled the small area. Evidently lots of the students had seen me in the halls but had been too shy and polite to approach me. Irene was a very shy girl who was curious and bright but also someone who was somewhat reluctant to test the waters of downtown Moscow life. We occasionally went down to the Red Square area and one time I decided to take her over to the Intourist Hotel that she knew had been traditionally off limits to Russians. She said they would not let her in but I had her put on my clearly Western-style Swedish outdoors jacket and I put my arm around her and told her to smile as we gaily walked by the hotel security man. It worked and once in she had a great time watching the tourists as we drank our Cokes at the bar that was located in the lobby.

Vera Zabotkina was my other good friend. She was a linguist and lexicologist and the head of one of the English department majors at Kaliningrad University on the Baltic Sea. She was the author of books and articles on new English words and was at MGU getting her second doctorate degree. She was divorced and her twelve-year-old son lived with her parents in Kaliningrad where her father was a retired Soviet navy lawyer. In her own words she said that over the months of our relationship she had "experienced the heights of pleasure" while bathing in my native American English with my generous sprinkling of down home expressions, slang and new expressions. Sometimes she actually took written notes. She had tremendous energy but needed all of it to deal with the endless complications created by the Soviet bureaucracy as she tried to make arrangements for her third trip to the United States. In addition to the writing of her dissertation she worked six evenings a week for a Soviet conglomerate company teaching their employees the use of English. She arranged for Sydna to do a workshop on business writing that resulted in a surprising 200 rubles of pay, and I spoke for a half hour on American political culture.

Vera had a somewhat glamorized view of Americans because she had only socialized with the upper middle class, well-educated elite in the Washington, D.C., area. She did agree that Russians were in love with the lowest aspects of American culture including consumerism: make up, glitz, youth culture, etc. While strongly supporting glasnost and perestroika she feared that Russian culture was in danger of losing its dignity and other positive things as competition and capitalism came to the U.S.S.R. Despite how hectic her life was she also would save her sugar ration and give it to a train conductor who would then give it to her mother in Kaliningrad so that she could do her blueberry canning. While my wife was there Vera got us great tickets to cultural events in Moscow and sometimes joined us and translated the Russian language performances. We went to the Bolshoi twice and saw two operas; the Moscow Musical Theater where we saw three modern ballets; the beautiful Moscow Conservatory where we saw a second round violin performance of the 9th International Tchaikovsky Competition; and the amazing Moscow Circus.

The Season's End: Baseball, Gorbachev, 28th Congress CPSU

Near the end of June the Mendeleyev Chemical Institute of Moscow won the Major League Baseball Championship of the Soviet Union after a close race with the runner-up Soviet Army Sports Club from nearby Balashiha. In descending order of finish the remaining teams that would make up next year's Major League were Simferopol, Tiraspol, and the Odessa Dockers all from near the Black Sea, the Vladivostok Forest Tigers from the Far East, Kiev from the Ukraine, Tashkent from central Asia, and two teams from Soviet Georgia. Our MGU team finished in thirteenth place which meant they would not compete in next year's reduced ten-team Major League. Directly under this Major League was the "First League," whose first and second place teams each year compete against the ninth and tenth place Major League teams in a post season play-off that could result in the worst Major League teams being replaced by the best "First League" teams.

At the end of June the flags of Japan, South Korea, the Soviet Union and MGU had fluttered above our stadium during the Second Annual International Baseball Tournament. In the opening game our underdog MGU team played the CCCP National Team, which was an all-star team of the best players in the Soviet Union, and which right after this tournament would depart for the United States to represent the U.S.S.R. in the Goodwill Games in Seattle.

I can remember that as the game progressed I was of two minds. It was frustrating to watch our familiar bonehead base running and botched bunts and relays. I thought of what might have been, if only I could have been in charge of team practices for all four months of my stay, rather than just one month in the spring. At the same time I recognized that before that one spring month, the MGU team didn't seem to use any bunt, steal, or take signs, never bunted or knew how to bunt, had no understanding of relays or cutoffs, and seemed to think the purpose of a rundown was to see how long you could keep the runner in it. So from this latter perspective it was satisfying to see us at least attempt these baseball maneuvers even if the results were not always pretty.

To the surprise of everyone including myself, MGU trailed by only two runs going into the seventh inning when we suddenly scored twice to tie the game. Then in the eighth after a single by catcher Vladimir Tarasov, our second baseman Dima Krugler, a former wrestler who did beautiful back flips, hit a sacrifice fly scoring brother Lorsha, our shortstop, with what proved to be the winning run. After the game the joyful MGU players bounded about the field and seemed as shocked by the 3 to 2 upset as the losing CCCP National Team. Despite their embarrassment the red and white clad National Team bit their lips and assembled along the third base line to exchange the traditional shouts of "Hurrah!" with MGU on the first baseline. Then the two lines moved in counter directions with the players shaking hands in a Soviet end of game ritual.

There were a few grumbles after our surprise victory about the key role played by the pitcher from Soviet Georgia that Halid had recruited just for the tournament. "Ringers" however, were not new to Soviet baseball, as during their drive to the National Championship the Mendeleyev Chemical Institute had supposedly paid 500 rubles to recruit a talented Lithuanian pitcher after his Lithuanian team had withdrawn from the Soviet Major League for political reasons. Also I was told that the Moscow Red Army team had arranged to have the star shortstop of a top Soviet team called back to active military duty so he could play for their team. Then, of course, there were the continuous rumors about the Georgia teams paying umpires and opposing teams to throw games, and maybe even "poisoning" Russian players so they were too sick to play up to par. I never knew exactly what to believe, but the old saying "where there was smoke there must be some fire" might be applicable, and it was not a stretch to say that there was considerable skullduggery involved in Soviet baseball.

In other tournament games both the Koreans and Japanese crushed MGU and the National Team by twenty or more runs, and South Korea decisively defeated Japan 9 to 4 to win the trophy. It was interesting that both the Korean and Japanese teams huddled into a perfect circle or semi-circle in front of the dugouts at the end of each inning to hear brief comments from their coaches and at the end of the game as they left the field most Japanese players turned back toward it and doffed their caps and bowed. The most interesting innovation was the South Korean practice of after every pitch all their fielders, except their pitcher and catcher, would shout something and jog about twenty steps in a tight circle. It was obviously the design of the coach to keep them alert and nimble and made sense, but I thought to myself, you would have a hard time selling that to American ball players who spend their time worthlessly spitting or gazing around the ballpark.

Head coach Halid fawned over the Japanese and acted like he was their valet. He even ordered three of our substitutes to unload the Japanese bags from their bus. He also put on a baseball uniform for the games for the first time all season that I saw. He left before the end of our CCCP game to change into a tight fitting blue suit, tie, white socks and white shirt with a curled up collar that he wore when he went to lunch with the Japanese. MGU had a Japan trip scheduled for the fall so Halid treated them like royalty and at the same time made sure they had no contact with me whom he kept at a distance during the tournament as I sat on the far end of the bench with assistant coach Valeri.

It might have been my imagination but I also thought the Japanese coaches were a bit distant on their own concerning my presence, as they considered MGU their turf where their money had built the stadium and their coaches had preceded me. The South Korean coaches and journalists were very friendly and sought out conversations with me despite Halid's efforts, which also included not inviting me to the post tournament banquet. It was only because other baseball officials and an angry and embarrassed Valeri insisted that I go to the banquet, that Sydna and I were driven out to the 1980 Olympic Village site where it was held.

At the banquet the cultural differences were very evident. The Russians with their toasts seemed on a mission to get themselves and everyone else drunk, and they generally succeeded in their own case, as even one MGU player lay unconscious on the floor. The Japanese drank enough to lose their inhibitions and join the singing and swirling all-male dances. The South Koreans, although they had a good rousing time and did drink the obligatory toasts, sometimes with slight grimaces, never lost their composure or sense of discipline. For my wife Sydna, who was only one of four females present (the others being waitresses), it was a rare look at a traditional cross-cultural male bonding ritual. In addition to the abundance of vodka and champagne there was a band and lots of male dancing, but Sydna also had a number of dance partners and was the recipient of two bouquets of roses, one from an umpire named Albert and the other from MGU designated hitter Philip. The party ran until well after midnight and Albert and another umpire, my friend Arkady from Tiraspol, got Sydna and me a ride back to Moscow in a Moscow Militia patrol car. It turned out that the two umpires followed in another car and when we got to MGU Albert insisted the party continue up in our room. Once upstairs the drunken Albert produced a bottle of champagne and also an offer to me to come back the next summer to coach in his Youth Initiatives Program. Arkady was embarrassed by his friend's behavior and we finally got him downstairs and out to where they could get a taxi.

During the first week of July the world focused its attention on Moscow and the long anticipated 28th Congress of the Communist Party of the Soviet Union (CPSU). President Mikhail Gorbachev had been under siege from all sides and there was fear that there might be an open split within the CPSU, or that this might be the last party congress, and even some talk of Gorbachev resigning from his party leadership position. His policy of glasnost had achieved great success in opening up the society for the free flow of information and political criticism of both the past and present. Even Radio Moscow ridiculed the past by saying that "under the previous ruling philosophy whatever was not allowed was prohibited." My Soviet intellectual friends cherished these changes, but the average Russian was more interested in the failures of perestroika to improve economic conditions for consumers. There were more shortages and lines now than in the past, and a cynical joke making the rounds in Moscow said, "Let's return to the days of stagnation when we had clothes and caviar to buy in the shops." Despite his popularity in the rest of the world, it seemed to me at the time that President Gorbachev might not win a popular election in the Soviet Union.

Gorbachev opened the Congress with a three-hour speech that systematically responded to each of the criticisms. Despite continuing attacks on his policies, by the week's end it was clear that most of the reform communists on the left and conservative communists on the right felt they had no other alternative except to support his orderly program of change toward some type of modified market economy. Each evening the hundreds of delegates would walk through Red Square on their way between the Kremlin and their rooms in the Hotel Rossiya. Although there were about a dozen policemen scattered about in the general vicinity of the hotel, they made no attempt to stop the small groups of protesters or individuals from engaging the returning delegates in discussions or sometimes lengthy debates.

One night we introduced ourselves to Alexander Zakharov, a second secretary of the Leningrad Communist Party, which my Soviet friend described as a high party position. He looked a bit like Gary Cooper at age forty and was easy going with a sense of humor. He kissed my wife's hand and then proceeded to talk with us for forty-five minutes as we wandered through Red Square. Among other things, he said he had no problems with a multi-party system but felt that the CPSU was the only organization strong enough to administer the changes of perestroika. That afternoon he had exchanged views with a priest at a monastery in nearby Zagorsk, and he and other delegates had just seen a new Soviet movie *We Can't Live Like This Anymore*, which he said was depressing but left them in a thoughtful mood.

In the evenings at around 11 p.m. in Red Square, Dan Rather and the other news people from CBS, ABC, NBC and CNN taped their reports for the evening news back in the United States. We had an interesting midnight conversation with CBS analyst and Princeton professor Stephen Cohen, the night that hard line conservative Ligachev made his surprise attempt to defeat Gorbachev's man for the position of deputy secretary of the CPSU. Cohen had just finished a tape for the evening news but said that he and Rather would have to return to Red Square at 2:30 a.m. (6:30 p.m. New York) for a live feed if the election results were announced that night. He commented that Gorbachev would win either way, because if Ligachev were to win, Gorbachev would have made good on his promise to bring democracy to the CPSU. He also confirmed what was obvious, that democracy was breaking out all over the society, but that few would live long enough to see the end of perestroika, and that there will be no final victory, just skirmishes in a long process of profound change. Ligachev failed in his bid but the late evening fireworks forced the cancellation of an early morning meeting I had scheduled with Soviet and American TV personality Vladimir Posner. Since he had to leave right after the Congress for the Goodwill Games, we agreed to try again to get together in New York to talk about Soviet baseball.

On the last night of the Congress we watched Gorbachev's closing speech on TV. When he finished there was a standing ovation but relatively quickly he seemed to become uncomfortable and indicated he wanted it to end. As the applause died away it was replaced by the rising swell of the delegates' voices as they sang their way through all the verses of the "Internationale." Gorbachev then leaned to the microphone and made a brief and apparently humorous comment that had the delegates chuckling as they left their seats.

The political origins of the Cold War date back to a period right after World War II, a time when my youthful attention was riveted on the exploits of Jackie Robinson, Pee Wee Reese, Carl Furillo, Gil Hodges, Roy Campanella, Duke Snider, Carl Erskine, and the other Boys of Summer. By 1968 however, the Brooklyn Dodgers were nothing but a fond memory, and the central focus of my life was by then organizing opposition to the Vietnam War, which was just one of the many tragic consequences of the Cold War mentality which would continue to shape world events for another twenty years.

In early August 1990 as I adjusted my old blue and white Brooklyn Dodger baseball cap on the dugout steps of the Moscow State University (MGU) Baseball Stadium, I reflected back on the rapidity of events that had brought an end to the Cold War and me to Moscow in April to coach baseball. It was like the realization of two intertwined fantasies, the first political, and the second personal, an incredible opportunity to return to my youthful field of dreams with the boys of summer of the Soviet Union.

The day before my August departure I took one last look at our Moscow State University field of dreams. I wondered if perestroika and baseball would take hold quickly enough for Mikhail Gorbachev to someday throw out the first ball on opening day. I was fifteen pounds lighter than when I arrived in April, but my mind was bulging with rich memories and I knew that the challenging and exciting last five months might have been the high point of my life. I also thought a lot about my Soviet friends and couldn't get the tearful words of my young undergraduate friend Irene out of my mind. "What will happen to my country?"

Perestroika and Ideology

John J. Neumaier

Thanks to the opportunity given to contributors by the editor of this book, my friend Dorothy S. McClellan, I am adding brief comments to the 1991 Foreword to my essay collection, *Perestroika and Ideology*. In a sense, they are an "afterword," with twenty years of hindsight.

My original newspaper reports were written during the tumultuous times of Michael Gorbachev and Boris Yeltsin, a period marked by the ideas of perestroika, the restructuring of Soviet governance along more liberal lines, and of glasnost, the loosening of restrictions on citizens' freedoms. As it happened, those events were closely related to the subject of my research project, which was to study the changing ideological currents in the Soviet Union.

"Ideology," a term popularized by the 18th century enlightenment *philosophes*, is a complex concept, used by scholars (particularly sociologists, social theorists, and philosophers) as well as by politicians, journalists, and folks generally, to denote and connote the value system(s) of people of diverse groupings, including nation-states.

In general parlance, the term "ideology" is used rather loosely, often with a negative connotation, especially when it is applied to groups which are alien from one's own. My own use and understanding of it is explained in my final essay. Here I want only to express my view that no one is free of ideological assumptions, including myself, of course.

In addition to my comments on ideological trends during the perestroika period and on how the expression of opinion was affected by glasnost, you will find reports on everyday Soviet living conditions, particularly in major Russian cities like the capital. In this connection, I need to point out that it was nothing new to hear Muscovites' complaints about their dismal living standards as compared with what they perceived to be far superior conditions in the West, particularly the United States. I had heard such criticism in the years before perestroika, especially from academics and professionals. However, I should add that at Moscow State University, we also heard orthodox *partinost* (party-minded) professors, as well as many citizens, give high praise to Soviet improvements of social conditions, indeed of Communist Party achievements in every sphere.

Given the contrast between the ubiquitous Soviet propaganda aimed at the *tovarishchi* (comrade-citizens) and the more sophisticated ways in which the mass media in the United States support our "national interests" and U.S. nationalism, I was surprised to note that in spite of the Communist government-controlled media, education, and communication outlets, Soviet citizens knew significantly more about life in our country than our people knew about Soviet life.

For example, while millions of Americans are familiar with the Kremlin fur-hatted line-up on Lenin's tomb reviewing the Red Square military parade (reminding the Soviet *tovarishchi* and the world of their victory over Nazi Germany), few Americans are aware of the generally high level of Russian educational achievements in history, science, and literature. I was amazed at how many Soviet graduate students I met who knew foreign literature and philosophy, including U.S. authors and philosophers. They had accomplished this in spite of the omnipresent emphasis on Communist doctrine and the censorship in libraries.

As I look back on my experiences of some twenty years ago, just preceding the dissolution of the U.S.S.R., I can't help but think that the emergence of a capitalist Russian Federation and the adoption of its version of parliamentary democracy were not inevitable. However, I will not engage here in speculation about iffy historical alternatives.

Instead, let me recall some aspects of what I believe to have happened after Gorbachev initiated perestroika. The final transition period was dominated by Boris Yeltsin (a former Communist apparatchik) who in June of 1991 was elected president of the Russian Soviet Federative Socialist Republic. After the dissolution of the U.S.S.R., it was replaced by the Russian Federation, of which Yeltsin was the first president. Under Yeltsin's authoritarian type of decision-making, his deputy prime minister Yegor Gaidar administered the so-called shock therapy, the method by which Russian capitalism was introduced.

The most prominent Western expert called in to help shape the new economic system via shock therapy, was the young American Harvard economics professor Jeffrey Sachs. The main characteristics of the transition from the highly controlled Soviet system to that of the Russian Federation were its top-down direction and the fervent fostering of the type of competition which created the "oligarchs" who profited so immensely from the new socioeconomic conditions.

It soon became common knowledge that many of the anti–Communist leaders, including some of the wealthiest oligarchs, were former Communist apparatchiks. In fact, in the years that have elapsed since those days, I have received letters from several Russian friends who were strongly anti–Communist, but were now telling me how disillusioned they were with some of the injustices and corruption of the new system.

In contrast, in 1991, the trend among academics of my acquaintance was to readily adapt their long avowed Communist ideological orientation to that of "democratic capitalism." The rush to embrace the new orthodoxy of private enterprise in place of partinost orthodoxy included many prominent Moscow State University professors of philosophy. I knew some of them well, yet I avoided naming examples of such "conversion" in order to protect the not-so-innocents. It is in this sense that the political becomes the personal and vice versa. After all, most of us philosophers are better versed in theory than in practice.

It reminds me of the German philosopher and activist, who concluded from his scholarly, personal, and political experiences that "philosophers have hitherto only interpreted the world in various ways; the point is to change it" (Karl Marx's eleventh thesis on Feuerbach).

In the years before perestroika, one of the ways that dissidents circumvented censorship in the Soviet Union was with "samizdat," self-published manuscripts, that were passed surreptitiously from hand to hand. If perpetrators were discovered by the authorities, the consequences could be severe.

In this country, where social control is far more subtle and widely diffused, "samizdat" is quite a different thing. In fact, most U.S. intellectuals are unaware of how the dominant ideology shapes their social perspectives and limits their alternatives (in sharp contrast to the Soviet Union, where the ideological hegemony of the Communist Party was no secret). Dissidents here are not put into an asylum; they are seldom even labeled "dissidents." If they insist on calling themselves dissident, they are apt to be dismissed as "nutty" and in need of therapy. Still, there is a kind of samizdat, American style, and it is often done with flair, utilizing the latest desktop publishing technology or the more costly vanity press. Its authors have manifold motives and reasons for trying to get their materials published. Sometimes it's because of unsatisfied pride of authorship, sometimes, because they're writing against the ideological grain. I like to think that my own case is closer to the latter than the former.

All of the material in this essay has been previously published, thanks to the publisher and executive editor of the *Daily Freeman* of Kingston, New York, Ira Fusfeld. (It didn't hurt that he was the student editor of the college paper at New Paltz while I was the "chief custodian" there.) For several years I have been writing a monthly column for the Sunday *Freeman*, which appears on the first Sunday of the month. Sometimes it is also published in other newspapers. The six columns which make up this essay, however, were written especially for the *Freeman*, and were sent to Kingston from Moscow (except for the last one datelined Poughkeepsie).

I was in Moscow from February 7 until June 26, 1991, with my wife and colleague, Dr. Sara (Sally) Fletcher Luther. I was there officially, as part of the State University of New York—Moscow State University (SUNY-MSU) exchange program, she, unofficially, doing much of the work while I got much of the credit (a long established sexist division of labor). Our host department was the "kafedra" of the History of Foreign Philosophy, one of the fourteen departments at the University's school of academic philosophy.

My research focused on the changes in ideology and in the theory of ideology that have occurred since perestroika and glasnost. My lifelong scholarly interest in ideology and propaganda has its roots in my experiences as a youth in Nazi Germany. Along with the physical brutality and terrorism of the Hitler regime, total ideological hegemony was the chief means of social control, perfected, by Hitler's German Minister for Propaganda and Popular Enlightenment Joseph Goebbels.

When I came as a German-Jewish refugee to the United States in 1940, I continued to pursue my interest in ideology and propaganda, sometimes with full awareness, sometimes intuitively. I studied and was concerned with its many manifestations in human relations, especially in the pervasive climate of racism and discrimination against women, and in the subordinate status of workers. For several years I worked in a Minneapolis factory, and then served in the U.S. Army. After the war I was graduated with a Ph.D. in philosophy from the University of Minnesota. For a time I taught humanities there, and later I served as head of three institutions of higher education: Hibbing Community College (1955–58), Moorhead State University (1958–68), and State University College at New Paltz, New York (1968–72). Since 1972 I have been a professor of philosophy and social theory at Empire State College, SUNY, in New York City. I am looking forward to retirement as of October 30, 1991, having been ready for it ever since leaving high school.

Standing in Line in Moscow: Moscow, February 25, 1991

After a comfortable eleven-hour flight on Aeroflot, with a refueling stopover at Shannon, Ireland, we landed smoothly, mid-afternoon, February 7, at

Moscow International Airport. Customs clearance went quickly and as Sally and I wheeled our luggage past the waiting crowd our eyes fell on a large sign with my name on it. It was held by an attractive fur-hatted young woman who turned out to be a graduate student from my host department at Moscow State University (where she is specializing in the theory of knowledge of the German philosopher Husserl). With less than perfect English (but decidedly better than our Russian) she gave us a warm welcome and led the way to the University van.

During the long ride (28 kilometers) to the city, the cheerful driver, apparently undaunted by a badly cracked windshield, pointed out the sights, including the commemorative barricade that marks the point at which the Soviet army stopped the Nazi advance on Moscow in 1941. He commented on the long lines of people standing in front of various shops and asked if we had such lines in the States. I said no, but that we too had our problems, whereupon he assured me that they were nothing compared to Soviet problems (a widely held view here). He then asked with obvious pride whether we knew that the Soviet orbiter *Salyut–7*, having completed its mission, had fallen to Earth in flames the night before. It is not uncommon to hear bitter complaints about Soviet living conditions right alongside expressions of national pride.

Moscow State University

When we sighted the gigantic main building of Moscow University (which was to be our home away from home), our young guide remarked with some amusement on its "Stalinski baroque" style. (In fact, during the postwar years, Stalin ordered the construction of seven such buildings in Moscow, all of them looking much alike, to the consternation of lost tourists.)

We are beginning our third research trip under the joint sponsorship of the academic exchange program of the State University of New York and Moscow State University (SUNY-MSU). In 1979–80 I concentrated on the organization, curricula, and teaching of philosophy in the huge MSU philosophy "fakultet" (160 philosophers) and interviewed professors in each of its fourteen departments (such as Logic, Ethics, Foreign Philosophy, and History of Marxism-Leninism). In 1984–85 (we flew home the day Gorbachev assumed office) I studied Soviet philosophers' evaluations of Western social philosophy, especially of Critical Theory. This time I will be exploring new developments in philosophy and ideology since glasnost and perestroika, as well as changes in the larger society.

The most prestigious university in the U.S.S.R., Moscow State University (sometimes called the Harvard of the Soviet Union), rises above the Lenin

Hills of southwest Moscow, forming a complex that is almost a city in itself. Its main building alone has dormitories for some 9,000 students, along with restaurants, cafeterias, theater ticket booths, movie theater, discotheque, post office, newspaper and book stalls, administrative and faculty offices, classrooms, a four-story museum of Earth sciences, and tailoring, laundry, barber, grocery, and shoe repair shops. The grand hall, decorated with a large mosaic of Lenin, was the site of Ronald Reagan's 1988 address to wildly enthusiastic MSU students.

Changes at the University

As we entered the building, changes were already noticeable. The two militiamen at the door were no longer checking identity cards ("propusks"), nor were the two supervisors stationed at the double desk by the entrance to our dormitory zone. A less welcome change was that none of the four elevators was working, although the next day one was, and still is (with occasional lapses). Our floor lady ("djournaya"), an old friend from previous stays, later told us that we had to press the elevator's down button to go up and the up button to make it stop on the way down. It was a new demonstration of Einstein's theory of relativity. Our quarters are Spartan but adequate, indeed, by local student standards, luxurious, and, wonder of wonders, we have for the first time a telephone. Getting it to work is an art form that we are determined to master. Dormitory facilities do not compare to those in American colleges, but, given the shortage of habitations in the Soviet Union and in Russian history, they are much in demand, which partly explains the presence of guards at the entrances.

Waiting in Line

In Moscow's present straitened conditions, the University is a kind of food oasis where students and staff can buy supplies that are not readily available in stores (though of course in most respects the universities tend to mirror the universe that surround them, and on which they depend). Off-campus shopping is far more difficult. There are usually very long lines and goods are severely limited. At one fruit and vegetable store we found no line, but all you could buy was rice, little green onions (still with the earth around their roots), cooking onions, a Soviet version of apple juice (not to suggest that ours is the "correct" version), tomato juice, honey, and sacks of black seeds, the use of which has become part of my research project. The green onions went like hotcakes. On a Saturday, at a barren "supermarket," we found the usual lines, though nothing was for sale but milk, kefir, rice, sugar, canned tomatoes, bottled soda, and one lonely piece of salmon. In order to shop at any of these stores, one is required (since last October) to carry a special identity card (Kartochky). The rule is aimed at keeping non-Muscovites from coming in to buy up food.

You also have to line up at the University to collect your stipend, to check your coat, to get on the elevator, to get your textbook, to receive clean linen, to eat at the students' cafeterias or the modest professors' restaurant, to buy movie and theater tickets, bread, snacks, or a newspaper. In the unregulated private markets lines are shorter and supplies are more plentiful, but prices are considerably higher than in state stores. At a state florist shop near the subway station Park Caldera, there were no flowers, only house plants, and a sales lady engrossed in her book (many Soviets are avid readers). Just a few steps away were private stands with beautiful flowers (tulips, roses, carnations, calla lilies, daffodils). Bunches sold for 3 to 7 rubles per flower, plus a ruble for the cellophane wrapper. Right now the official exchange rate is 5½ rubles for one dollar.

Demonstration Against the War

Another change that we witnessed was a street demonstration that was not sponsored by the government. About 150 people protested the Gulf War on Sunday, February 17, in front of the U.S. embassy. Organized by an Arab-Soviet committee, the crowd also contained elements of the extreme right (before glasnost these were pretty much suppressed). While Sally was shooting video pictures, a woman who appeared to be part of a strongly anti–Zionist contingent asked me whether we were for or against the war. I explained in my elementary Russian that we opposed the war and also the Iraqi invasion of Kuwait. She repeatedly lamented the terrible cost in human lives. I expressed our own deep concern with the bombing and the mounting casualties. She asked us if we were Americans; I nodded and informed her that I also happened to be Jewish. She was dumbfounded.

Public opinion on the war appears to be divided. Many academicians have told us that they supported Gorbachev's efforts to put an end to the killing. Others completely agreed with U.S. military and diplomatic policies in the Gulf region. But most Soviets are primarily preoccupied with domestic problems, particularly economic ones, and with the relationship between the Union and the republics, especially the Baltic states. That there is wide diversity of opinion is illustrated by the fact that Moscow now has some fifty newspapers, most with sharply differing points of view. The study of ideological change is going to be a big challenge!

The Intelligentsia and Perestroika: Moscow, March 31, 1991

It is difficult to assess the long-term consequences of the March 17 referendum on Gorbachev's plan for the preservation of the Union (which was approved by 76.4 percent of the voters, representing an 80 percent turnout). But it is clear this country is experiencing a veritable flood of ideological crosscurrents. You can see it every day in the very labels that people and political movements use to identify themselves and each other as they engage in battle for public support.

MAKING IDEOLOGICAL WAVES

One trend is represented by *Moscow News* (MN), a formerly Communist weekly, founded in 1930. It appears in seven languages, including Russian and English and is distributed worldwide (with a claimed circulation of more than two million). Its editors view it as "democratic," and it is generally referred to as "liberal" or even "left." An excerpt from a commentary in the February 10–17 issue provides a good summary of MN's present orientation. It is an example of how the many anti-communist critics here are looking at the recent history of their country. The author writes that

> perestroika in its first stage was viewed by its initiators as a "reform from above" aimed at renovating the country's political, economic and social systems. To this effect it was necessary to curb the arms race which had completely exhausted the Soviet economy, to give up confrontation with the West and China, to rebuff the Brezhnev doctrine and paternalism in relations with East European allies, to put an end to the Afghan war, to stop supporting "progressive" dictatorships in the Third World, and to create favorable conditions in order to concentrate on domestic problems. This kind of new thinking suited almost everybody, except perhaps diehard Marxist fundamentalists who still held the supremacy of class-oriented values over commonly-held human values.

But toward the end of 1989 things changed considerably, the writer argues. The Communist Party began to attack Foreign Minister Shevardnadze's foreign policy toward the West, and sharpened its criticisms of the "dismantling of socialism" and the "disintegration of the Union." The commentator continues: "In the current political situation, there is an imminent threat that the policy of new thinking may be reviewed. The conservative and reactionary forces now under the President's patronage or perhaps vice-versa are not interested in preserving [the] former foreign policy to the same extent." They harbor "aspirations to keep the old system intact at any price, apart from minor alterations," he concludes.

This portrayal of the U.S.S.R. and the "decline of perestroika" is not unlike what one reads in the U.S. mass media, except that *Moscow News* goes even further than most Westerners in criticizing President Gorbachev and his "turn to the right" (which here is taken to mean the Communist Party). On the other hand, MN and other Soviet papers also have depicted Gorbachev as a "centrist," who is trying to steer a middle course between "party apparachiks" and "democrats" (the latter are often called "radicals"). Although the people here know that the West condemns Soviet military action in Lithuania, they also know that Gorbachev is much more popular in the West than he is in the Soviet Union.

The Intelligentsia

Many in the Soviet intellectual establishment, certainly in Moscow, are strongly opposed to Gorbachev's administration and policies. In conversations with Soviet academics, I found some bitterly accusing him of making what they believed to be a planned linkage of the referendum on preserving the Union with the larger issue of preserving its socialist orientation, thereby reinforcing the dominance of the Communist Party. Still, the question of the socio-political and economic future of the Soviet Union is extremely complex, even for Soviets. And because of our very different historical backgrounds and institutions, it is even more difficult for Westerners to understand.

Criticisms, opinions, and Weltanschauung differ widely, not only among those outside of the Party, but within its membership as well. There are many Communist Party members, for example, who strongly oppose the orthodoxies of the past, which they call "distortions and deformations."

In this country dissent has a long history. It predates the Revolution by centuries and is connected in many ways with what is called the "Russian intelligentsia," an influential stratum that reflects literary, spiritual, philosophical, and political traditions. As it happens, most of the people I have met are part of the "Intelligentsia," some of them intellectuals and academics, others technocrats and administrative functionaries. One professor, whom we had known from our previous research at Moscow University, told us that during the long years before perestroika he and many of his colleagues had to lead a double life (it seems to me some of them still do). He felt oppressed by the requirement that he think in terms of the collective, the "we," and that he had to keep quiet about the personal, the "I." He implied that such silence was necessary for career advancement, if not also for personal security. Others have agreed, describing themselves as having had split personalities—their public postures and their real values and ideas. When I mentioned this to a young woman professional, she accused such people of being opportunists and asserted that she and others like her were able to get professional work without belonging to the Party. Her political views happen to be to the left—in the old sense of "left"—of most contemporary Soviet Communists. In any case, while plenty of dissident criticism of the regime was expressed to us during our two previous visits, it was seldom as explicit as what we are hearing now, under glasnost.

Sausage Lines

There is another dimension to the widespread alienation among intellectuals. Several of the professors who are particularly strong in their condemnation of the past ideological emphasis on the concepts of "class" and "class struggle" feel that ever since the Bolshevik revolution the contributions of the intelligentsia have been downgraded in favor of the masses, whom they describe as ignorant and materialistic. Various categories of workers have higher salaries than academics. One full professor complained about receiving a monthly salary of 400 rubles while party functionaries, many of whom he felt lacked adequate cultural and educational backgrounds, receive higher salaries and all kinds of privileges, including foreign travel. He also bemoaned the fact that while the people form long lines for sausages and other goods, he could see no such lines to buy tickets at the Tchaikovsky Concert Hall. The challenge of perestroika should be to improve not only the material conditions of life but the spiritual as well, he said. I mentioned that I had seen plenty of academics standing in "sausage lines." Indeed, in the prestigious academic institutes the lines of customers waiting for hard-to-get-items consist almost entirely of academics. The same professor, perhaps expressing more freely what some of his colleagues only hint at, recalled with some contempt that Lenin once said any washerwoman could fill a government post (though Sally and I haven't seen any women at all in high government positions).

Celebrating Women

Which brings me to International Women's Day. One of the major Soviet holidays, it was celebrated here on March 8 with great popular enthusiasm. Many took the occasion to congratulate Sally. One professor gave her a bouquet of tulips, and she, along with thousands of other women on Moscow streets, could proudly display this token of recognition. As I was cooking rice that evening in our communal dormitory kitchen I observed the women preparing huge dinners. I hoped that they did not have to work too much harder than usual in celebration of their day of honor.

"Your Problems Are Our Dreams!" Moscow, April 29, 1991

As various political factions, nationality movements, labor unions, and breakaway republics struggle for power here, it sometimes seems that the very existence of the Soviet Union is in question. There is a pervasive pessimism about living standards and the immediate future of the economy. Many Soviet citizens view the day-to-day business of fending for themselves and their families as the most serious problem in their lives. Intellectuals also share in this basic concern for material well being, despite their bitter attacks on the old Marxist and Leninist emphasis on the centrality of the economic factor in human life.

Pervasive Pessimism

Complaints center on the inadequacy and poor quality of food supplies and services and on the recent sharp rise in prices, on top of the 5 percent sales tax imposed in February. Scarcities range widely, from matches to cheese, from shoes to light bulbs, from decent phone service to automotive repairs (for the few who own cars, about 50 per 1000 compared to 580 per 1000 in the U.S.). And, of course, there is the continuing problem of having to wait in line for just about everything.

Adding to the atmosphere of gloom and doom are the many Moscow newspapers, which lament the state of the economy in story after story, week in and week out, and repeatedly compare conditions here to the way things are in "normal" countries. Even Radio Moscow echoes this pessimism, in stark contrast to its old ways when it saw almost everything through rose-colored glasses.

If you ask for an explanation of the shortages of goods and the inadequate services, the usual answer is "Ya ne znayoo" (I don't know), which is followed, nonetheless, by assorted hypotheses. Sometimes the problems are attributed to the difficulty of switching from a centralized economy to a market-oriented economy (the term "capitalism" is seldom used). Another answer is simply: "74 years of communism" (more specifically, of social egalitarianism and the absence of the profit motive). Others tell you that it is the lack of hard currency, or financial mismanagement by the state, or the ineptitude of the Party bureaucracy, or the indecisiveness of Gorbachev and government agencies. Some have said it is the overall lack of skill in business management, coupled with large-scale corruption, incompetence, inefficiency, and technological backwardness. Two explanations that seem to be favored by the intelligentsia are the "laziness of workers" and the "traditionalist mentality of the peasantry" from which the present population sprang.

In fact, despite the widespread discontent, we have noticed that people are better dressed than they were even five years ago. And notwithstanding the current food shortage, there appears to be a greater variety and supply of fruits and vegetables than we saw in 1979 and 1984. Nevertheless, self-flagellation, pessimism, and negativism are clearly in fashion. "Understanding that everything is bad is good" (quoted from the column of a humorist in the April issue of *Business in the USSR*). One friend told us that she prefers to stay at home most of the time just to avoid the "constant frustrations of daily life." On the other hand, an old Party loyalist told us that public morale has been made far worse by the "Western-oriented" Moscow press and its hyper-critical attitudes—not only toward present difficulties but to all Russian history, ignoring the many positive achievements both before and since the revolution. Despite the deep ideological differences however, everyone agrees on the difficulty and frustration entailed in shopping.

Time Out for Shopping

When it comes to this matter of shopping, you have to see it to believe it. I don't speak in derision, but in recognition of the grim reality. Take, for example, the hundreds of Moscow food stores, most of which specialize in only one kind of product—such as bread, vegetables, dairy products, cakes and cookies, or meat. First, customers crowd each other trying to get up to the counter to see what there is to buy. Sometimes this means you have to line up successively at several counters. Once you have selected your items you receive from the salesperson a chit that itemizes the prices, without specifying the commodities. Then you shift to another line for a wait of up to twenty minutes, in order to pay the cashier. She adds up the figures, often on the traditional abacus, and issues a receipt which you carry forward to a third queue (often identical with the first) to wait for the clerk to hand over the selected items.

Frequently, what you want may not be available. Or if it is—maybe a shipment of shoes has just arrived—there is a line of shoppers who have heard the good news and are out in the streets waiting to get admitted to the store. The sales "system" varies somewhat with types of stores, that is, between those selling food, books, clothing, hardware, furniture, household goods, office supplies, watches, department stores, etc., but the general pattern is the same.

All of this gives more ammunition to the parade of columnists and editorial writers who criticize the authorities for being too slow to make the transition to a "market economy" and too quick to raise prices, and regularly compare Soviet economic performance with the standard of living in "civilized" countries. Unlike the past when journalists concentrated on urban decay and poverty in the West, especially the United States, they are now at the other extreme, writing as if U.S. streets were paved with gold. They laud without reservation "the tremendous progress made by contemporary Western Society." As one acquaintance put it to me, "Your problems are our dreams."

In this volatile climate it is easy to understand why there are not too many prominent politicians (apart from Yeltsin) who are eager to replace President Gorbachev. Nor have his numerous critics been offering much in the way of politically viable proposals to solve the economic and nationality crises. Not that this has diminished the intensity of the attacks on Gorbachev, who paradoxically was the one who paved the way for making such attacks possible.

Still, the outlook is not all bleak. There are a small but growing number of joint ventures that are taking shape. They consist of U.S.S.R. and Western businesspeople who are seeking to develop the kind of market economy favored not only by the "radicals," but also by various levels of the government, the Party, and many of the constituent republics.

"New Thinking" and the "New Economic Policy": Moscow, May 28, 1991

Almost everyone here agrees on the need to switch to a more market oriented economy, but that is where the agreement stops. The difficult period of transition—which forms the centerpiece of Gorbachev's perestroika and "New Thinking"—is enormously complicated, not only by the traditions and history of Russian and Soviet society, but also by today's political and social struggles. It would take a superior economist and social analyst to figure it all out, let alone find a solution. Professionals here give you a pained smile when asked which Soviet or Western expert is best qualified to help this huge country make the transition from a centrally controlled to a market economy. A reply I have heard more than once is that there is no such expert because it has never been attempted before.

Conflicting Views

One need not be an expert, however, to recognize some of the obstacles. Foremost among them is the struggle between those who want to preserve the framework of social relations developed over the years since the Bolshevik revolution and those who want to abolish as many socialist institutions and traditions as possible. Of course there are many, particularly outside of the intelligentsia, who do not think in terms of a clear choice between socialism and capitalism. What the people on the street seem to mean by a market economy is more and better goods on the shelves, greater choice of products, improved housing, in short, a higher standard of living, a condition which they identify with life in the West. They are not concerned with the finer points of economic theory, nor do they want to hear about the existence of poverty in the West, as compared with what they perceive as the incredible affluence of the West's middle classes.

Another issue here is the deep division between mental and manual workers. For a long time class struggle in the Soviet Union was said to be nonexistent, or, if acknowledged, it was regarded as "non-antagonistic," because the means of production were owned by the state. But the evidence is clear that inter-class conflict is alive and well. In fact, its overt expression has become much sharper since the introduction of glasnost. Members of the intelligentsia tend to see themselves as having been systematically underpaid and not sufficiently appreciated ever since the founding of the workers' state. While there is much debate on whether the Union of Soviet Socialist Republics was really socialist or even a workers' state, the intelligentsia ruefully point out that many of them receive the same salaries as street cleaners and often less than skilled workers. Still, it would be a mistake to think that the resentment is coming only from the professionals. One soon becomes aware of the less than comradely feelings of some tired wardrobe women, kitchen employees, and other non-academic workers toward those who are privileged to read, teach, research, and deal with ideas for a living. Obviously, such social tensions are not confined to Soviet society, though many Soviets sometimes talk as if that were the case.

A Window of Opportunity?

Despite dissatisfactions and complaints, there are many who are ready to take advantage of this time of ferment and transition. They see the promising economic potential of an unleashed market. One person commented to me that it could be compared to the Wild West or the time of the "robber barons" in the United States. At the cutting edge of the "New Thinking" are those who are getting involved in a special form of doing business called "joint ventures." Under a decree of January 3, 1987, Soviet and foreign partners may now co-own and jointly manage a business corporation. The purpose is to develop the relatively untapped Soviet market, utilizing Western business know-how and management techniques and, most important of all, to attract foreign capital. It is not an easy undertaking, given the great shortage of "hard currency" (meaning Western currency, particularly dollars) that is needed for essential imports and for the development of Soviet industrial production for export. U.S. trade barriers continue to stand in the way of Soviet-U.S. commercial relations. And many U.S. firms are reluctant to do business in the U.S.S.R. because of past Soviet restraints on commerce and foreign operations.

My understanding is that even now there still are no clear-cut legal distinctions between legitimate business operations and fraudulent business manipulations, an uncertainty that can have tragic consequences for business people engaged in what Westerners might regard as acceptable commercial activity.

Actually, major Western banks and financial institutions have maintained at least token representation in Moscow for many years. An article in *Moscow Magazine*, appropriately entitled "Risky Business," calls attention to "the thorny issue of the ruble, which according to most experts, is years from convertibility." Paradoxically, the West's traditional business opposition to socialism, let alone Communist Party control, is now counter-posed by nervousness about present developments in the U.S.S.R. Alan Cooper, Moscow group representative for National Westminster Bank, is quoted as saying: "We applaud glasnost and perestroika, but from a purely banking point of view, it raises the credit risk, it allows strikes to happen, it allows people to start talking about all the problems in the society, and at the end of the day it all adds up to a bad credit rating." This view is echoed by John Minneman, Moscow representative for Chase Manhattan Bank: "The market is nervous because of the pace of political change. Clients are covering their bets, but it's a damn difficult time to finalize contracts."

In spite of the problems, contacts between budding Soviet entrepreneurial types and Western businesses are growing rapidly. And, despite the uncertainty arising out of presidential decrees and the ongoing process of amendments and refinements in the laws governing joint ventures, there seems to be an unwritten rule that private initiative is to be encouraged throughout the economy. It may be of interest that some of the supporters of the "New Thinking," including Gorbachev himself, have not infrequently made the point that it was Lenin's NEP (New Economic Policy) of the early twenties that pioneered the idea that incentives were needed to improve Soviet performance and provide openings to the West.

Private Enterprise at the University

Here at Moscow State University I have found that private commercial initiative is in full stride. Vendors of hard-to-get items, including caviar, set up their stands on university grounds, inside and outside of the dormitories. Private bookstalls are opening up, at least one a month, offering art books, novels, journals, and sometimes souvenirs and sweatshirts. Recently I purchased a beautiful volume of Tretyakov Gallery paintings, priced by the state publishing house at 25 rubles and 10 kopeks, and sold by eager entrepreneurs for 250 rubles. Of course, at the new tourist exchange rate of 27 rubles per dollar, this is a bargain for foreigners but not for Soviet academics, many of whom get that amount as monthly salary. At the same time, it should be pointed out that comparisons between salaries here and in the U.S. are difficult, since here such expenses as rent and transportation often constitute no more than ten to fifteen percent of a family's income. Incidentally, bookstands at the University now sometimes sell foreign newspapers like the *Wall Street Journal*, *International Herald Tribune* and *Frankfurter Allgemeine* for about two rubles, and *Time* and *Newsweek* for four rubles. I have not yet been able to find out whether this low price is being subsidized by the University, the State, or the Western media—in hopes of opening the glasnost curtain ever further.

A major challenge for perestroika is the absence of business experience. An increasing number of institutes are offering classes in principles of economics, business management, sales techniques and business ethics, and the competition for admission is stiff. One such institution is the Russian-American University founded by Soviet émigré Edward Lozansky, a prominent physicist-businessman residing in Washington, D.C. Located here at Moscow University, the school has just finished its first year. It is headed by U.S. economist Edward Dolan. I sat in on one of his lectures, in English, on inflationary cycles. Judging by the students' questions and comments, they followed his difficult themes with remarkable understanding and interest.

Even more impressive is the Soviet talent and creativity surfacing in the field of computer science. I have met three computer scientists who have developed advanced programs for scientific and business use, working out of small offices at the University. The mixing of public and private enterprise is not uncommon, and seems to operate with the encouragement of the authorities.

It may take a long time before the Soviets catch up with the West in developing and applying advanced technology in the civilian sector, but I for one am confident that they will eventually do so, not only for their benefit, but for that of the world.

Problems and Paradoxes in Moscow: Moscow, June 23, 1991

As our departure nears, I am increasingly conscious of how difficult it is to understand this huge country, its diversity and paradoxes, and the momentous changes now unfolding. Unfortunately, most of our stay has been limited to Moscow itself. Though it is the capital of both the Soviet Union and of the Russian republics, and has a population of eight million (which swells to 11 million with daily visitors from the countryside), it is no more representative of the Soviet Union than New York City is of the United States.

Elections in the RSFSR (Russian Soviet Federative Socialist Republic)

We observed with interest the June campaign to elect a first president of Russia. Each of the six candidates got 200,000 rubles to finance his campaign. Nomination required 100,000 signatures or 10 percent of the votes of the Russian parliament. As everybody predicted, Boris Yeltsin, the sixty-year-old chairman of that parliament, was the winner, with 57 percent of the votes. The runner-up was the former Soviet prime minister Nicolai Ryzhkov, 61, with 17 percent of the vote. None of the minor candidates received more than a few percentage points. Pluralism was the dominant theme. In fact, the voters had a much wider choice than is usually the case in the United States.

Like almost all of the candidates, Yeltsin rose to prominence through a career in the Communist Party, though his present populist position stresses anti-communism and the free market rather than the virtues of Brezhnev and Bolshevism. In fact, support for free market principles is today as common as support for Marxism-Leninism once was.

We were present at a campaign rally of one of the minor candidates. He had made a name for himself by using rather strong language on television and also by his promise to bring down the price of vodka. The audience was wildly enthusiastic, but we were not always sure whether they were laughing with him or at him.

Meeting People

Every day is crowded with new experiences, although they don't seem to help us much in penetrating the cultural curtain that still separates the East from the West. It has been a tumultuous five months, not only for the world and the Soviet Union, but also for Sally and me, as we have trekked from place to place and interview to interview. The list reads like a Baedeker: the offices of the patriarchate at Danilo monastery, the holy city of Zagorsk, the Central Moscow Synagogue, the offices of Radio Moscow, the Soviet Women's Committee, a score of museums, galleries, libraries, academic institutes, concert halls and theatres (including the Bolshoi), and the famous Spasso House (the U.S. embassy), where Ambassador Jack Matlock presided over a seminar on federal-state relations, Soviet-style. Not forgetting our main task, which has been to interview professionals and academics about changes in Soviet ideologies since perestroika, an inquiry we have supplemented with informal conversations with dozens of non-academic Russians, from our dormitory plumber to an elected people's deputy in the regional city council whom we encountered on a trolley-bus. We have also enjoyed the rare opportunity of visiting families in their homes, talking about life and politics around the living-dining room table, and even at their dachas (we're told that 50 percent of Muscovites own one of these little summer cottages—most of them within a fifty mile radius of Moscow).

At a conference on worker-management relations sponsored by Hofstra University, the Moscow Academy of Labor and Social Relations, and the Soviet Sociological Association, I heard a Xerox Corporation executive declare that he was not here to give advice since he realized how little he knew after only 72 hours in the country. I reflected that I had had the opposite experience; I felt far more knowledgeable after my first 72 hours here than I do five months later.

Soviet Education

On another subject, much has been written on the high quality of educational achievement in the Soviet Union. It is no doubt a factor in the social mobility we have observed. For example, the son of the woman who sells newspapers in our dormitory lobby is a graduate student in chemistry and electronics. This fall he will be an exchange student in the U.S., very likely at MIT. Another success story is our dormitory floor inspector's daughter who is a member of the University geography faculty. Understandably, the two mothers are very proud of their children's accomplishments.

Alongside the excellent education that many Soviets receive in their universities and institutes is the desire of many people to emigrate to the West. No wonder that Gorbachev and others are worrying about the brain drain that may occur once the new legislation opens up the exit gates on January 1, 1993. Already a significant exodus has occurred as a result of the accelerating emigration of Soviet Jews.

Anti-Semitism

We have discussed the issue of Soviet anti–Semitism with several acquaintances, both Jewish and non–Jewish, and have found a wide diversity of views. Most of the Jewish people we have met are not practicing Jews, except for those we encountered at the Moscow Central Synagogue. There too, views differed, though most that we talked to showed great concern with what they said was an upsurge of anti–Semitism since glasnost. They said that many of their members had emigrated. As a side note, one of the women whom Sally met in the women's gallery said she wanted her daughter to meet our young Dutch bachelor friend whom Sally had pointed out in the men's section downstairs. She withdrew the offer when she learned he was a Catholic chaplain.

Our guide on the trip to the synagogue was a young man whom I had asked for directions on the subway a few days earlier. He turned out to be a businessman, and, of all things, an "eighth generation Schneerson." The Schneersons are a well-known rabbinical family, he told us, whose most prominent member is Menachim Mendl Schneerson, the 7th Lubavitcher rabbi, who lives in Brooklyn and is leader of the Chabad chassidic movement. Like others who have talked with us at the synagogue and elsewhere, young Schneerson and his family will emigrate to the United States. He is very worried about the uncertain future of Jews in the U.S.S.R. and sees greater opportunities in the U.S.

We spent several evenings with a Jewish person who has a very different outlook. He is an expert on race relations in the Western hemisphere and has written several books on the subject. His father disappeared in a labor camp in the thirties. He told us how his career had suffered because of his being Jewish. In the fifties he was accepted into the Communist Party, but he is very critical of some of its past practices, and, of course, of the anti–Semitism of some of its leaders, including Stalin. Still, he is not ready to turn in his card and is one of the very few who have expressed to us the view that Gorbachev is providing constructive leadership. He believes that socialism has a future, but that it must be carried on democratically, and according to him, it will take a long time before the world is materially and spiritually ready for it. I should add that unlike most of our Jewish friends, this man was critical of the Israeli government's policies toward the Palestinians.

We also made friends with a Jewish philosophy teacher from Baku who was terribly disheartened by last year's catastrophic events in Azerbaijan. He told us that the ethnic conflict there, between Azerbaijanis and Armenians, led to some 300 deaths and that about 250,000 people were made refugees. Of the 15,000 Jews who used to live in Baku, he said 14,000 had left, including his own family, which now resides in Israel. He wondered why Western media had given so much more attention to the events in Lithuania and the other Baltic republics than to what had happened in the Baku region. He also told us of an incident in which his aunt was hassled in a Moscow metro by a stranger who identified her as Jewish. In spite of all of this, he has decided to stay, at least for the time being, because of his deep attachment to Russian literature and culture and the rich array of cosmopolitan traditions that characterized the Baku he used to know. Another paradox.

We have heard and read about other manifestations of anti–Semitism, including a verbatim report of a debate between a representative of the fascist *Pamyat* organization and a leader of the Jewish community. In addition to the long history of Russian anti–Semitism, including the time of the horrible pogroms, there appears to be continuing envy of Jews. This is illustrated by comments on the fact that many emigres from the Soviet Union are Jewish. I have been told more than once that some Russians succeed in getting their passports stamped with the Jewish "nationality" so that they will become eligible to apply for emigration. On the other hand, one finds Jews highly placed in the country's academies and in other prominent positions who are in no way interested in leaving their country. But they too (like members of some other minorities, for example Armenians) are envied for their cultural, educational, political or material achievements.

It may well be that the current economic crisis has heightened the problem of anti–Semitism just as it has fanned other inter-ethnic conflicts. Unfortunately, glasnost itself has had the effect of unleashing ethnic prejudice and even acts of open hostility. Still, it may be a mistake to speak of a purely Jewish problem, for here, as in the United States, prejudice and discrimination against Jews is symptomatic of social problems that go well beyond the victimization of certain groups.

My next column will come to you from Poughkeepsie with further reflections on this mysterious and fascinating country.

The End of Ideology in the U.S.S.R.? NYET! Poughkeepsie, New York, July 30, 1991

Back from the hustle and bustle of Moscow, I am still pondering the enormous changes that have occurred since perestroika, especially in Soviet ideology, the focus of my research. What I learned in my many interviews does not lend itself to simple exposition. But as I have always believed that theory must not be left to the theoreticians (any more than war should be left to the generals!), I will try to summarize some of the theoretical problems and findings, at the risk of oversimplification.

Problems of Ideology

I will not go into the logical distinction that is made between "theorizing about ideology" and "having an ideology." But I need to mention some related complications. One is the disagreement that exists concerning the meaning of the term "ideology." The other is the problematic fact that commentators on ideology are not without their own ideological assumptions.

In the United States, as in other Western countries, there are many definitions of the term "ideology." Some give it a primarily political meaning, some economic, some moral; others emphasize religious values or cultural orientations. At the same time, many agree that, generically, "ideology" refers to whatever set of values underlies the socially and historically conditioned ideas of a person, group, or culture. Clearly, these kinds of definitions allow for varying and even competing ideologies. In contrast, in the Soviet Union in the past there was only one approved ideology and that was Marxism-Leninism.

ON BEING SCIENTIFICALLY CORRECT

As for the problem of interpreting someone else's ideology in terms of one's own, Marxist-Leninists freely admitted that they were no more free of ideology than anyone else, but claimed that theirs was the one that was "scientifically" correct. In the West the problem is not always acknowledged, and when it is, it is handled quite differently. Some Western professionals, for example, journalists claim that their reports are "factual," "objective," "dispassionate," and "nonpartisan," including their sensational reporting on current struggles in the Soviet Union. In the same way, Western Sovietologists often claim a privileged status for themselves, purporting to adhere to universally valid and objective criteria of rationality as they critique Soviet institutions and history.

In short, both Marxist-Leninist ideologists and Western "non-ideologists" have traditionally claimed that their own inquiries are objective and valid, but not the other way around. During their Marxist-Leninist years, Soviet academics viewed their Western political science colleagues as having been systematically misled by "bourgeois" ideology. Their own political investigations, the Soviets felt, were grounded in an ideology that was scientific. Western political scientists ridiculed that view, claiming the very opposite, namely that their Soviet colleagues were misled, indeed rigidly controlled by orthodox Marxist-Leninist ideology, which, they argued, undermined the kind of scientific approach practiced by Western political scholars, as implied by the very name of their discipline—political "science."

CHANGES IN SOVIET IDEOLOGY

As a result of today's sweeping ideological changes in the U.S.S.R., the discipline of "scientific communism" is disappearing from Soviet academia; in its place are courses in what is called "politology." In fact, the new paradigm of Soviet politologists is Western political science. The situation is similar in other social sciences, including economics and sociology. Indeed, many Soviet intellectuals, and certainly the majority of philosophers and sociologists I met in Moscow, have gone from one extreme to another. In the past they insisted that Marxism-Leninism was the only correct ideology and that it also provided the only correct way to theorize about the concept "ideology." Now they just as passionately reject Marxism-Leninism and openly condemn the way it shaped their lives and scholarship during decades of repression. They aver that the time has come to get rid of ideological influence altogether and to substitute for it science, moral values, political pluralism, and the disinterested search for truth. Such a turn of events, they believe, will bring an end to ideology.

All of this is music to most Western ears. Its melodious harmonies come through loud and clear, devoid of dissonant variations on the theme of "ideology." Still, I am no more convinced by the present passionate testimonials of the newborn anti–Marxists than I was by the pre-perestroika Marxist-Leninist fundamentalists (all too often the very same people). The abrupt turnabout reminds me in some ways of student Maoists that I met in the sixties. When they eventually became anti–Maoists, they held to their new beliefs with the same dogmatic intolerance and fury that they had shown before their conversion.

What about myself? Can I claim to be free of ideology as I observe and interpret the present Soviet scene? Of course, not. Do I claim that my own ideology is scientifically proven or constitutes an unshakable commitment to sacrosanct values? No. I must be just as willing to learn from new experiences and to reconsider my own perspectives as I expect others to. At the same time, there are indeed some issues upon which I am fully decided, as, for example, my hatred of concentration camps, in the Soviet Union or anywhere else. It was in a concentration camp that my mother was killed, by people controlled by the Nazis and by fascist ideology.

Ideology and Propaganda

By the same token, I am not convinced that the mainstream ideology which becomes dominant at different historical periods—be it German, Soviet, or American—ought to be sheepishly followed, whether in the hallowed name of patriotism or religion or socialism or capitalism.

I freely admit that in holding these sentiments I am strongly influenced by my experiences in Nazi Germany. Hitler's potent propaganda appealed to the traditional and uncritical patriotism of the German people. (Similar propaganda has blinded other peoples before and after Hitler, including our own.) In spite of his views on religion, Hitler commanded the allegiance of the majority of German churches. The Nazis called it *Gleichschaltung* (getting everybody into line). His cunning use of the term "socialism" misled millions to follow the Fuehrer of the National "Socialist" party. Nor could Hitler have come to power without the financial backing of beguiled capitalists.

In the sixties, the U.S. sociologist Daniel Bell was naive and mistaken when he announced "The End of Ideology" in his book by that title. (He later claimed that he was misunderstood.) Similarly, various Soviet academics and journalists are making a mistake when they interpret the present turbulent transition in the Soviet Union as foreshadowing the end of ideology. Instead,—as was just demonstrated at the recent Communist Party meeting by the leader of that transition, Mikhail Gorbachev—it marks the revival of ideological struggle, a struggle with national and international dimensions, profoundly affected by ethnic and class division.

Russia Between the Union and the Commonwealth: New Carpetbaggers and Old Dreams

Carla Lipsig-Mummé

I went to Russia between December 7 and December 17, 1991, an incredible period in Russian history. I had been invited to participate in a conference convened by Alexander Buzgalin, leader of the Marxist Platform Group and professor in the Economics Department of Moscow State University, in conjunction with several trade unions and research institutes. The formal purpose of the conference was to discuss the current state of economic restructuring and to examine critically alternatives to Yeltsin's "wild west marketization." The unofficial purpose was to acquaint progressives from a number of Western countries with the (then) current state of the political spectrum.

People of various political hues from Greece, Spain, the United States, England, Canada, Hungary, and Poland, and about sixty Russians and Byelorussians, worked together for a week, the week in which the Commonwealth was crystallizing and the Union was dying. We were based in a sort of resort owned by the (then) Soviet Ministry of External Affairs, some 37 kilometers outside of Moscow. By some feat, they managed to feed us meat every night and provide an open bar in which vodka flowed freely. Our hosts insisted that we dance—1950s, Dick Clark, *American Bandstand*–style. Given the ages and pedigrees of the Western participants, we were uniquely able to fulfill their expectations.

The Russian and Byelorussian participants at the conference were particularly concerned with self-management. There is some current thinking within the anti–Yeltsin, post–Party forces which believes that self-management may offer workers in the goods-producing sectors a way to avoid the kind of highway robbery that is occurring in East Germany and Poland, where the managers of enterprises are selling them off for peanuts and pocketing the profit.

The idea of self-management, which is not—or no longer—central to our thinking, is being grasped as a lifeline by the Russians, and seems to be approached on three levels. *The first level is* self-management in the organization of work on the shop floor. Here, Buzgalin and his colleague Kolganov focus on two issues: the opening of the books and the running of factories without any employment of managers, technicians, or experts. I have to say that the last idea surprised the hell out of me, because there are very few in Canada who believe that getting rid of technicians and specialists in complex work organizations is a realistic priority.

On the next level, worker self-management as a form of property ownership attracts a great deal of Russian attention at the present time. There is a tendency to romanticize the U.S. Employee Stock Option Plans (ESOPs) and to present them as worker-directed capitalism or industrial democracy (which sent me into a frenzy). However, after some discussion with a Canadian journalist based in Moscow and a thoughtful political economist from the Institute of the U.S.A. and Canada, I understood that it is possible that the Russians may be able to adapt one or another of the U.S. worker buyout models as a way of continuing to own their factories. At present, workers are still defined by law as the collective owners of their workplaces. It is hoped that if this law is not changed, some form of worker buyout may buffer them against the East German debacle. It is important, however, that they harbor no illusions about the limits and possibilities of worker *buyins.*

Finally, *the third level of self-management,* the linking of self-managed enterprises into regional or larger systems of exchange and distribution, remains very fuzzy in everybody's mind. Everyone was enchanted by the paper presented on Mondragon, but for obvious political reasons no one had begun to think about how it might be applied to Russia or one of the other republics. Ironically, however, some haphazard microeconomic systems of distribution and exchange are already developing outside the urban centers, as strategies of survival. However, even if these micro-systems remain self-managed in the sense that they exist without centralized regulation, it is not clear that they will be composed of worker-owned enterprises.

Beyond self-management, a number of other ideas were floated, including the idea of the New Economic Policy (NEP), Bukharin's market socialism. It is generally understood, however, that it is too late for that now. What is feared is what is already eventuating, a market economy so lacking in state regulation, or suffering from incoherent, uneven regulation, that it will not only impoverish workers, but will give rise to a new elite formed from elements of the old party elite-turned-businessmen, military leaders, and the semi-criminal business elite which is growing by leaps and bounds in the black economy. It is referred to as *nomenklatura capitalism.*

The outlawing of unions is also feared. Unions remain the only mass democratic force still organized in the country (although the relationship between levels of union structure is becoming unstuck), and the unionists fear that when they are able to organize real pressure on the government against inflation, against the wholesale robbery of real estate in Moscow, Leningrad, and other big cities, when that pressure becomes effective, they will be driven underground. At least one speaker at the conference, an influential trade union economist, called for a political coup against Yeltsin, but no one took the idea seriously in discussion. Which is just as well, since there were journalists, at least one of whom came from Radio Liberty (formerly Radio Free Europe), at this conference.

One of the things that became clear during the conference and my subsequent stay in Moscow is that the non-capitalist, post–Party groups are experiencing an astonishing renaissance of radical ideas that I, at least, assumed had been destroyed after 1929; ideas like Bukharin's market socialism, like direct self-management, like the creation of mini–economic systems of exchange based on small regions or neighborhoods and operating without state intervention, like community and neighborhood-based cooperatives. I understand that what is now being dismissed as Stalinism (stretched to describe seventy years rather than twenty-four), was truly a permafrost, trapping below the ice a range of both pre-revolutionary and early revolutionary ideals on the one hand, and pre-revolutionary hatreds on the other, both of which are now re-emerging, alive and astonishingly unchanged. On the one hand there are the ethnic and racial hatreds, the smaller xenophobias, and anti–Semitism. On the other hand there are the earlier dreams of a different, liberating socialism, the dreams of certain groups within the Second International as well as the first ten years of the Third.

However, if you ask me how important these ideas are, in political terms, I cannot clearly answer. It is clear that the left of the political spectrum is burgeoning with a number of small political groups that choose to call themselves parties. Most are aligned with some level of the trade union movement (more on this later), each has a charismatic male leader who would not willingly subordinate himself to any other charismatic male leader, and each is developing programs and platforms before it is organizing its base and mobilization strategies. When I was there, the anarchists called a demo against the slow pace of reform—100 showed up. The unions and Kagarlitsky and the Socialist Party called another demo the next day, then half-countermanded it, and only 200 showed up. A general strike was called by the Moscow Federation of Trade Unions without consultation with its political allies, but scheduled for December 25, then countermanded when Gorbachev resigned. Oy.

Indeed to Westerners it is quite noticeable that there is little concern with rank-and-file democracy, or rank-and-file appropriation of ideas, but there are lots of cafe socialist intellectuals referring to the "low cultural level" of the workers. There is also little or no preoccupation with patriarchy, nor even recognition that women are simply not equal in many, many of the aspects of their daily lives. For both men and women (not all women, but an astonishingly large number of the thoughtful), pride in the admirable efforts of the Soviet regime to provide day care, to educate women well, to open job categories, etc., blocks recognition of the continued, pervasive inequality of women in the home, the family, the double day of work. Of the core ideas that distinguish the newer progressive movements in the West, only ecology and community control have resonance in Russia. Not feminism, not really, not among men, and not among women.

The political "location" of these nonaligned forces is particularly delicate and volatile at the moment. Perhaps the only thing that links its diverse elements is (ex post facto) respect for Gorbachev and what he is seen to represent is carefully left unspecified, and dislike for Yeltsin (but what he represents is all too clearly understood). But if any fragment or coalition of fragments is to become credible and effective, it must articulate a program, a strategy, and tactics which will allow it first to provide alternatives to Yeltsin's marketization, second to distinguish itself from the nostalgic Communists, and third to coalesce into a viable fighting force capable of pushing its options forward.

As of December 1991, there were two main political groupings on the post-party left. One, the Socialist Party of Workers, is identified with Roy Medvedev. Medvedev, in an October 1991 interview, described his party as "the heirs" of the CPSU, seeking a "renewed socialism," to be distinguished from Marxism-Leninism while "guarantee[ing] maximum internal democracy." I think that a number of Gorbachev supporters will gravitate here. The other, the Party of Labor, is identified with Boris Kagarlitsky and the Socialist Party, fragments of the Marxist Platform, and was supposed to be coming into being in late December. It is impossible for me, from the outside, to evaluate these two would-be parties. I do assume, however, from the frenetic factional activity taking place within both, that the alliances underpinning each and the relations between them will change considerably over the next few months. At present they do not look to be in contact with each other and are not organizing joint actions.

It is even more difficult for me to tell you with any assurance what the links between these parties and the unions are. At least one reason for this is that the union structure is like a kaleidoscope now. I do know, however, that the Moscow Federation of Trade Unions and the Party of Labor are allies. The structure of unionism is, of course, undergoing mind-boggling change, in ways and at a speed that I find difficult to get my mind around. The long-time official structure, capped by the All-Union Congress of Trade Unions is now called the General Confederation of Trade Unions. It is now composed of a small number of big branch or sectoral industrial unions, as well as of regional groupings based on the republic, the city, and the region. It has now fragmented but not disappeared. In every industry, the inter–republican industrial union (e.g., the Textile and Light Industry Workers of the U.S.S.R.) has become a union based on its industry in each republic separately. Because union offices were centralized in Russia, this breakdown of inter–republican union structures causes fewer problems there than it will in the other republics, where the industrial union structure may have to be rebuilt almost from scratch. In Russia, at least, a great deal of the dynamism seems to have flowed away from these industrial unions. And the inter–industrial Federation of Russian Unions is restructuring internally, in its ways of operating as well as in who holds key posts. I have been told that it is reflexively pro–Yeltsin, but I have not seen much sign of its activity.

You see dynamism in the city labor councils, though. The Moscow, Leningrad, and Volgograd labor councils are particularly active and particularly critical of Yeltsin. For the near future, I expect trade union action to be municipally or regionally based. However, it is important not to underestimate just how unstable things are in the union world. This instability comes not only from the ravages of inflation or the breakdown of production in many sectors or the fragmentation of the distribution and exchange networks into mini-systems relying heavily on barter. It comes as well from a very real uncertainty as to who will own the places of employment, what legal rights unions will have, and how they will learn to exercise those rights.

It also became clear to me, after discussions with the Moscow Federation of Trade Unions, that the relationship between different levels of the union structure is itself in volatile evolution, and few if any of the original relationships between the *levels* of union organization are still in operation. Among other questions, the issue of who owns the really considerable union resources is quite important. Under the Soviet regime, the unions played a much broader social role than unions do in Canada or the U.S., and as such are the owners of health camps, resorts, educational facilities, guest houses, and buildings galore. It is estimated that the old All-Union Congress of Trade Unions had some 60 million rubles that are now being fought over. But if it does not succeed in recreating a pan-republican union structure (which seems most likely), and if union levels and groupings which had not been of particular importance or particularly well-funded in the old dispensation begin to grow and take on a life of their own, as is becoming the case with the municipal labor councils, how is the allocation of union funds and other resources to be decided?

Surprisingly, to me, the independent unions such as SOTSPROF (a coalition of trade unions not formed out of the official unions), as well as the miners and a few others, have remained small, although in some cases strategically crucial. Except for certain sectors, it would be incorrect at the present time to assume that these independent unions could become the core of Russia's next labor movement. Rather I think that the next labor movement will emerge from within the rapidly transforming present labor movement. And it is no longer correct to refer to it as the official movement, because the internal changes it has already undergone make it virtually unrecognizable. I think we have to think of it as the re-forming labor movement.

There is, in addition, an interesting new grouping, the Inter-Republican Council of Works Collectives. It seems to be drawing on leadership which did not come up through the official union ranks, to be oriented toward problems of ownership and the representation of workers in a conflictual setting. It is one of the groups that is examining self-management as a desirable form of property ownership in the post–Soviet economy. I know little about it but it warrants being known better.

During the conference outside of Moscow and the rest of my trip, I was able to meet with trade union leaders from the Moscow Federation of Trade Unions, the Inter-Republican Council of Work Collectives, the Byelorussian Federation of Unions, and the Textile and Light Industry Union of the U.S.S.R. I also had a lengthy discussion with the deputy director of the Institute for the Study of the U.S.A. and Canada, Plekhanov, as well as with two leading economists at Moscow State University and a number of Canadian journalists, on the subject of what help Canadian trade unionists and union-university partnerships like the Center for Research on Work and Society (CRWS) could offer. Uniformly, the trade unionists were enthusiastic about the possibility of Canadian unions and intellectuals getting involved in a systematic labor education effort within Russia.

Two sorts of help were repeatedly mentioned. The first, which all identified as crucial, was intellectual in nature: "help us to prepare ourselves to defend workers in a conflictual system." The second sort of help was technical: help in developing a modern communication net within and between unions, in computerizing internal administration, in setting up a system for dues collection, for negotiating and bargaining a collective agreement, for doing the research necessary to back their demands both to employers and to the government. One trade unionist said to me simply: "help us to get through this transitional time as a union defending its members."

I also think there is a third level of help that needs to be offered: working with the Russian unions to develop links between *their* academic researchers and *their* unions, developing the kind of union-academic partnership that centers like CRWS in Ontario and the Institute for Applied Labor Research (IRAT) in Quebec have created, but adapted to the Russian reality.[1] As the unions are cut off from their traditional state sources of economic data, as they are marginalized in the social-policy formation process, as the problem of collecting and analyzing information about workers and working conditions becomes—as perhaps it always has been—highly political, unions in all the republics are going to need the skills of trained, friendly researchers who can tap into the considerable intellectual resources of the universities and quasi-independent research institutes. During this December trip and my earlier trip to Moscow, Leningrad, and Kirov last June, I found academics in Russian universities and institutes fascinated with the idea of working with Canadians who worked with Russian unions, but they had not made the direct links themselves. One union told me that part of the trouble was the marketization of union research: when they approached a research institute to prepare a demographic portrait of their membership, the researchers demanded an impossible fee.

This, then, is the essence of what I did during those ten days. There is much more I could relate, for example, about the new breed of carpetbaggers descending on Russia, filled in equal parts with greed and contempt for the Russians about to be fleeced. Take the bankrupt Virginia real estate man come to Moscow to remake his fortune via a shady real estate deal with the manager of the Moscow Zoo (hoping to sell off a plot of land) and with the National Union of Journalists (looking for American interior finishes in their new building). Or going with my friend Helena to buy one cup of coffee each and one toasted sandwich and spending the equivalent of two months of her salary. Or trying to get around the Moscow subway when they are *de-Marxizing* the station names: they have gotten around to removing names that are no longer politically correct (like Prospekt Marxa), but have not gotten around to replacing them with anything. Even Muscovites were going a little crazy. I just got lost, repeatedly.

Enough.

Note

1. CRWS, Centre for Research on Work and Society, was established as an Organised Research Unit at York University, co-governed by Canadian unions and academics from a number of universities. Working in English and French, from 1990 to 2001 it researched

the wide range of issues that confronted trade unions in a volatile, global political economy. CRWS researched on and with unions and academics in France, Germany, the U.K., Sweden, South Africa, New Zealand, Australia, the U.S., Latin America, and former Soviet bloc countries. IRAT, l'Institut de recherche appliquée en travail, based in Montreal, was also a think tank with academic-trade union governance. It, too, researched with and for trade unions, in academic-trade union collaboration. Like CRWS, IRAT retained intellectual independence while carrying out applied research. IRAT focused its research mainly on Québec.

Worker Self-Management in Soviet Theory and Practice

AARON BINDMAN

INTRODUCTION BY DOROTHY S. MCCLELLAN

Aaron Bindman was invited to the U.S.S.R. as a visiting scholar in the State University of New York and Moscow State University exchange program to study worker self-management. In this essay he discusses the challenges he faced gaining entrance to industrial production facilities in the Soviet Union. Having studied worker self-management in Yugoslavia, he was more than a bit surprised by the roadblocks he encountered in pursuing his research in the U.S.S.R. Factory managers and government officials no doubt questioned the wisdom of allowing him to visit their enterprises. They were reluctant to let foreign, peering eyes examine the day-to-day deeply troubled operations of factories in this centralized sector of their already failing economy.

His persistence paid off only slightly with a last minute visit to a factory's museum. He did, however, have opportunities to talk with fellow researchers and union officials. He discovered the concerns that underlay the reluctance to grant him entré. His essay provides priceless insights into why perestroika and glasnost were greeted with such widespread support by critics of the centralized economy, already in the early days of perestroika and glasnost as dissent concerning centralized planning emerged.

After the elevation of Mikhail Gorbachev as general secretary of the Communist Party of the Soviet Union (U.S.S.R.) and head of the Soviet government (1984) and his advocacy of perestroika—renewal and democratic reform of Soviet society—I applied for and received an appointment as university exchange professor in the Faculty of Philosophy at Moscow State University (MSU). Ernest Boyer, chancellor of the State University of New York, established the first university-to-university exchange program between Russia and the U.S. in the 1976–1977 academic year in the midst of the Cold War. The appointment afforded me the opportunity to pursue the research in labor relations that I had been involved in all my adult life.

Shortly after I submitted my application in September 1985, a committee from SUNY's International Program Office interviewed me and instructed me to submit a *nauchnye plan* (prospectus), which I did. In it I outlined my objectives: to lecture on labor-relations in the United States and to do an "on-site" study of labor-relations in U.S.S.R. factories producing wood products. My request to do an "on-site" research project in factories producing wood products was to continue the line research on labor relations in worker self-managed factories that produced wood products that I had carried out between 1979 and 1983.[1]

A month after I submitted my prospectus I was notified by IP-SUNY that IP-MSU affirmed my appointment as a Visiting Professor but they requested a more detailed *nauchnye plan* spelling out the contents of my proposed lectures and research objectives. I complied and finally, early in February 1986 I was notified by IP-SUNY that they received our travel visas and were making airplane reservations for all of us, professors and students, who were selected in that year's exchange program.[2]

During the long wait for the necessary papers to go to MSU, I made contact with U.S.S.R. trade union leaders and officials of U.S.S.R. labor relations research organizations with the assistance of Ernie DeMaio, the U.S. trade union representative on the Board of the World Federation of Trade Unions and Lou Gordon, Legislative Director of the United Paper Workers, AFL-CIO. Both of them, U.S. trade unionists, had recently been to the Soviet Union for trade union conferences and gave me the names of Soviet trade unionists and leaders of organizations doing labor research they met at those conferences. I wrote to two of them: Mihail Kuleshov, president of the Central Committee, Timber, Paper and Woodworker Union, and Professor Dr. Alexander Belchuk, deputy director, Institute of the International Labor Movement, Academy of Sciences of the U.S.S.R. I received replies from them in which both suggested that I contact them when I got to Moscow and they would arrange to meet with me.

The day after we arrived in Moscow, I was introduced to my advisor, Nikolai Driachlov, who had very recently been named Deputy Chairman of the newly formed Department of Sociology in the Faculty of Philosophy. He had not been told that I was coming nor did he receive either of the prospectuses that I had submitted through IP-SUNY. Fortunately, I had brought with me copies of both previously submitted prospectuses in both English and Russian. He took them and asked me to come back in two days in order to give him time to read them. When I returned, instead of discussing my proposals for lecturing and research with me, he handed me a new *nauchnye plan* that he had written.

The plan he drew up (in English) included visitations with the two trade unionists I had previously contacted and with some of the academics involved in labor relations research that I had suggested. But he omitted any reference to my lecturing to sociology students and faculty or my engaging in on-site research in wood products enterprises. When I called his attention to the fact that I was under the impression that their invitation to me was based on the prospectus that I had submitted which included lecturing and doing on-site labor-relations research, he said, "It would be impossible for me to arrange for you to do research in another institution, but I will arrange for you to lecture here in this department." He told me to be patient and he would make arrangements for me to lecture to his students and faculty and he would try his best to arrange for me to meet with academics involved in labor relations research. "But," he added, "it will be difficult and take time."

It wasn't long before I found out why "it will be difficult and take time." Shortly after we arrived the major event of the decade for the Soviet people—the 27th Congress of the Communist Party—was called into session by its new leader Mikhail Gorbachev. On the radio, in English, we heard excerpts of Gorbachev's report and hourly summaries of floor discussions. One of the central themes of Gorbachev's report called for the decentralization of the bureaucratic planning structure that controlled every aspect of Soviet life. In it he specifically pointed to the restrictions on direct contact between units of organizations, industries and agencies at all levels. It was clear that Gorbachev recognized that the rigid bureaucratic rules that governed communication between units of production were stifling initiative and productive activity between people, agencies, factories and collectives.

What Gorbachev was decrying, and what my advisor Driachlov found difficult to breach, were the bureaucratic procedures that required that all communications and contact between units of institutions and agencies go from the initiating unit to the top level of its organization, then over to the top level of the organization contacted, and then down to the level the initiating unit desired to contact. Every step of the way from echelon to echelon, each unit had to put its stamp of approval on the request. At any point the failure to approve ended the process and the request for contact was denied. Worse yet, there was no reply and no reason given for the denial.

These rigid bureaucratic rules and procedures governing all forms of communication and transaction were, in my opinion, the Achilles heel that generated the adverse consequences that brought down the U.S.S.R. Here is a brief description of what one encountered in the pursuit of any and all activities: All agencies were rigidly segmented, each performed its own specific functions that were set forth in the book of rules and regulations. To do almost anything—from coming to Moscow for a job, to obtaining a library card (a separate one for each library used within the university) or to get an apartment, one had to go to three, four or more agencies to get approval for different services. At each step in the procedure, the clerk acting for the agency scrutinized the application, forwarded it to the next echelon of authority, all the way up to the head of the agency for his/her approval. The applicant was asked to return in a day or two for the decision and then, if approved, one was asked to take it to the next agency for the same physically tiresome procedural treatment, on and on until final approval was given or denied.

The procedures in and of themselves were but the tip of the iceberg. People who were the agents in these agencies, we would assume, aspired to higher positions and advancement in their careers. They, too, had to go through the same bureaucratic procedures of application, examination and approval through all the higher echelons of their own and other agencies. To improve one's status one had to make application, and if approved, had to serve as a candidate for a year to demonstrate ability, good character, moral conduct, devotion, and intention to promote the interests of the agency and through it the social and political objectives of the country. One would suspect that in such a merit system agents would act very cautiously in handling applications and reluctantly give approval for fear of making a mistake in judgment that might cut short one's own career aspirations. Additionally, imagine the power that heads of departments had over their underlings. Indecision and ritualistic job performance or "hard-nosing" was more than likely the consequence of that type of merit system. Each worker and those with aspirations for promotions and leadership positions had to satisfy his "boss" before being recommended for a promotion.

In addition, each agency had as an integral and functioning part of it three organizations—the Communist Party, the Komsomol (youth and young adult organization) and a trade union. The workers in an agency, factory or farm collective were members of these organizations and elected from among their ranks leaders to represent them in these organizations. These local leaders also served a period of candidacy, however, only after having been recommended by the district leadership of the three controlling organizations that based their decisions on the candidate's past performance, good works and high moral character. The authority of the leaders was derived from the "vanguard role of the Communist Party," a theory and practice instituted by Lenin after the revolution and that was rigidified in the Soviet bureaucracy under Stalin's autocratic rule. When the "vanguard role" was instituted the country was in shambles; its economy was operating at 5 percent of capacity with a minuscule working class and a large peasantry, 90 percent of whom were illiterate. The only possibility for establishing a stable political economy was through a strong centralized bureaucracy, led by a carefully selected, dedicated and loyal leadership cadre that was tried and tested in revolutionary struggles. It was this vanguard of educated and dedicated people who had a plan that they promulgated in the interest of the working class; this earned them the respect of the people who came to accept the "dictatorship of the proletariat" as necessary for their survival.

These cumbersome procedures and dependence on an all-knowing decision-making elite became enshrined in all institutions and agencies. It became a dictatorship *for* the proletariat and not *by* the proletariat. Graduate students and faculty whom we got to know well would consult with their "leader" before making and acting on what they regarded as an important decision. Rather than "buck" for change, many people went along doing their work ritualistically. It dampened their innovative spirit resulting in mediocre performances and made inoperative any meaningful attempt at scuttling the rigid bureaucracy. In a word, few protested the endless rigid procedures; instead they accepted them as necessary. They came to rely on the wisdom of the elite who occupied the top posts.

Such a system reinforces the notion that to succeed or advance you must ingratiate yourself to those who head your agency, institution, factory, collective farm and government office. The consequence of such a system of rewards and promotions was that it attracted opportunistic, self-seeking individuals who understood that to acquire a leadership position, one must join the party and "work the system," whether or not one agrees with the ideological orientation of the government. In a review of David Kotz and Fred Weir's *Revolution from Above: The Demise of the Soviet System* (Routledge, 1997), Stanislav, a Russian economist, wrote:

> The Soviet economy did not fall apart by its own momentum. It was intentionally destroyed by members of its own elite who became increasingly anti-communist and pro-capitalist.... The basic thesis of Kotz and Weir's book is rooted in a well established left ... tradition ... which accused the Soviet leadership of transforming itself into a bureaucracy that would eventually become state capitalist rather than socialist.... The largest portion of the top new Russian businessmen came from the Soviet economic elite—industrialists and bankers amounting to 37 percent. The "other" category represents the former underground economy and constitutes another 18 percent.... "Scientists" are those new entrepreneurs who mostly came from the applied research institutes closely associated with industrial enterprises. One of them, Mr. Berezovsky is estimated by "Forbes" to be worth $3 billion....[3]

The above quote clearly suggests that the former Soviet ruling elite used their positions of power and authority in a rigid bureaucratic structure and were able to abscond with the wealth and resources of the "working class" who were taught to accept the wisdom of the elite as "the vanguard of the proletariat" in a "dictatorship of the proletariat."

Due to these rigid rules, procedures, and restrictions, my advisor, Professor Driachlov, who was more than willing to assist me in gaining access to a factory, was unable to fathom the complicated bureaucratic structure to get from the Sociology Department of Moscow State University to a factory in the wood products industry. But even on his own turf, it took him six weeks to arrange for me to lecture to his students.

Driachlov provided me an interpreter and a week to prepare my lecture. It was agreed that I would write out my lecture entitled "Philosophical Systems of Analysis in American Sociology." I gave a written copy to my interpreter (a very pleasant and bright female graduate student who spoke English very well) to translate and then read to the audience. It turned out that three students appeared for the lecture together with Professor Driachlov. After my interpreter read the contents of the lecture, I, through the interpreter asked for questions, and answered them. Five or six questions were asked and answered. I asked Driachlov why there were so few students in attendance and he replied, "Frankly, this was a test to learn what you would say. I am pleased and will arrange for more lectures." A few days later he asked me to prepare a lecture for graduate students and the sociology faculty. This time I was given an English Ph.D. candidate, Maria Bobrova, who was assigned to be my interpreter during my stay and facilitator in getting appointments for me with sociologists doing on-site research in factories studying motivational factors to improve workers' attitudes and increase production.

Professor Driachlov was able to make arrangements (since it was within the "academic enterprise") for me to meet with Professor Alexseev of the Institute of Sociological Research and author of the article "The Interrelationship of Social Factors Determining Work Attitudes."[4] The article was "based on the results of a comprehensive social and economic study conducted in … 536 … collective fisheries between 1969 and 1971, under the direction of the author, by researchers of the Plekhanov Institute of Economics; the survey covered 2,942 members of these collectives, including 2,016 fishermen."

The study sought to ascertain those social factors that determine a worker's attitudes, satisfaction and productivity. Professor Alexseev drew the following conclusions from the study:

> Thus we can say that after the system of payments, the next most important social factor shaping a person's attitude toward work is his participation in the management of the life of the production collective of which he is a member.

According to Professor Alexseev, the study found that

general participation in conducting the collective's affairs consists of two important factors for both the individual worker and the work collective: first, management of the process of production itself during the course of which the individual worker is both organizer and executor of his work; second, management of the distribution of the results ... by means of a system of material remuneration that provides the most objective and fair equivalence between the measure of individual-collective labor and the measure of its material remuneration.

He further concluded that

participation in management is of decisive importance for the shaping of an optimally positive attitude toward work activity among members of the collective. However, this participation is still inadequate in actual practice and the skillful utilization of this factor is an important source for raising labor productivity and increasing social production.

Professor Alexseev recommended that

to be specific, the role of the rank and file members ... in deciding fundamental questions must be increased. This conclusion is in full accordance with the need for further intensification and stricter observance of the basic principles of economic accounting in all branches of collective production as the chief economic mechanism for managing the economy and as the basic form for managing labor activity, stimulating initiative and fostering the creativity of collectives engaged in production; the possibility of such a system relies on a highly developed and functioning democracy within the collective units.

The reason for extracting such a large quotation from this early (1969 and 1971) research of Professor Alexseev is that it is very similar to what I was told by all the researchers I met or had read in their work. These suggestions were precisely those which Gorbachev was promulgating in his perestroika speeches and which were enacted into legislation in 1985. However, my Russian colleagues told me in confidence that their research recommendations, despite the laws mandating them, were not being implemented, but were instead being shelved by the bureaucratic elite who were supposed to put them into practice.

The researchers whom I met could not get me into a factory to observe and interview participant workers, managers and leaders of the three organizations in each factory. The only opportunity I had to visit a factory was provided by Alexander I. Belchuk, deputy director, Institute of the International Labour Movement, Academy of Sciences of the U.S.S.R. After two days of successful meetings with him and his staff, he arranged what amounted to a tour of the Second Watch Factory two days before we were scheduled to leave for home. The following day my interpreter, Maria, and I were given a tour of the watch factory. A tour guide took us through the factory museum and told us everything about the operation of the factory, but did not take us where workers were working. All we got from that visit was the tour guide's perception of worker participation in running the factory. I had read numerous times in Soviet literature about workers' rights and participation in the operation of their factory. By this time I knew what he was saying was far from the truth; it was a canned presentation.

The two days of meetings with Deputy Director Belchuk were highly productive. On one of the days he invited me to make a presentation to his staff on my research on workers' participation in Yugoslavia's system of worker self-management and to field their questions. On the second day members of his staff discussed the research they have done and were doing on worker participation in decision making in Soviet factories and I asked the questions. Their findings and conclusions were similar to mine: worker participation in the decision making processes increased worker satisfaction and involvement, induced creativity, and improved the quality and quantity of production. Belchuk and his staff were impressed by the fact that I, a foreigner, an academic from the U.S., was given free access to Yugoslavian factories.

A day before we left Moscow State University and Moscow, Driachlov arranged for me to meet with the Dean of the Faculty of Philosophy under whom he served, Professor Anatoli Kosichev. After some superficial discussion about my work in the U.S. and about conditions of the workingman in the U.S., he asked me my impressions of the Soviet Union and my activities as a visiting professor. I demurred and said that I would give him a thorough appraisal of my impressions in writing. (Actually I had already written my critique and had given it to my interpreter to translate with instructions to give the translation to the Dean and Driachlov.) Below, in part, is the substance of what I wrote:

> My major disappointment was not having had the opportunity to visit factories, talk to managers, functionaries, and workers, or to meet and chat with sociology graduate students doing research in my area of interest, or to gather empirical data on workers' reactions to advances in technology and the effect on their attitudes, satisfaction, and productivity. Every research scholar and trade unionist with whom I had met told me about new legislation that mandated worker involvement in the management of their collectives, but I never had the opportunity to even observe, let alone to study, its relationship to worker attitudes, satisfaction, involvement and productivity.

The reason for making an issue of the failure to make arrangements with a work collective to interview their managers and workers and to get permission to collect empirical data is not simply that it has reduced the validity and credibility of my research; that is but a minor and insignificant matter. The failure reveals a far more serious problem for Soviet society, namely, that it is just about impossible for one work collective to make direct contact with another work collective to resolve a mutual problem. According to the *Moscow News*, "Mikhail Gorbachev stressed that it is necessary to give proper attention to those who work at related enterprises to reach accord and cooperate with them. We must develop and strengthen a good socialist tradition of cooperation among collectives."[5]

My observations have led me to conclude that the barriers to direct contact between lower levels of organizations are not the result of either malfeasance or malevolence; they are the outdated and counterproductive formal-legal procedures adopted and instituted in the distant past to deal with entirely different social and economic conditions that prevailed then. Under present modernization efforts the old authority structure and bureaucratic procedures impede and "choke" the flow of information and activities and inhibit cooperation between collectives. It is not that bureaucracies are bad; they are absolutely essential, particularly in advanced scientifically-oriented and planned systems to effectively organize and efficiently accomplish large scale, social, economic, and political tasks. It is when the bureaucracies are so structured as to impede the fulfillment of the goals and purposes of the organization, that the time has come to reexamine, reassess, and revise the bureaucratic authority structure. Mikhail Gorbachev (as reported in *Moscow News*, April 20, 1986) clearly called for such revisions when he said, "We must begin with changing the way we think, our psychology, organization, the style and method of work."

If I may be permitted to use my "sociological imagination," I would point to an aspect of the authority structure that has outgrown its usefulness in the U.S.S.R.; namely, the "vanguard role of the party." When the "vanguard role" was first instituted, the newly established Soviet state was in great distress. Now, however, with a highly developed industrialized economy, with a gigantic pool of well-educated, trained, skilled professional working class about to launch the massive implementation of the U.S.S.R.'s advances in science and technology to produce goods and services for the Soviet people, it is mandatory that the base of leadership and control be extended to include workers at every level of organization and production.

However, if workers and work collectives have to request permission and wait for approval from higher authorities before they initiate any productive activity, they will not be engaged and involved in the collective effort, instead they will become discouraged and lose interest in their work and resort to ritualistic behavior. Such withdrawal behavior by workers was described in the *Moscow News* article that reported on a speech of Mikhail Gorbachev to the people of Togliatti, Italy as "a desire to do everything 'in the proper way' according to instruction 'not to stick out' meticulously to fulfill instructions from above.... Today such an approach is particularly intolerable because it undermines the very idea of economic growth on the basis of accelerating scientific and technological progress" (April 20, 1986).

It was the unanimous conclusion of the Soviet scholars with whom I discussed workers' behavior and attitudes that "active influence by workers on decision making promotes successful operations of plants and ... offers extensive opportunities for developing workers' creative activity [even] outside the immediate work function." In *Pravda* on April 12, 1983, the Soviet Union Council of Ministers and the All-Union Council of Trade Unions proposed legislation (which has since become law) "designed to raise socialist democracy to a new level by increasing the authority of labor collectives at all enterprises, institutions and organizations." Their draft stressed that "every worker must consider himself manager of his enterprise and a representative of the entire country."

More of the findings and conclusions of Soviet scholars with whom I met were included in my report to Dean Kosichev and Professor Driachlov. It was translated into Russian by Maria Bobrova, my interpreter, and delivered to them in person by her. It has been eleven years since they received my report. To date I have not received from them any comments or acknowledgment of receipt.

Prior to leaving Moscow in June of 1986, a Soviet party member who had been a delegate to the 27th Congress took me for a walk in the Lenin Hills, a beautiful area near MSU. While walking he pointed to a large fenced in enclave of some 30 acres. He said critically, "In that enclave live the top party leaders; they have good apartments, their own hospital, doctors, a shopping center well-stocked with food supplies and clothing." But he expressed the view that this type of special treatment was dealt with at the Congress and would soon be a thing of the past. People who pass the enclave either make derogatory remarks or deny its existence—but none were proud of its existence. Since then I have read the abundant literature coming out of Russia. None confirm that the laws enacted changing the procedures of the bureaucratic structure or the laws mandating worker involvement in decision-making processes have been implemented.

Notes

1. Studies were done in the Republic of Slovenia at Meblo, a work organization of seventeen Basic Organizations of Associated Labor (BOAL's) in 1979, in the Republic of Bosnia-Herzegovina at Sipad (the largest factory complex in Europe with 77,000 workers in twenty-two work organizations in 1981, and in the Republic of Croatia at Slavonija, a BOAL of about 200 workers in 1983.

2. In my application I made it known that my wife would be accompanying me and set forth her qualifications as an occupational therapist and a teacher of multiply handicapped children. Others who had received appointments at MSU were either denied

the right to bring their spouses with them or had to insist as a condition of acceptance of the appointment that their spouses be permitted to accompany them. I made it clear to the review committee that I would not go without my wife and when my invitation arrived, it included a visa for my wife.
 3. *Monthly Review*, vol. 49, no. 5, October 1997.
 4. *Sotsiologicheskie Issledovaniia*, no. 3, 1975, pp. 112–21.
 5. *Moscow News*, April 20, 1986, no. 16, 3212.

The Crisis of Soviet Legitimacy

HERMAN SCHWENDINGER *and*
JULIA SCHWENDINGER

We participated in the SUNY-Moscow University exchange program during the 1988 fall semester. The committee that approved our participation in the program had reservations because we were incapable of speaking Russian fluently in spite of exposure to an introductory course in that language. But we promised them that if we couldn't understand Russian, we would have a good time dancing around a samovar.

We arrived in Moscow when perestroika and glasnost encouraged free speech and hope for a better future. We had a great time at Moscow State University. We also visited law schools in St. Petersburg and Alma Ata, Kazakhstan, as well as Julia's relatives in Riga, Latvia. In Alma Ata, the dean met us with open arms. We partied with students who were pioneering in environmental reforms.

On return to Moscow, the university's international division tried to prevent our trip to visit Julia's relatives in Riga because of the rise of the Latvian's People's Front Movement. But a member of a Moscow legal collective helped us get around this problem by purchasing our railroad tickets to Riga for us. We told the university authorities that we'd sleep in the railroad station among the peasants if we had to. The image of Julia in her beautiful leather coat and fur hat, Herman in his blue cashmere coat, his hair prematurely white under a hat that was fashionable among American working-class men during the Great Depression sporting white sneakers with no place to stay must have convinced them and they arranged for elegant hotel accommodations.

In Moscow we gave lectures in the foreign language department in return for their translation services. Julia talked about crimes against women in the U.S.A., Herman about civil liberties. Julia's talks produced energetic and animated responses. Despite the fact that Herman's lectures proved to be a dud, the language department gave us a send-off party. We socialized at the university with visiting scholars from around the world. When we left a Lithuanian economist, a Chinese judge and an MSU academic saw us off at the airport. Our daughter had even flown to Moscow to ensure we got on the right flight.

The Russians we encountered were extraordinarily friendly. We had terrific experiences. *Of course, we tried to understand what was going on.* We certainly inquired about corruption, Stalin's crimes against humanity, and civil liberties.

In this essay we trace the crisis of Soviet legitimacy from the 1920s through the 1990s noting the contradictions between theory and practice that led to the economy plummeting downward in a never-ending slide. The crises of the 1980s swept away the illusions that kept many from seeing the antisocialist facets of Soviet life. Years later, we concluded that the extremely rapid economic transformation and oligarchy produced by the *privatization* of state enterprises in 1991 was fueled ironically by the ruling class control of *public* property.

We have always had faith that someday people would create a society without exploitation, poverty, unemployment, homelessness and crime; without ethnic, gender or racial oppression. Almost everyone agrees that the Gorbachev period finally eliminated any remaining illusions about the Soviet system providing a model for that society. Spending a semester in the U.S.S.R., we learned a great deal. We hope some of this learning will be imparted to the reader in this article.[1]

When we were exchange scholars at Moscow State University, the Soviet Union seemed like a playground in Dante's inferno. The economy was plummeting downward in a never-ending slide. Party leaders seesawed frantically over a boiling cauldron of ethnic strife. Stalinists, social democrats, nationalists, monarchists and liberals were grappling on every rung of the jungle gym to keep each other from its commanding heights.

Decades of bureaucratic policy-making resulted in this inferno. Josef Stalin had turned the Soviet Union into a barracks-room society. Yet, while he ran the country like an army, its officer corps was composed of party apparatchiks, enterprise managers and civil bureaucrats. V.I. Lenin had detested these bureaucrats but Stalin continuously fed their voracious appetites. He never had enough personnel to run the economy, terrorize people, censor artists and gag intellectuals. During his rule, the bureaucracy swelled to monstrous proportions and helped orchestrate the Soviet Union's catastrophic finale.

After Stalin's death, Soviet society veered off on another tangent, to some degree. On becoming general secretary of the Party in the 1950s, Nikita Khrushchev reined in Stalin's bureaucratization of terror. In addition, overriding Central Committee objections, he openly denounced Stalin's crimes at the 20th Party Congress. While such organs of repression as the secret police and forced-labor camps still operated under Khrushchev, the relentless carnage ceased.

However, after sweeping out some of the worst of Stalinism and encouraging economic reforms, Khrushchev was forced out of office. A conservative backlash, its muscle concentrated in the bureaucracy, replaced him with Leonid Brezhnev in 1964. Brezhnev symbolized the heavy industry, production-oriented engineers, who dominated the central party apparatus and government ministries (Hough 1977). The Central Committee also seems to have favored his appointment because he would not dominate them. Khrushchev reportedly said that Brezhnev's peers had nicknamed him "ballerina," when he was the Dnepropetrovsk province party secretary, because "anyone who wanted to could turn him around" (Khrushchev 1990, p. 32).

Collaborating with provincial party conservatives, Brezhnev's neo-Stalinist regime suppressed criticism of Stalin, ended Khrushchev's limited experiment with free speech, and reasserted control over artists and intellectuals. The reformers, who had ripened during the Khrushchev Spring, now withered in the cold.

When Stalin had taken control of the party apparatus, he rebuilt the state to fit his own particular needs. But, after his death, his bureaucracy continued evolving, now according to its own needs. Ironically, as Nikita Khrushchev's son, Sergei, observes, his father's denunciation of Stalin gave the bureaucrats greater freedom to protect their own interests because their fear of imprisonment or execution at the hands of an all-powerful leader had died down (Khrushchev 1990, pp. 25–28).

Paradoxical Trends

On the other hand, noteworthy paradoxical trends also occurred in the Stalin and post–Stalin periods. During the 1930s and postwar years, schools and universities educated millions and, to a certain extent, inculcated communist ideals. The economic and educational strides in urban areas also created an optimistic spirit and faith in communism among youth. Many people were not disillusioned by Stalin's terror. They focused instead on national accomplishments.

Though Stalin demoralized many and undermined their patriotic sentiments, the feelings of national solidarity and pride in country surged upward during the Great War. The victories over Germany and its allies weakened cynical reservations about socialism and doubts about the cult of Stalin.

The words and thoughts of Aleksander Yakovlev, originator of glasnost, critic of Stalinism and son of a Russian peasant, reflected these changes. When asked about Stalin, Yakovlev admits, "I will tell this: We believed very strongly and sincerely in what then existed." He explained, "In general, we young fellows went off to war with an absolute, one hundred percent faith in Stalin. And I will tell you that the moral state of Soviet society—from the point of view of attitudes, honesty, decency and good conduct—was on the whole very high. Now they say there was a universal fear in those times.... Clearly it did exist, particularly among those people hit by or touched by the repressions. But I remember that at *Komsomol* meetings after the war, and at party meetings, people bore themselves patriotically and bravely" (Keller 1988).

Positive feelings about Soviet society were also sustained by sensational leaps into the modern era. Some older members of national groups such as the Kazakhs from Central Asia have memories of a nomadic or feudal existence when the Soviet Union was founded. A Kazakh professor in his late fifties or early sixties humorously told us he was "born on the back of a camel." He was using a popular expression meaning that he was raised as a child in a nomadic family and lived in a *yurt*, a nomadic tent. He related how his people, in a few short decades, made astounding progress in economic and scientific development.

We viewed examples of this progress when we visited the University of Kazakhstan in Alma Ata, only a few hundred miles from the Chinese border. We saw photographs of graduating classes dating back to the 1930s when the university began. We noticed after careful examination that compared to the Russian students, the proportion of Kazakhs, who are Asian but look somewhat like Native Americans, increased steadily from the 1930s to the present in each class. Alma Ata is now an educational, scientific and industrial center. In our conversations with students and faculty at the Law School, we sensed pride in the socialist accomplishments that had, at that time, withstood the overwhelming disillusionment seen in Moscow.

Furthermore, it should be noted that urban centers like Alma Ata had not been exceptional. Boris Kagarlitsky, a sociologist and activist, indicates that great industrial cities sprung up from the 1930s onward and that rural people settled into them. By the 1970s, a new generation of workers and intellectuals had grown up, completely shaped by the conditions of urban life. "The average conditions of life for a majority of people approached those of the 'average European'—and so did their psychology," Kagarlitsky (1990, p. 285) reports. Cultural experiences had been rapidly altered by state policies. The numbers of well-educated people soared and stimulated a huge increase in the sale of newspapers and books. Sociologists in the 1970s found that people had accumulated a vast fund of books amounting to 30 million volumes. G.G. Dadamyan, a leading expert on the Soviet sociology of art, observes that millions of people supported the art booms, attending the galleries and other showplaces for visual art. From the 1950s to 1978, attendance at theaters, concerts and museums increased significantly as well. Dadamyan concludes that "a fundamentally new cultural situation" had emerged in the 1960s and 1970s (Kagarlitsky 1990, pp. 291–92).

Kagarlitsky appropriately remarks: "Though we may doubt how *deeply* the new culture has penetrated the masses, the *breadth* of its dissemination is beyond doubt." He supports the idea that "a qualitatively new situation unprecedented in Russian history" had emerged. In a startling reversal, "the cultural level of the masses" he surmises, "became on average somewhat higher during the 1970s than the cultural level of the elite" (Kagarlitsky 1990, p. 292).

Other far-reaching changes have been reported. In the 1970s, Soviet studies were discovering that skilled and professional workers in the West required a greater general and technical education to deal with jobs created by higher technology. These Western workers also needed "significantly better conditions of work, housing, nutrition and variety of leisure opportunities." Similar requirements, the studies found, were being demanded by Soviet workers as the complexity of their work increased, and some of these demands were being fulfilled (Kagarlitsky 1990, pp. 284–85).[2]

These and other psychosocial trends contributed to political stability until the mid–1970s. Then, as economic growth declined and dissatisfaction with ruling policies increased, the trends themselves undermined the system. For example, well-educated, skilled and professional workers were being produced in large numbers to deal with technological advances but the decline in economic growth denied these workers the opportunity to get appropriate work. Toward the end of the 1970s, thousands of engineers could find no jobs matching their education and training. Many were forced to lower their sights because of the deceleration in technological progress although not all engineers became skilled workers involuntarily. Their wages were frequently so low that many opted for jobs as skilled workers.

At that time, *Literaturnaya Gazyeta* observed: "It now takes on average seven years for a skilled worker to rise in status. And for a typical engineer the step up to the next rung of the ladder of responsibility takes ten years. Some reach pensionable age without having gone beyond even the stage of 'ordinary' or junior research officer." This erosion in individual mobility, *Literaturnaya Gazyeta* noted, was causing frustration and anger.

Previously, semiskilled workers could, through hard work and technical training, look forward to improved conditions of life. These workers in the

1950s compared themselves to their parents who were mostly peasants, living under austere conditions. Therefore, small advances in living standards satisfied them. Later, however, from 1965 to 1970, living standards among semiskilled, skilled and professional workers improved sharply, and this increase created higher expectations. Toward the end of the 1970s, the higher aspirations resulted in workers being extremely dissatisfied with the declining growth in living standards and job opportunities.

In addition, working-class parents were experiencing decreasing opportunities for their children. In the 1960s, a majority of young people believed all roads were open to them; but in the 1970s, they began to feel the growing inequality in real opportunities. With prestige institutions favoring admission of the children of bureaucrats and intellectuals, many working-class parents now believed their children could not get ahead in life regardless of their ability.

Increases in education, culture and living standards during the 1960s and early 1970s also changed the structure of consumer demand. It stimulated a general demand for even better standards. Housing conditions, for instance, had changed radically as most families moved out of communal apartments and dormitories into private flats. In the 1970s, however, people wanted even larger flats than they had. Their education and tastes recognized the potential benefits of industrialization and fully justified even higher standards than before.

On the other hand, certain strata and groups were discontent because their conditions had scarcely changed for the better. Many Siberian coal miners were living in dormitories and makeshift housing in highly polluted communities. They had experienced few improvements in general living standards despite comparatively high wages. Other workers also lived in substandard conditions. These workers included the very poor such as the Moscow *limitchiki* who led a precarious existence, caught in a vise with no permanent jobs or residency permits. They also included poverty-stricken people in the Soviet Union's "third world," Uzbekistan, Tajikistan, and other underdeveloped republics. In the 1980s, when censorship was lowered, the statistics on poverty came out—40 million people survived below the poverty line.

Workers also suffered from the deterioration in social services such as child care, medical care and pensions. Some Western countries held Soviet social services in high regard in the 1950s and 1960s but Brezhnev cut them back and they sharply deteriorated. Meanwhile, Western countries such as Sweden and Germany had rapidly improved the quality of their services. This improvement made the Soviet deterioration appear especially shameful.

Working conditions produced even greater shame and resentment. Workers were demoralized by bad management, bureaucratization, and the "lack of rhythm in production" caused by shortages in material supplies. Workers hated making useless products nobody wanted. *Izvestia* correspondents reported that large numbers of skilled workers left the factory that produced Vega refrigerators because nobody would buy them. Women working for an overcoat factory were depressed for the same reason. A seamstress, V. Niul'chenko, said angrily, "Why do our technologists agree to put such absurd patterns into production? We wouldn't wear such overcoats as the ones we make. So why do we offer them to a customer? I'm ashamed to work like this" (Kagarlitsky 1990, p. 305).

When *Literaturnaya Gazyeta* surveyed discontent among young people, in 1985, it discovered that younger workers were reacting more strongly than older ones to irrational production targets. Traditional managerial methods were proving ineffective. Young workers were more likely to refuse overtime. They were demanding greater self-respect and they wanted their work to be managed properly and utilized intelligently. They expressed anger about the idleness caused by shortages in material supplies and the frantic "storming" to make up time lost in meeting the monthly plan (Kagarlitsky 1990, p. 305). While the quality of the labor force had rapidly improved in the 1970s, the opportunities for self-actualization in the workplace did not.

The Legitimacy Crisis

Although initially confined to conversations between trusted friends and to "kitchen politics," a crisis of legitimacy had arisen at the end of the Brezhnev era. Such a crisis occurs whenever masses of people give up trusting their ruling groups, their economic and political systems that are no longer credible. Writers at the close of Brezhnev's reign reported a marked decline in the effectiveness of government propagandists. By 1983, the Central Committee and political journals were also complaining about the widespread rejection of party propaganda. Old slogans were losing credibility in the face of the oncoming economic crisis.

Throughout the Brezhnev period, propagandists and censors had kept a lid on popular awareness and resentment. But when the economic crisis under Gorbachev escalated and glasnost had become established, these demagogues could no longer convince people that "actually existing socialism" upheld the standards that were supposed to make socialism morally superior to Western capitalism.

When glasnost drew attention to real differences between the Soviet Union and the West, communist dogma shriveled up. At Moscow University we met a young man who had just received a doctoral degree in "scientific communism," and he told us that many students now believed his field to be completely worthless. At mass demonstrations, people showed contempt for official communist ideology and its dogma about the inevitability and superiority of socialism. They derisively shouted at speakers who talked of "the triumphant achievements of socialism" to justify the Soviet economy and the Party.

Even party members had become contemptuous of party hacks using oversimplified Marxian ideas to deny that Western economies were better off, that they had left the Soviet economy far behind. Dogmatists had long prophesied the imminent collapse of capitalism, saying that Western nations were caught in the "primary contradiction" of capitalism because its class system had become a fetter on economic development. But this prophecy was completely out-of-joint with current realities. The political and corporate rulers in Japan, Europe and North America had overcome one international crisis after another and had taken their countries into a new technological era. By contrast, the Soviet bureaucracy had stalled scientific breakthroughs, technical innovations, and economic reforms that threatened its interest. How, then, these disillusioned communists asked, could the dogmatists continue to justify bureaucratic centralism after it had strangled the forces of production?

Communists and non-communists alike became furious with the central economic ministries because they were responsible for administering the economy according to five-year plans. Economists had touted central planning and administration as the socialist panacea for technological backwardness, shortages, economic imbalances, unemployment and poverty. Yet *Gosplan*'s (the ministries' planning agency) own policies were being held responsible for the backwardness, shortages, imbalances and poverty in the Soviet Union.

Even the positive effects of central planning on employment were deniable. Full employment, where it actually existed, was being achieved through over employment and inefficient production. Extra hands were desperately needed to catch up to planning quotas after workers stood idle for days or weeks waiting for supplies to arrive. Also, over-employment prevented cuts in enterprise budgets by the ministries. If labor costs were reduced, the central ministries first appropriated the savings and then cut enterprise budgets. So enterprises hired more workers than they needed to pad their payrolls.

Thus, as the 1970s drew to a close, Soviet society had become an ideological minefield ready to explode during the following decade under the increasing weight of economic and political crises. Western observers at that time took note of the growing number of dissidents, *samizdat* (underground) publications, and other indications of challenges to the legitimacy of the Soviet system hurled by political movements above and below ground. These movements were constructing the foundations of a new Soviet-style civil society in the 1970s and 1980s.

By the 1980s, economists started to accuse the ministries of creating the opposite of what they were intended to do. They had produced a Frankenstein monster, an economy that could neither be planned nor managed. Planners did not know how to control this monster nor did they intend to get rid of it.

Throughout 1989 and 1990, opinion polls showed that the federal government had lost its credibility. Most people no longer trusted it. They felt that their country could not create a market economy unless both *Gosplan* and the ministries were abolished and the prime minister (N. Ryzhkov) and his cabinet resigned. Striking Siberian miners made these two political demands in the summer of 1989. One year later, many legislators in the Supreme Soviets of the Russian Republic and the Soviet Union made the same demands.

However, this emerging civil society was barely influenced by class-conscious working-class movements because the repressive organs of the government and the organization of production relations had, for decades, co-opted, confined and crushed these movements. Even "socialist" property relations restricted working-class consciousness. Though socialism meant social ownership of the means of production, workers in any given enterprise did not actually own their enterprise nor were they generally given the authority to use its profits to upgrade equipment or expand capital assets. Since the central ministries appropriated a state enterprise's profits and subsidized its losses, they had an important effect on the working class. As a result of this ministry control, worker self-interests centered around the negotiations between work collectives and management over wages, hours, tempo of work, etc., rather than productivity, profitability and enterprise planning. Consequently, the Soviet organization of social ownership had paradoxical effects on workers. Although the ministries operated in the name of socialist property relations, their policies actually weakened the worker's sense of collective responsibility and strengthened his or her interest in private aggrandizement.

Loosely organized social movements headed by nationalists, populists, fundamentalists, demagogic apparatchiks and free marketeers filled most of the political vacuum created by the legitimacy crisis. As consumer shortages became general shortages and as real incomes declined, discontent increased; but the consciousness of workers, who were fed-up with the system and its unfulfilled promises, was usually confined by economistic horizons.

Thus the new civil society was sharply divided but it was largely composed of movements that opposed the system for reasons having to do with individual social mobility, expanding consumerism amidst consumer shortages, dissatisfaction with wages and working conditions, and the deterioration of living standards. Even the nationalist movements drew supporters from people who were discontented with the system's inability to satisfy their private aims. The legitimacy crisis, under these conditions, devoured hopes for socialism and replaced them with the idealization of American capitalism.

The party-state bureaucracy was also split by the crisis. While ruling classes in the West are regenerated by the private accumulation of property and inheritance, the bureaucracy reproduced itself through cooptation. It selected young people from all social strata and classes, winning their initial allegiance through appeals to careerist interests as well as socialist ideals. As the legitimacy crisis grew worse, those who had kept or revived their ideals cut the ties that had compromised them. They no longer conformed like robots to party dogma and expediency. But the careerists also broke away in large numbers as bureaucracy constricted and their opportunities for advancement declined.

In the 1980s, the spiraling economic and legitimacy crises fractured the Party horizontally and vertically. Disagreements on all party levels between radical, technocratic, and conservative party reformers had flared into the open. Neo-Stalinists quickly distanced themselves from the outright Stalinists. Democratic movements within primary party organizations turned against the party *Apparat*. Nationalists in the Soviet Republics began to tear the Communist Party apart though it had dominated the empire since the Civil War.

Until 1985, the Party had successfully maintained the illusion that party, government and managerial authority were bound together in an indestructible monolith. But the fractures hidden by this illusion rapidly widened after perestroika was launched. Like a block of steel struck repeatedly in sub-zero temperatures, glasnost and perestroika shattered the legitimacy of central authority into a thousand pieces.

The Nomenklatura

The class character of Soviet society must be considered to appreciate another dimension of the legitimacy crisis having to do with inequalities in living standards. At first glance, the Soviet Union did not appear to be a class society because the party-state bureaucracy did not totally annihilate the socialist relations envisaged by Lenin. The people who controlled the bureaucracy used their power to establish exploitative conditions but this exploitation was never fully consolidated through a legal transformation of property relations. These people did not seize and claim ownership of state property in the name of individual members or groups of members. In other words, they were members of an embryonic ruling class whose bureaucratic characteristics set them apart from ruling classes in the West.

This embryonic class was unique because its members were much more dependent on bureaucratic status than personal income, property or inheritance. Actually, as Alec Nove (1983) has pointed out, the members of this class couldn't even pass on really significant wealth to their children unless they had managed to get this wealth illegally and to have hidden it from the government. So they usually applied the power of their office, for example, to getting their children admitted to special schools, universities and jobs; and a large number also greased the way to a better life with substantial *blat* (bribes) and black market transactions.

Still, according to party dogma, the rulers of the Soviet Union were simply bureaucrats who managed resources in the public interest. They were not officially a social class. Theirs, after all, was supposed to be a classless society. Yet class realities belied their devotion to the public. While emphatically denying that their country was composed of antagonistic classes, these rulers had actually insinuated exploitative relations into everything.

This contradiction between class realities and public rhetoric, between actual aims and professed aims, was built into the system. And it also eroded the system's legitimacy. In an attempt to repair this erosion, the *Nomenklatura* in the post–Stalin period relied on propagandists who manipulated public opinion, mystified the power of the party and government—and actually changed nothing.

As glasnost unfolded, the president of the Soviet Sociological Association, Tatyana Zaslavskaya, called the ruling group within Soviet society "the *Nomenklatura* stratum." The *Nomenklatura*, as indicated previously, were people in authoritative positions. They had been vetted by party organs that controlled appointments of administrators and specialists. This system of personnel selection produced an overarching bureaucracy—"an all-inclusive Soviet establishment," in the words of Nove—because it covered every significant post.

The foremost representatives of the *Nomenklatura* stratum were the functionaries and administrators in the party, state, and state-owned institutions, namely party secretaries, state ministers and enterprise managers. But support networks composed of other types of personnel such as high-status artists and intellectuals were included on the periphery of this offspring of the bureaucracy. Even editors of publications such as *Pravda* were included because no establishment can maintain its rule without artists and ideologists who control people's minds.

M.A. Cheskov (1989) argues that the *Nomenklatura* is a "class-like group" and that the Soviet Union is not a socialist society at all. He uses the term *statocracy* to characterize economies with bureaucracies based on nationalized productive resources.[3] He observes that, internationally, state-owned corporations are frequently established to cope with the political and economic forces unleashed by the global economy. These state-owned assets include such firms as Fiat in Italy and the Thomson Group in France. (Fiat is one of the largest motor vehicle companies in the world and the Thomson Group is an electronic firm which, in 1990, ranked number one in television and video cassette recorder sales in the United States.) State entrepreneurship has often been used by governments in underdeveloped countries to accelerate the pace of economic development.

However, there are also partial statocracies, such as certain capitalist countries and the Soviet Union during the New Economic Policy (NEP) period, because nationalization, in these cases, is cramped by private property relations. Stalin, in due course, destroyed NEP and put an *absolute statocracy* in its place when he nationalized almost all productive resources and placed them under the control of a centralized bureaucratic system.

Cheshkov contends that in this process Stalin created a qualitatively new class structure. The rulers of this structure have been bureaucrats, but they are not just bureaucrats alone. Their exploitative relations transcend discrete party and government institutions, and they operate as the de facto owners of the nationalized resources. They can do virtually whatever they want with factories and state stores, including shutting them down. The Soviet class system may not be similar to class systems in the West today, but this difference does not detract from its ability to dominate people's lives. The Soviet ruling class exploits their whole society through the collective appropriation of surplus production through control over the nationalized sector of the economy and the state institutions.

Because the ruling bureaucrats operate as de facto (if not legal) owners of the nationalized resources, Cheshkov believes that the Soviet Union has not, after all, had a socialist economy since Stalin took power.[4] Soviet enterprises represent "universal private property" rather than property that is genuinely "socialized" and controlled by workers for non-exploitative ends. The Soviet economy, therefore, is in this view not even implicitly a "state socialist" economy because its means of production were not owned and controlled by workers.

Cheshkov's opinion about who ruled these enterprises has been shared by socialists in the Soviet Union and elsewhere. They disagree, however, on the status of the rulers: Are they a social class, a stratum or an elite group? There is also disagreement about the socioeconomic system—is it a statocracy, state socialism or state capitalism?

Alternatives to "statocracy" such as "state socialism" seem valid because they are vaguely similar to the professed aims of Soviet rulers and long-held technocratic and utopian socialist ideas about how a socialist economy should be organized. Furthermore, the prototype of the command economy, War Communism, was instituted during the Civil War and it was originally endorsed by Bolsheviks such as Lenin. These Bolsheviks changed their minds in 1921 when they realized what harm War Communism was doing to their revolution; but some continued to believe that socialism meant taking direct command and running the economy like a large factory.

On the other hand, even though the economic chaos and dislocation during the Civil War encouraged the Bolsheviks to rely heavily on War Communism's command methods, the need to win the war did not make the command economy inevitable. Lenin said as much when he repudiated War Communism and confessed that the Party had gone too far in nationalizing trade and industry. Consequently, the command economy was, at most, a "quasi-socialist" economy because it violated fundamental principles of socialist thought. Furthermore, this quasi-socialist economy did not merely rely on the nationalization of productive resources. Its origination and reproduction were necessarily dependent on political mechanisms that integrated the productive resources. If public enterprises had been forced to compete with other public or private enterprises in a market economy, the integrating functions performed by the party-state bureaucracy would have been superfluous. Consequently, the way in which the nationalized resources were *integrated* by party and state agencies was as important as nationalization itself for the dominant mode of production.

Of course, the extraordinary complexity of Soviet society makes the disagreement about the nature of its system understandable. Zaslavskaya suggests that Stalin imposed antisocialist relations on a society when only the very first steps had been made toward socialism. Some socialist mechanisms were allowed to continue operating while others were modified, destroyed or forced to degenerate.

Menshikov (Galbraith and Menshikov 1988) points out that *Gosplan,* the central planning agency, for instance, continued to operate under Stalin. But it was devastated by his purges. From Stalin onward, *Gosplan* operated differently. It was originally designed to predict the overall development of the economy and estimate investments to be made in industry, agriculture, housing, schools and defense, based on legislated priorities. If *Gosplan* had done its job properly, these estimates would have helped create strategies for using resources to expand the economy and eliminate poverty. But *Gosplan* had merely become another cog in the bureaucratic machine and a huge gap separated planning ideals from reality. The ministries had determined *Gosplan*'s work and their assigned tasks had little to do with either forecasting or developing strategies for effective use of resources. It's no secret now that *Gosplan* helped the ministries ensure their own survival at the nation's expense. Consequently, criticism during the legitimacy crisis was being directed at a planning agency that was very different from what socialists had envisaged.

The degree to which high status bureaucrats were rewarded represented yet another difference from the way socialists had envisioned things. While the Brezhnev regime tightened the bureaucracy's grip on society, for example, it also increased the numbers of large apartments, country houses, special shops, chauffeured limousines, superior medical facilities and other services available only to higher-status bureaucrats.[5]

The lower-status bureaucrats were taken care of, too. A comprehensive system of small privileges turned many lower echelon bureaucrats into extreme conservatives. While Stalin had executed these bureaucrats if they got out of line, and Khrushchev had moved them around from one part of the country to another, Brezhnev let them stay in one place. They sank their roots deep into their local communities. To protect their cushy jobs, these ward-heelers presided over patronage systems and actively sabotaged reformist initiatives from the top. Political corruption spread everywhere and promoted inequality.

Brezhnev's policies increased the real income gap between privileged and unprivileged groups. This gap was examined in a 1982 study of Latvian savings banks which found only three per cent of the deposits contained half the overall sum of the deposits (Kagarlitsky 1990, p. 274; Izvestia, July 24, 1984). Victor Zaslavsky, a sociologist, observed that the major depositors were apparatchiks, high-ranking military officers, famous artists and eminent scholars as well as commercial entrepreneurs. These groups had special opportunities to get scarce goods at low prices that meant that officially sanctioned privileges enabled them to save most of their legally earned incomes.

A second way the income gap was widened was through corruption. Corrupt party and state officials siphoned off millions of rubles through swindles and bribes. Commercial entrepreneurs, mostly speculators and black marketeers, took advantage of the official corruption and shortages. Their real incomes were much higher than most people's because they were able to turn millions of rubles into jewelry, gold, and hard currency that they kept hidden rather than in banks.

The government had created the shortages, economic imbalances and corruption that had made black markets inevitable while factory managers, in collusion with workers, enlarged their incomes by producing or trading for this market. One study on corruption in the U.S.S.R. proposed that Georgia had been more prosperous than other republics because of the size of its black markets. It estimated that some Georgian factories had exceeded their quotas by 40 percent, and then channeled this unreported above-plan production into the black market (Mars and Altman 1983; Lampert 1983). Such studies imply that black markets comprised the largest sector of free market activity and were an important source of economic inequality in the Soviet Union though their exact magnitudes were impossible to determine.

Brezhnev's contribution to the life style of affluent citizens was not lost on those in high places. Though Brezhnev had become senile and could no longer even walk unaided, these colleagues maintained him in office until 1982. As his power was preserved, corruption was flowering. And although their economy had expanded faster than ours in the United States, it became more erratic and unmanageable as it grew. In the final years of Brezhnev's reign, the growing inefficiency of the command system and the priority given to the military-industrial complex stalled economic growth.

Taking the Surplus

As indicated, the functionaries, officials and managers within the *Nomenklatura* stratum were in control of the productive resources of the economy. They were de facto owners of U.S.S.R. Incorporated. Still, the *Nomenklatura* never achieved anything like the status of proprietied classes in capitalist societies. Merely having power to control state property in its own selfish interest did not mean it could justify these interests in public. As a result, its members had to resort to massive deception and censorship to hide the exploitation, privilege, and economic inequality produced by their control of public property.

Another avenue to economic privilege was paved with public funds. Enormous budgetary outlays were spent on networks of sumptuous party buildings, sanitaria, estates and perks that were not financed by party dues. In addition, the *Nomenklatura* adopted a Machiavellian strategy for appropriating the surplus wealth produced by workers. Since commodity markets were extremely restricted, they had to find ways of enriching themselves primarily through payment in concrete goods and services rather than money. They created a broad network of institutions that provided their families with superior medical services, better quality yet cheaper food, and superior apartments, dachas and hotels. The network underwrote the costs of automobiles, vacation resorts, travel to foreign lands, dining rooms and other privileges. Professional associations of elite cultural workers such as the Writers Union were also in this network.

The new stratification system even increased the privileges provided on location in industrial plants. At the great complex of steel mills in Magnitogorsk, for instance, there were five levels of dining rooms. The top level included the plush places for VIPs that served caviar and sturgeon. On the bottom were canteens serving bread and thin gruel to convict laborers. The top-level dining room served superior quality food but its clientele paid the same low subsidized prices that people on wages and salaries in the other dining rooms paid for lower quality food.

The *Nomenklatura* created these networks for distributing concrete goods and services because it was difficult to enrich people legally by giving them a great deal of money. They usually funded these networks from a variety of public sources such as enterprise income, construction ministry budgets and social consumption funds. Social consumption funds, however, were created to serve everyone equally. These funds, among other things, provided subsidized housing, subsidized food, free medical care, free child care, free vacations, grants to families for raising children, educational stipends, free education at all levels, and pensions whose costs were not directly paid from personal property taxes or income. The government greatly expanded these funds in the postwar years and their magnitude in the 1980s was astonishing. Per capita income in 1987 increased as much as 42 percent when these funds were added to wages and salaries.[6]

The *Nomenklatura*'s use of social consumption funds was a wily answer to the general leveling of wages and salaries in the Soviet Union. It introduced economic inequalities that were not disclosed publicly. By using the funds this way, the *Nomenklatura* corrupted a widely legitimated communist principle of social justice. This bizarre mutation of social consumption fund use reveals just how thoroughly the party and state had betrayed socialist ideals.

Consequently, social consumption fund policies were shaped by a social contract that, along with virtually guaranteed employment, also marked the mutation of socialist standards. These standards certainly justified subsidized basic living standards for poorer members of society. However, since housing, food, transportation, medical care, etc., subsidized the well off more than the poor, the allocation of these funds violated the principle that people should only enjoy a living standard they have truly earned. Old Bolsheviks such as Lenin never believed that socialism should guarantee employment to everyone regardless of how unproductive they (or their enterprises) were. And he certainly did not contend that socialism entitled individuals in more advantageous class situations to receive a greater share of the surplus wealth acquired by the state than others.

Inevitably, workers discovered how the *Nomenklatura* was cheating them—appropriating the economic values they had been creating. Since social consumption funds were a main channel through which wealth was appropriated, the effect of this corruption on socialist ideals was profound. It promoted demoralization and cynical attitudes toward socialist ideals.

Areas of agreement between Boris Yeltsin and Yegor Ligachev, two major political antagonists, show that no party official could justify this corruption in public. Yeltsin, in a speech at the 19th Party Congress, in 1988, declared that there are "secret questions, such as the Party's own budget" which maintains "luxury houses, villas, sanitaria on such a scale that one feels ashamed when representatives of parties" from other countries visit these facilities. "We must," Yeltsin bitterly added, "finally liquidate the food parcels for, so to speak, the 'starving Nomenklatura.'" The conservative party leader, Ligachev, also spoke before the Congress. Although he showed contempt for Yeltsin on other grounds, he emphatically agreed that official data on the privileges afforded party functionaries should be published openly. He insisted that "people should know the truth," rather than "the *erzatz*" from the liberal newspaper, *Moscow News* (Nove 1983, pp. 164–66).

In November 1988, we interviewed a Moscow book editor who was an ardent advocate of perestroika. During the interview, we used the idiomatic American term, "bureaucratic hacks," for mediocre office holders who opposed perestroika. The editor smiled and, playing on words, told us that the word "hack" was not appropriate and was an insult to honest workers. He explained, "A butcher is a worker who hacks meat but the bureaucrats and party officials are *exploiters* not workers. They sit like kings on thrones and tell people how important they are." He pulled himself up in his chair as he spoke, assumed a haughty demeanor and lampooned a pompous bureaucrat commanding subjects at his feet to serve him. He then went on to proclaim that socialism did not do away with exploitation because the bureaucrats exploited the people.

In 1990, Vladimir Kabaidze, the general director of the famous Ivanovo Engineering Production Association who visited the United States for business and pleasure, also knew the truth. During the visit he showed a fine sense of humor when swapping jokes with Americans. When asked about the differences between his social system and ours, he replied: "What is the difference between capitalism and socialism? In capitalism one man exploits another. But socialism is exactly the opposite."[7]

The crisis of legitimacy in the 1980s swept away the smoke, mirrors and Potemkin villages that kept many from seeing the anti-socialist facets of Soviet life. The Soviet model was a complex tangle of socialist and anti-socialist relations whose appearances often belied their content. Some Soviet social scientists have attempted to untangle these snarled relations, "but even now," admits Zaslavskaya, "it is by no means easy to determine what sort of social organism this was, one that oddly mixed elements of a society in transition from capitalism to socialism, Asiatic despotism, state-monopoly capitalism and, perhaps, some other types of societies."

Notes

1. We were exchange scholars during the fall semester, 1988. This article was begun while the Soviet Union still existed. It was finished during a 1991 sabbatical, spent at the Institute for the Study of Social Change, University of California, Berkeley.
2. These standards however could not be achieved by the average worker. Soviet econ-

omists estimated that at best average workers could only satisfy 70 percent of their rational needs (Kagarlitsky 1990, p. 297).

3. Cheshkov uses the term "class-like groups" rather than social classes when he refers to the bureaucrats.

4. Cheshkov says Marx warned that such a collective form of exploitation would occur if barracks-type communism came into existence.

5. Policies providing substantial perks go back to Stalin. Documents circulated among central committee members by leaders who were executed during the early 1930s by Stalin (along with a million and a half other members of the Communist Party) were indignant about these corrupt policies.

6. This is the Union average. It was 44 percent for industrial workers. Our calculations utilized data from: *The USSR In Figures for 1987. The State Committee of the USSR on Statistics,* Moscow: Finansy i Statistika Publishers, 1988. See Table entitled "Average Wages and Salaries of Workers and Employees with Allowances and Benefits Received from Social Consumption Funds" (pp. 202–203).

7. This quip was expressed on American television two years later by a Russian who had migrated to the U.S. and become a comedian.

References

Cheshkov, M. A. 1989. "A Conception of Bureaucracy: The Necessity and Possibility of a Reformulation." *Soviet Sociology* (28): pp. 61–80.

Cohen, Stephen F. 1980. *Bukharin and the Bolshevik Revolution: A Political Biography, 1888–1938.* London: Oxford University Press.

Galbraith, John, and Stanislav Menshikov. 1988. *Capitalism, Communism and Coexistence: From the Bitter Past to a Better Prospect.* Boston: Houghton Mifflin.

Hough, Jerry F. 1977. *The Soviet Union and Social Science Theory.* Cambridge: Harvard University Press.

Izvestia. July 24, 1984. No further information available.

Kagarlitsky, Boris. 1990. *The Dialectic of Change.* Translated by Rick Simon. London: Verso.

Keller, Bill. 1988. "Moscow's Other Mastermind: Aleksander Yakovlev, Gorbachev's Little-known Alter Ego." *The New York Times Magazine,* February 19, pp. 30–44.

Khrushchev, Sergei. 1990. *Khrushchev on Khrushchev: An Inside Account of the Man and His Era, by His Son Sergei Khrushchev.* Boston: Little, Brown.

Lampert, Nick. 1983. "The Whistleblowers: Corruption and Citizen's Complaints in the U.S.S.R." In *Corruption: Causes, Consequences and Control,* edited by Michael Clark. New York: St. Martin's.

Mars, Gerald, and Yochanan Altman. 1983. "How a Soviet Economy Really Works: Cases and Implications." In *Corruption: Causes, Consequences and Control,* edited by Michael Clark. New York: St. Martin's.

Nove, Alec. 1983. *The Economics of Feasible Socialism.* London: George Allen and Unwin.

Zaslavskaya, T. 1989. "On the Strategy of Social Management." *Soviet Sociology* (26).

Moscow Memoir: On the Status of Women

FREDA CASNER

INTRODUCTION BY DOROTHY S. MCCLELLAN

Through a personal lens, Freda Casner's essay examines the changes and challenges women in the Soviet Union faced as the country entered the uncharted waters of glasnost and perestroika. Having served as a faculty exchange scholar in the State University of New York-Moscow State University program in 1983, returning in 1988, she had a baseline from which to measure the effect of these political events on women. Being fluent in Russian she interviewed and read the work of major Russian feminist thinkers from which she gained insights that she shares with us. Her examination begins with Gorbachev's 1985 accession to the post of General Secretary of the Party that brings "new openness, literally, to the negative aspects of women's lives." At the twenty-seventh Party Congress in 1986 he expressed his concerns about family issues and called for major reforms to improve women's lives by enabling them to more easily combine motherhood and career. She shares feminist responses to Gorbachev's reform and wonders aloud what might have been had his plans not been brought to a halt by his fall and Yeltsin's rise to political power.

Background

Already in 1884 with the publication of *Origin of the Family, Private Property and the State,* Engels considered changes in the role and status of women that would result from transforming society from the rule of private ownership to collective ownership of the means of production. Engels argued that when women were able to participate fully in the productive process, they would achieve true liberation. Bound by love rather than economic ties, the relations between men and women would take a new form. Women would take their place in the workforce and in the family as full equals.

The Russian Revolution of 1917 provided the opportunity for redefining the relationship of men and women and women's place in the world of work. Alexandra Kollontai, a militant member of the Russian feminist movement, was nominated by Lenin to be a people's commissioner with the title Commissar of the Department of Social Security. As first woman member of the Bolshevik cabinet, she played a pivotal role in getting women the right to vote three years before women were granted the right to suffrage in the United States. The *Zhenotdel* (Women's Section) of the Central Committee was established in 1919. Kollontai, along with Inessa Armand who headed the Women's Section, drafted many key pieces of family legislation for the new Civil Code. By 1923 these laws secularized marriage, permitted divorce by mutual consent and first-trimester abortions, and granted women equal rights of custody to their children, inheritance, and choice of residence and work.

The Civil War that followed the Revolution had far-reaching consequences: millions of homeless, orphaned children needed supervision in the many children's colonies that were established and workers in factories were needed to replace the men who enlisted in the Red Army. Women were drawn into the world of work and succeeded in making great advances in their emancipation. Unlike the situation in the U.S. after World War II when Rosie the Riveter was laid off as men returned home, Soviet women retained their positions in the workforce. The loss of 28 million people in the war made everyone's work a necessity. Figures suggest that of males born in 1922, only 20 percent were still alive at the end of the war. Since World War II Russian women have comprised 50 percent of the employment sector. Women were almost equally divided between agricultural, service and industrial sectors, where they generally held low paying positions. But the situation improved as a result of the feminization of higher education. While in 1927 28 percent of students in higher educational institutions were female, by 1986 it was 51 percent.

What we saw in the U.S.S.R. was "a real transformation of female roles, although living conditions and the far slower evolution of male mentalities did not always allow these new aspirations to be manifested fully" (Kerblay 1996, p. 462). A study conducted by Hansson and Linden in 1983 suggested that "women are demanding two things: freedom in love, modeled on a certain image of femininity" and "the ability to establish themselves in a circle less narrow than the family" (Kerblay 1996, pp. 462–463). As is true in the West, "women attempt to equal men in the workplace and they revert to being wives and mothers in the home. They dream of not having to choose" (Kerblay 1996, p. 463). While women had to a certain extent achieved equality in the workplace, this was and is not true at home. The dramatic economic crisis in the period of transition to a market economy hit women particularly hard: "70% of the registered unemployed in Russia on 1 January 1993" were women (Kerblay 1996, pp. 474–475).

References

Engels, F. 2010. *The Origin of the Family, Private Property and the State.* London: Penguin.
Kerblay B. 1996. "Socialist Families." In A. Burguiere, C. Klapish-Zuber, M. Segalen, and F. Zonabend. *A History of the Family, Volume II, The Impact of Modernity.* Cambridge: Belknap Press of Harvard University Press.

I will never forget the ambiance of Moscow in the spring of 1988. I had arrived late one evening in the middle of February at Sheremyetevo Airport. The cold clear air was a bracing change as we disembarked from the heated Aeroflot plane and boarded the van that was to take us to the *passa-ZHIR-sky zal ozid-DAN-iye* (passenger waiting room). I had come as a faculty exchange scholar from the sociology department of the State University of New York at New Paltz to spend a semester at Moscow State University. I had been an exchange scholar under the same program five years earlier, but this time it was different: it was Moscow in the time of perestroika. In the three years since Mikhail Gorbachev had acceded to the office of general secretary of the Communist Party, perestroika and glasnost had become household words worldwide. As much as I could at home, I had followed this exciting and historic movement, which Gorbachev had called revolutionary. Now I would be seeing, experiencing it for myself.

Inside, the dimly lit corridors seemed dark and mysterious, but not uninviting. I had always liked the dark wood contemporary decor, so typical of northern European airports at that time. So here I was pushing and pulling my two heavy suitcases towards customs inspection, wishing that my husband had been able to come with me, annoyed that Sheremyetevo had no porters. Suddenly, striding towards me I saw my *konsultant*, Professor Nikolai Driachlov, chair of Moscow State University's sociology department, and his son, Dima. We had been corresponding, but I had to leave before receiving his acknowledgment of the date and flight number of my arrival. It was an exuberant and embracing reunion. Dima, who had been a gangling adolescent five years ago, was now a handsome twenty-one-year-old, beaming as he handed me six plastic-wrapped yellow tulips, luminous in the dim light. Then father and son each seized a suitcase and we proceeded to the customs tables. I did not look forward to the ritual of opening suitcases. But much to my surprise,

Professor Driachlov flashed a card at the customs officials and we sailed right through without having to open anything. Once we were out of the building the suitcases were strategically fitted into the rather small trunk of the Lada sedan, at that time one of the most popular Soviet-made cars. I sat in the back seat surrounded by boxes and bags of food: bread, cake, jars of cooked fruit, cooked meat that dear Mrs. Driachlov had prepared for me, "to get you through the first few days of getting settled."

The warmth expressed in that auspicious arrival was, more or less, typical of those extended to other Americans. It resonated from an attitude some Russians had towards Americans, an attitude of hospitable friendliness and admiration that almost bordered on deference. I appreciated it, but somehow found it sad and sometimes embarrassing, as when I was marched to the front of a long line of prospective buyers outside a shop or past people lined up for theatre tickets.

The next day, despite all the unpacking left to do, I took a walk towards the metro. Everything seemed exactly the same as it was five years earlier. Nothing had changed, even the huge rusting girder I remembered tripping over near the trolley station was still there. But as the days passed, it was the ambiance that seemed different. Everywhere, in the streets, in the halls and restaurants of the University, there seemed to be an electric, almost palpable air of great expectations. Much of it, I thought at first, was due to my own eager anticipation to be where I now was. But weeks later a Russian friend whose specialty was English literature was to tell me that many Muscovites felt the same way. "Let's hope," he joked, "that the great expectations won't be followed by hard times." Little did we realize then the grim prescience of that Dickensian word play in the years to come.

During the following two weeks I got rid of the welcoming *tar-a-KAN-y* (cockroaches) in my apartment by sprinkling boric acid powder in appropriate places. The apartment consisted of two rooms and a bath off of a small entry hall. Originally planned for two occupants, each room was furnished with a daybed, small table, two chairs, and a combination desk-cupboard. After I unpacked, set up some family photographs and other personal objects, the effect, my friend Tanya said was "*ooDOBno i ooYUTno*," comfortable and cozy. She lived near the university and had come to help, have tea and talk. But most of the time was taken up by an endless list of bureaucratic procedures that all foreign newcomers had to follow, procedures that seemed to have been deliberately designed to consume maximum time and effort. Upstairs to the tenth floor to *Inotdyel*, the international department, for an assortment of ID cards; the most important one was the "*Pro-pusk*," the pass to get into the University. Downstairs to relinquish passports for ten days. The final trip was a ten-minute walk outdoors to the humanities building called *Gumfak*, the acronym for *Gumanitarniye Fakultet*, the Humanities Faculty. (There is no letter "h" in the Cyrillic alphabet; it is transliterated as "g") Russians seem to like acronyms as much as Americans do. For some reason that building was where students and faculty collected their monthly stipends. That came to 400 rubles a month, a princely sum considering the prevailing rate of exchange and the low cost of food and other items.

At the end of the second week, Nikolai Ivanovich asked if I would be willing to lecture on university life in the United States to a group of eighteen interested students. (Professor Driachlov was always so formal I found it difficult to use his patronymic when addressing him. But I did after he specifically requested me to.) I demurred claiming it was not my field, no proper research sources at my disposal, etc. "Use your own experiences," he insisted," whatever they are it is more than what the students know." I finally agreed, but not until I had checked and found two good sources in the library of the American embassy. It turned out to be an enjoyable and productive experience on both sides. I think I learned almost as much about Russian university life as they did about American. What they seemed to like most were the participatory discussions. From my subsequent classroom observations such procedures were rarely followed. Although Nikolai Ivanovich was no longer part of the philosophy department and had increased authority as chair of a new department officially named *Trud* (Labor), I marveled at his flexibility, scheduling my lecture without, it seemed, prior approval from the Rector of the University. I wondered whether it resonated from the *NOV-i-ye MISH-len-i-ye* (New Thinking) of perestroika.

My own research centered on a comparative critical analysis of Soviet society using two time frames: the three years of the perestroika period and the last three years of the Brezhnev era (Gorbachev's predecessor). One variable was the workplace with gender distributions as to wages, hours, hours spent at work, at home, managerial access, etc. After several interviews I was struck by the acceptance by both men and women of the immutability of stereotyped sexual roles—the word "gender" was totally new. As a result I decided to change my research to the status of women in Soviet society. The decision had its basis in previous developments. My scholarly interests and studies in Russian/Soviet culture had coincided with the growth of the women's movement in the United States. Paraphrasing Simone de Beauvoir's 1949 statement in *Second Sex*, "One is not born but rather one becomes a woman," I, having been born and become a woman, found myself becoming a feminist (de Beauvoir 1961). So my change of research at Moscow State University seemed logical. It did not seem so to Professor Driachlov, my *kon-sul-TANT*. He agreed to the change but not with much enthusiasm. "This feminism is not an issue here in the Soviet Union," he said. "And don't American women have all possible rights and privileges already?" I told him that we were lobbying for equal pay for equal work. "*Zhe-LA-yu Vam us-PYEKH*" (I wish you success), he commented, dryly.

That comment, positive in content but so disapproving in tone, reflected the strong patriarchal attitudes that defined both personal and public relationships between Russian men and women. During Leonid Brezhnev's tenure as General Secretary, journals and newspapers had begun to discuss the "woman question" extensively. Such discussions actually spurred systematic research on the subject. Natalia Rimashevskaya (1987, 1993), head of the Institute for Socio-Economic Studies of the Population, was one of the first to research and write about women's problems. A report based on her ongoing research in the city of Taganrog included data on the "unfavourable status of women." It was the first time that a serious scholarly report described negative aspects of women's status in Soviet society rather than stressing their achievements.

Gorbachev and Perestroika

The 1985 accession of Gorbachev as general secretary of the Party brought new openness, literally, to the negative aspects of women's lives. At the twenty-seventh Party Congress, February 1986, Gorbachev voiced concern about family problems: the high divorce rate, the deficit of adequate housing, and the declining birthrate. His solutions, however, were not too different from those that Brezhnev had proposed: improvement in working conditions (flexible hours, part-time employment, take-home food service) and provision of more adequate domestic services (public laundries, home appliances, etc.) to "enable women to successfully combine motherhood with active participation in the workforce."

Gorbachev's 1986–90 Five-Year Plan pledged increased part-time work for women, a shorter workweek, and development of work opportunities for women at home. Maternity leaves were extended and plans made for increasing kindergartens. The emphasis was, as it had been under Khrushchev and Brezhnev, to alleviate but not alter women's dual roles. Addressing the demographic problem of the declining birthrate and prevalence of the one-child family, Gorbachev advocated early marriage and early childbirth. Students were urged to marry and have children and not wait until their education was completed. Students with children received the usual family subsidies, as well as educational stipends (Buckley in Kruks et al. 1983, 269–278). The halls of the graduate student dormitories at Moscow State University, replete with prams and kiddy cars, were evidence that students were heeding Gorbachev's exhortations.

Already under Brezhnev, some sociologists suggested the need for all family members to contribute to housework. Others said the answer was to increase services and improve housing. Brezhnev himself at a Trade Union Congress said that men had not done enough to ease women's dual burden. In the late seventies, some social scientists began recommending what had rarely been mentioned previously, that negative male attitudes towards sharing household work and rearing of children needed to change. They advocated an early educational effort to avoid stereotyping of male and female roles. New legal codes, they argued, should emphasize the "joint and equal responsibility of both spouses for the maintenance of the household and the rearing of children" (Lapidus 1978, 290–330 *passim*). So how did these enlightened debates affect the general populace? Unfortunately, the ancient patriarchal cultural norms again prevailed. There were some changes but most families reverted to the ideology of the "old days": household labor was "not man's work." Although the "woman question" was not solved during the Brezhnev era, women played an increasingly decisive role in the economy, especially in the fields of science and technology.

Fast-forward to 1987, concerned about rising juvenile delinquency, Gorbachev surprisingly resorted to an old ploy—women should get back into the home. At a 1987 international women's conference, he spoke of "woman's inherent functions: those of mother, wife, the person who brings up the children." In a television interview some months later he expressed similar sentiments, referring to "women's predestination as keeper of the home fires" (Smolowe 1987, 35). Given their strong legacy of seventy years of economic independence and their high educational levels, most women paid little heed to Gorbachev's words. Zoya Pukhova, chair of the Soviet Women's Committee, in a show of independence unusual for her office, spoke at the historic 19th Soviet Communist Party Conference: "Women have constitutional rights unequaled elsewhere, but the big problem now is guaranteeing their enforcement" (quoted in Bloice 1988). She told of women still doing heavy manual labor and working night shifts despite the illegality of such work. She attacked the by now popular contentions that many social problems like divorce and juvenile delinquency were caused by women working outside the home, and repudiated arguments that responsibility for home education and socialization of children were the responsibility of only the mother. The new economic reforms, she pointed out, had worsened the problems. "In the factories the conditions of *khozrachat* (cost accounting and self-financing) have put great pressure on women in the work brigades ... women are becoming undesirable labor power" (Ibid.). But after all that brave talk, she capitulated to history.

In 1917 Alexandra Kollontai began her campaign to get the Social Democrats to establish a separate women's commission. She agreed that such a move could be viewed as separatist and might diffuse the whole revolution, but she insisted that it would not in fact do so. She failed to convince the Social Democrats but the Bolsheviks accepted the proposal. In the autumn of 1919 the women's departments were reorganized as a formal section of the Central Committee and were given the name "Zhenotdel" (Women's Section), run completely by women. Seventy years later Pukhova recognizing that advocating for a special women's commission as had been suggested by some activist women might be viewed as divisive proposed the following:

> The solution to women's problems depends on the success of perestroika, and the success of perestroika is dependent upon the activity of women. That's how it was in 1917 and that's how it should be now [Ibid.].

Gorbachev's leadership will always have important historical significance because it ushered in the revolutionary perestroika process. But for women all it did was to broaden the parameters of public discussion. Few of the palliative measures he had proposed ever materialized. More freely than ever, women and men could speak openly about women's subordinate position in society. Although he frequently spoke about perestroika's "new freedoms," its "new democracy" and "new thinking," Gorbachev's most hortatory rhetoric gave women no choice: your "predestined role" is to go back in the home. Yet in many families two incomes were needed and in some better-off families women chose to combine home with work. No mention was made of "father's predestined role" even though fathers' abandonment of mothers with children is an urgent social problem and has been for many years. If Gorbachev's tenure had survived, would the status of women have improved? The answer was well-put by Anastasia Psadskaya-Vanderbeck, a leading Russian feminist, in a talk she gave at the State University of New York at New Paltz: "Perestroika was intended to expand individual freedoms, but for women it represented a post-socialist patriarchal renaissance" (1995). As it was, the disintegration of the Soviet Union was destined to bring on an unprecedented decline in women's status.

Russian Feminists and Non-Feminists

Tatiana Mamonova organized the first feminist *samizdat* (underground) journal in the 1970s in the Soviet Union. She was forced into exile in 1980 as a result. She has since lived in Europe and the United States and has always believed that the very fledgling feminist movement should not be subordinated to the "greater" fight of the pre-perestroika dissident movement and today's transition to a market economy. In a U.S.A. conference she reaffirmed this belief, urging "separateness" for women's issues in the new Russian economic order (Symposium, Westchester Consortium for International Studies, 1991).

Tatiana Zaslavskaya, a sociologist and well-known academician has made it to the top of her profession. A former president of the Soviet (now Russian) Sociological Association, she was one of Gorbachev's earliest top advisers on economic and social reforms. She was the director of a prestigious polling agency, the Center for Public Opinion and Market Research, the first of its kind in Russia. By Western standards one might expect a woman of such accomplishment to be a staunch advocate for women's equality in the workplace. Yet in a personal interview (Moscow, April 1988) the opposite seemed true. "Yes," she said, "women still suffer some inequities in the work place, but on the whole, most women do not have the interest or ambition in pursuing careers to highest levels." She herself, she added, and a few other women were exceptions. Her comments on gender differences would have raised the dander of even the least committed Western feminist: "Men are more varied in their inclinations and aptitudes, they are the innovators in the organization of life. Women are more conservative and stable precisely because they are the transmitters of life" (Ibid.). A factory worker and single parent of a three-year-old boy expressed somewhat similar thoughts on gender-differentiated roles:

> From very early on [a boy] must ... learn to be independent. That's much more important for a boy than for a girl. A girl can be spoiled with toys and finery and clothes. She has to learn from the beginning to be well-groomed, kind, charming and graceful [Hannson & Liden 1983, 107].

To many Russian women—and men—such sex-role stereotyping is part of the "natural order of things." Feminist theory and feminist scholarship, popularized in the West by the women's studies discipline, were virtually unknown in Moscow in the spring of 1988 (Taubman 1989, 211). And from my numerous conversations with Russian women, it appears that the word "feminist" itself still carries much of the pejorative aspect it acquired before and during the October revolution, when it was used to describe the bourgeois feminist movement. Generally, the Soviet media tend to reinforce such a view. There was little or distorted knowledge of Western feminism. Some women perceived it as reinforcing attitudes of hostility towards men and the family (Lapidus in Hannson & Liden 1983, Introduction, XV). Others saw it as a movement that creates "aggressive women" and "weak, effeminate men" (Taubman 1989, 206). Zaslavskaya pointed out that women make the really important decisions in family life and quoted an old Russian proverb: "Man is head of the family, but woman is the neck, and it is the neck that turns the head." At that time, in conversations and in the media (articles and letters from readers) there was much discussion about who should be the "head" and that it should be the man. Few expressed the opinion that "being the head" should be a shared responsibility.

Yeltsin: The Transition Period

Russia's transition to a market economy brought ruinously hard times to its people: rampant inflation, unprecedented increases in crime and corruption, a rise in hard-currency prostitution and pornography, widespread unemployment and poverty—mostly of women. There has been a drastic social, economic and political deterioration in women's status. How, why did this happen? The reasons form a complex web. Right after his election, Yeltsin eagerly embraced "shock therapy" as the economic method of the transition to capitalism. One of the first results was a massive reduction in the labor force with women being the first to be let go. Politicians have tried to console them: "First we'll turn the economy around. After that you women will have your rights" (Klimenkova 1992, 44). These words echo the objections of the Social Democrats when women tried to develop a separate women's agenda in 1917. But many women in this last decade of the twentieth century are no longer willing to accept the patriarchal norms of earlier times. Women comprise 53 percent of Russia's population. They are now experiencing disproportionately high rates of unemployment: 70 to 80 percent of all the unemployed are women. The result has led to the creation of a cohort of highly educated, skilled women, a population "that is eager to participate in the new formal economy and in political policy-making but is often denied access to [both]" (Dupar and Shaw 1995, 25). Employment discrimination against women is openly practiced by private and government employers. The government not only participates in discrimination, it does not enforce existing laws that prohibit gender discrimination (Khotkina 1995, 32).

Discussion of sexuality, long suppressed in Soviet times, is now a *cause célèbre* in the media. According to Klimenkova (1992), pornographic displays appear regularly on television and in the print media: "This regime propagates a crude and vulgar [approach] to sexual relations, completely dominated by a masculinized interpretation" (p.46). Employment of women reflects these new attitudes. The men in charge of the new jobs in the emerging entrepreneurial businesses (most of the new executives like the old party bosses are men) hire "very thin, young women who look as if they are straight out of *Elle* or *Vogue*" with little attention to job qualifications (Khanga 1991, op-ed page). Some secretarial want ads have specified that interview applicants must wear "miniskirts and have no inhibitions" (Ibid.).

Conclusion

Despite all these negative manifestations, women themselves have made dramatic changes. All across Russia they have formed autonomous organizations, grouped around similar interests (Business Women; Mothers of Soldiers; Association of Librarians; Women, Environment and Civil Society; etc.) and are raising women's consciousness about their subordinate position in society. Although they are aware that they did not have equal rights completely with men during the socialist era, they are beginning to fight to regain those rights, lost in the transitional period.

Summing up then, there is today, very definitely, an independent women's movement that speaks in a plurality of voices coming up from the grassroots level. These voices are much stronger, have more validity than the one voice that in previous years emanated from the top. And at the Moscow Centre for Gender Studies feminists like Anastasia Posadskaya-Vanderbeck, Olga Voronina, Tatiana Klimenkova and other scholar-activists carry on research, articulate women's issues, and reach out to women's groups in other countries. The Centre bears solid testimony that this time the women's movement won't go away.

References

Bloice, C. 1998. "The New Russian Woman." *People's World,* Moscow, July 3.

Buckley, M. 1983. "Women in the New Russia." In S. Kruks, R. Rapp, and M. Young, (eds.). *Promissory Notes: Women in the Transition to Socialism,* New York: Monthly Review Press.

de Bouvier, S. 1961. *Second Sex.* New York: Bantam/Knopf.

Dupar, M., and J. Shaw. 1995. "Small Grants to Support Large Goals." *Surviving Together,* Summer, Washington, D.C.

Hannson, C., and K. Liden. 1983. *Moscow Women.* Translated from the Swedish. New York: Random House.

Khanga, Y. 1991. "No Matryoshkas Need Apply." *New York Times,* November 28, op-ed page.

Klimenkova, T. 1992. "Reflections on Status of Women in Russia." *Alternatives,* Vol. 2, No. 2.

Lapidus, G.W. 1978. *Women in Soviet Society.* Berkeley: University of California Press.

Lapidus, G.W., ed. 1982. *Women, Work, and Family in the Soviet Union.* Armonk, NY: M.E. Sharp.

Mamonova, T. 1991. Comments at the Symposium, Westchester Consortium for International Studies, Westchester, New York.

Posadskaya-Vanderbeck, A. 1995. "Women in Russia." Lecture delivered at State University of New York at New Paltz, September 29.

Rimashevskaya, N. 1987. *Women of Taganrog.* Moscow: International.

Rimashevskaya, N. 1993. "Health Care Issues in Russia." Paper presented at American Association for Advancement of Slavic Studies, November 1993. Referred to in Susan

J. Linz, "Gender Differences in the Russian Labor Market," *Journal of Economic Issues*, v. 30:161–185, March 1996. Also referred to in article in *Financial Times*, March 1994.

Smolowe, J. 1987. "Russian Women Today." *Time Magazine*, November.

Taubman, W., and J. Taubman. 1989. *Moscow Spring*. New York, Summit Books.

Zaslavskaya, Tatiana. 1988. Personal interview in Moscow, April.

Perestroika and the Internationalization of Russian Higher Education: The Summer of 1990

Donald A. Biggs

with the assistance of Robert J. Colesante

This essay was initially prepared in the early 1990s following a series of visits to Moscow, Leningrad, Kiev, and the Kursk region of Russia. The trips were academic in nature, but involved colleagues in higher education, students, family, and friends. They spanned a ten-year period throughout which I attended conferences, served as a visiting professor, coordinated diplomatic visits of faculty, and traveled to "see the sights." In particular, they provided opportunities to see into the lives of citizens in Russia before and after the dissolution of the Soviet Union. The bulk of the chapter summarizes a study on the views of faculty and students concerning international exchange programs. Interestingly, this became a lens to listen to them talk about changes in the culture toward openness and reconstruction (glasnost and perestroika, respectively), and how these ideas were being interpreted by a variety of ordinary citizens.

As I talked with students and faculty from different parts of the Soviet Union, I heard a growing sense of uncertainty and angst about the future. Students often spoke pessimistically about new opportunities, and the possibilities for self-determination in the provinces from which they traveled. While some faculty saw the system they had "bought into" falling apart, others were trying to find a foothold in the new Russia by capitalizing on entrepreneurial opportunities.

At the time I began to write this, I was very much taken by Jerome Bruner's conceptualization of "Life as Narrative" (see Bruner 1987; 1990). My own perspective was also constructivist in nature, and very much attentive to the role of culture in shaping the lives people lead. Though my academic views and interests have changed somewhat, I haven't felt the need to change much of what I wrote at that time. I saw a people in transition, responding in ways that made sense to them given the culture and history of the place in which they told me their stories. Accordingly, this chapter reflects my interpretations of what was going on at the time. I also hope it reflects the voices of faculty and students who shared their lives with me.

This text reflects a collaboration of Professor Robert J. Colesante and myself. His contributions were important in developing the completed manuscript. He was a companion on my third trip to Russia, and helped in reworking and finalizing the essay.

My story begins in spring 1990 when my family and I were about to encounter our first Moscow spring. We were traveling from Helsinki to Moscow on a train that was a little late leaving and a little late arriving. Our first experience involved a lesson in the importance of punctuality, which was then a virtue of individuals and a test of responsibility in a well choreographed culture. On the trip from Leningrad, we met Russian citizens and tourists. Our conversations with them allowed us to get a sense of how they viewed the possibility of changes which would be linked to "glasnost" and "perestroika." When Gorbachev initiated reforms, the public press contained narratives which applauded democratic changes in the country. At that time, it was very difficult to ascertain whether or not these predictions about positive changes reflected "wishful dreams" or "solid commitments."

Leaving on the train, we heard different voices telling very different stories about the potential benefits and evils of glasnost and perestroika. Although some described the contributions that these changes could make to the political climate, others had reservations about Gorbachev's programs recalling that he had previously enacted statutes that were used for the repression of dissent. He was just starting the processes of establishing legal standards by which his government's actions could be judged. Still, it was very difficult for "ordinary" Soviet citizens to distinguish between legitimate and illegitimate public dissent and criticism of conditions in Moscow and the Soviet Union. In some cases, public criticism was viewed as a positive example of free speech in a democratic society. At other times, similar criticism was viewed as being motivated by "anti-perestroika" forces and was condemned (see Glynn 1989 for an analysis of political conditions in the Soviet Union at the time).

The Soviet system of higher education was expected to play a significant role in the implementation of Gorbachev's programs. They were to help his efforts to develop a competitive market economy that would have necessitated a number of changes in Soviet higher education including the initiation of international dialogue and cooperative endeavors. Several joint ventures had been developed with Western European, North American, and Japanese universities to educate a new class of Soviet managers and administrators, and to develop management courses in Soviet universities. The Soviet Union had recently developed exchange programs in sociology with a collection of North American universities. The goal was to educate Soviet scholars who could provide needed professional expertise in sociology, particularly in polling methods. Even though many foreign visitors in Moscow, Leningrad, and Kiev argued for increased efforts to internationalize Soviet higher education as a means of promoting both perestroika and glasnost, Soviet academics were not of "one mind" on this topic. Indeed some saw internationalization initiatives as being more like "Western threats" than "Western opportunities."

The prospect of developing extensive international exchange programs for Soviet students and faculty presented challenges to Soviet educators. Although these universities had extensive experiences in providing education for students from the former Eastern Bloc countries, they had primarily acted as hosts in these international exchange programs. An important aspect of both perestroika and glasnost would involve the internationalization of Soviet higher education and significant organizational and cultural changes in the various institutions of higher education in the Soviet Union (see Dunstan 1987). International exchange programs were envisaged by some Soviet faculty and administrators as providing an important catalyst for achieving needed changes in Soviet higher education. For international exchange programs to become positive forces in the internationalization of Soviet higher education, they needed to be viewed as culturally relevant and not as foreign intrusions. One educator in Moscow was less than excited about learning "Western ways." She had something that resembled an altar in her class recognizing great Soviet leaders she admired—statues of Lenin and Stalin were prominent. She reflected on the changes with sadness and uncertainty: "We thought that we were following the leaders in government. Now we find that we have been on the wrong track and we were not meeting the goals of these Russian leaders. We were not on the path to utopia, and the changes may not bring us closer either."

For new exchange programs to be effective means of contributing to perestroika, they would need to be a mechanism for improving Soviet higher education, and consequently faculty members would need to play significant roles in the development and implementation of such activities. This essay presents the views of a sample of Soviet faculty members and students from various disciplines in three major universities in the Soviet Union: Moscow State, Leningrad, and Kiev Universities. Faculty members and students were asked to discuss the strategy of developing new international exchange programs for Soviet students, the possible costs to their departments and universities, and potential models for organizing and managing such programs.

Interview Questions

The present study involved interviews and meetings with Soviet faculty members and administrators. In reporting the results of the study, I have attempted to interweave the actual results of interviews with interpretations, so as to present a more coherent and readable commentary. However, these results are not presented in detail because of the limits of space, and the fact that there was substantial overlap in the themes that emerged from the interviews. The choice of the results presented was mostly governed by the goals of the initial study as operationalized in the interview schedule.

The interviewer first briefly described four models for foreign student programs, their goals, and approaches.

The rest of the interview dealt with the following questions:

A. What will be the outcome or impact of foreign exchange programs for students, university, society-as-a-whole, as well as foreign interests and constituencies?
B. What are the major reasons for Soviet students to participate in foreign exchange programs?
C. What kinds of foreign exchange programs and experiences would be most valuable for Soviet students?
D. What problems might students have in adjusting to foreign study experiences?
E. How should Soviet programs be organized, administered, and financed? Who shall be responsible for making decisions?

The questions were modified from those questions used by Teichler and Steube (1990) in their Study Abroad Evaluation Project. The individuals who were interviewed were from the Moscow State University, Leningrad University, and the University of Kiev (Ukraine). They were from the following disciplines or academic fields: (a) Psychology, (b) Biology, (c) Mathematics, (d) Computer Science, (e) Sociology, (f) Philosophy, (g) History, (h) Journalism, (i) Physics, and (j) administrators and staff from international relations offices on the three campuses.

The Culture of the Universities

To understand Soviet views on internationalization of education, an observer must first try to attain some sense of the student culture and their perspectives on the changes in the Soviet Union (see Traver, 1989, for a popular description of the Soviet youth culture; see Avis, 1987, for a review of research on Soviet students). Soviet students, like the Soviet university, cannot be adequately described by generalizations or normative characterizations. Traver (1989) described young people in the Soviet Union as being focused on the pursuit of *kife*, a slang word which means "catching a buzz," or "having it all." *Kife* was the centerpiece of many Soviet jokes and could be a young person's concept of heaven or the definition of a good time. Soviet youth wanted everything their Western counterparts had and they wanted it immediately, and not in some Soviet utopia about which the party preached to them. *Kife* is in some ways directly in conflict with the official Soviet concept of *kollektiv* and its emphasis on conformity. *Kife* is also in conflict with an important goal of the education system which is to teach collectivism, or the value of it, to improve society rather than to improve a person's own well-being.

Avis (1987), utilizing data from two major surveys of Soviet students in 1973–1974 and 1977–1979, concluded that the priorities among first year Soviet students of all disciplines and backgrounds was to enjoy the advantages of student life. The humanistic values of personal development and cultural growth were uppermost in the minds of these students. Those sociological studies reviewed by Avis (1987) tend to support Traver (1989) in her impressionistic observations of the Soviet youth culture and her use of the term *kife* to describe their over-riding personal goals. It should not be surprising that the official and legal duties of students as found in the 1969 decree of the U.S.S.R. Council of Ministers and official Soviet publications differed considerably from the stated educational goals of many Soviet students who might participate in international exchange programs. Indeed, a significant percentage of these students seemed to be very uncertain about the importance of the vocational and academic purposes of Soviet higher education.

The Soviet Union was a pluralistic society that had discouraged cultural and ethnic awareness among citizens. The focus was on promoting a unitary party loyalty and a homogenous national identity. However, even before perestroika, ethnic unrest was a significant problem in the Soviet Union. The ethnic situation in the Soviet Union was very complicated. Nationalities in the various republics had very different goals. During ethnic unrest at the time of the interviews, about 90 percent of the demonstrators had appeared in three

Baltic and the two Christian Caucasian states and in Azerbaijan, which accounted for less than eight percent of the Soviet population (Glynn 1989). Goble (1989) described the political and ethnic unrest in the republics as a kind of negotiation process in which things move back and forth. Writing at the time, he cautioned that "on some days, things look oppressive and on other days, they appear to be opening up. The biggest mistake is to focus on a single facet of this phenomenon and ignore the others" (p. 17). Still, Soviet universities included students from different republics with very different ethnic backgrounds and consequently these "ethnic" issues affected the student culture in the universities. Skepticism and pessimism were a part of the Soviet youth culture. A 1989 Moldavian newspaper poll reported that 89 percent of the young adults who were polled believed that their country would still be poor and undeveloped in twenty years; 93 percent said that economic reforms were needed but they were not prepared to make sacrifices at work (Traver 1989). What follow are brief "clips" of encounters with some Soviet students whose skepticism and pessimism were obvious in their comments about ethnic, political, and economic conditions in the Soviet Union and their own goals and plans at the time.

Pessimism, Doubt, and Uncertainty Among Soviet Students

A Russian student in computer science described views about life in the Soviet Union. He was very concerned that rubles were not convertible in the international market. For him, this fact alone prevented him from ever being free to see what was going on in other parts of the world. Moreover, he was not confident that the government would ever be strong enough to solve the "problem of the Soviet ruble." Consequently, he felt doomed with no chance of achieving freedom to travel and see the world.

In another encounter, a Lithuanian postgraduate student described his thinking about the future for both himself and his republic. As we rode a bus to the Kiev railroad station in Moscow, he and another Lithuanian friend described their pride in the Lithuanian heritage and their anger about conditions in their republic and in Moscow. They felt strongly that Lithuanians needed to reestablish their lost cultural identity that the party had tried to eradicate in its attempts to create a homogenous socialist society.

In a quite different context the week before this encounter, a group of Armenian postgraduate students laughed and smiled as they told me of their fears for worsening political conditions in Armenia and their personal fears that they had nothing to look forward to as far as improvements in their own lives. There was a surprisingly frank discussion of the need for a revolution in Armenia. For them, more changes and faster changes were needed in Soviet society, as they shouted "Bravo for Yeltsin!"

I asked both the Lithuanian and Armenian students, "What kind of changes are needed?" Both thought their educational experiences in a Soviet university were inadequate and did not prepare them to work as physicists in the modern international world (see Traver 1989). They felt that they had been "locked up" and were not sure if the locks were ever going to be removed. They complained that much of their research equipment was inadequate and their laboratory skills were deficient. They particularly abhorred their required courses and examinations in Soviet communism and political ideology. Most of all they felt their education had limited them because their university experiences had been constrained by "ideological censors" and "international barriers" to knowledge. They romanticized, and even idealized, the United States and Western-type universities' free societies and capitalism. In listening to these students, I was not sure whether they wanted to "run away" from the stressful environment in the Soviet Union or "run to" some romantic image of European and North American societies. They were obviously being both "pushed" and "pulled" by their views about the present conditions and their feelings about the future.

A postgraduate student in psychology from Russia met me for coffee and a discussion of her student experiences. Her family was privileged, and she had lived in Europe for a year or more. Her opinions were more balanced than those of the other students. She complained that many psychology requirements at the undergraduate and graduate level were "Marxism-Leninism" ideology courses that did not contribute to her education as a psychologist. (I later interviewed a faculty member in psychology who claimed over 50 percent of the required courses in that department were not psychology courses but political ideology courses.) She said that she was preparing to be a psychotherapist. Since she was not a student in either clinical or medical psychology but general experimental psychology, I asked her how this program differed from that offered by the clinical faculty of the department. Her only answer was that she had to take fewer courses to qualify to become a psychotherapist than she would if she were a student in the clinical program. When asked about her future work as a psychotherapist, she was not quite clear as to what those duties might include, beyond "helping people with problems."

In spite of her criticisms, she painted a "positive" picture of the psychology department as being at the pinnacle of the University's "academic hierarchy" because of its high status faculty and its popularity among students. I asked her why psychology was so popular among students. Her answer was quite pragmatic. Graduates from the psychology department received job placements that often provided "high status" opportunities to practice psychotherapy.

The student culture in a Soviet university in June 1990 was in many ways a microcosm of Soviet culture. The voices of students representing the various geographical regions and ethnic groups raised questions about the future university and how it might respond to internal cultural differences. Yet these same students at night played "Western style" rock music from their windows and dressed according to international standards of the "youth culture." Moreover, many of those I met spontaneously expressed their "fond hopes" of seeing the United States and Western Europe because they felt they had "missed something" in their lives. Many believed that the Soviet economic "way of life" had failed and that their Stalinist history robbed their people of their culture and their human rights. Still, one sensed a growing loyalty to a Russian culture that predated the socialist revolution in the country.

The "Brain Drain" Issue

The concept of "brain drain," or the tendency of some foreign graduates to remain in their host countries, was a controversial aspect of proposed international student exchange programs. For instance, should students be expected to return to the Soviet Union following their international experiences? With regard to solving this potential problem, there seemed to be two different perspectives. Some argued that international exchange programs should have no restrictions regarding migration of talent because the manpower needs of the international community would achieve an optimal balance; while others took the position that exchange programs could, if not controlled, heighten manpower needs in the Soviet Union and negatively impact the social-political climate of regions which were most in need of educated and talented citizens. Many Third World graduates of universities in Western Europe and the United States have continued to live in host countries without plans for returning home. For example, the non-return rates for Indian, Chinese, and Iranian foreign exchange students were high compared to other countries (see Altbach 1990).

It seemed highly unlikely that the Soviet government, or its universities, intended for possible "international exchange" activities to be mechanisms for providing indirect subsidies to either the United States or Western Europe through "brain drain." For instance, the Philippines provided more money to the United States through the migration of well educated Filipinos than the United States provided in their foreign aid programs (Altbach 1990). However,

Soviet advocates of internationalization of their universities seemed to have little awareness about the potential costs to their universities and to their society of a potential "brain drain" as faculty and students chased their American and European dreams.

At the time, there were certain troublesome social and cultural forces in the Soviet Union that seemed to provide the psychological conditions for an almost panic response among students and faculty to potential exchange programs (see Traver 1989). The response to proposed exchange programs reflected the impact of frustrated personal needs, inadequate information, and naive benefits about the Soviet Union, Western Europe, the United States, and Asian university life. Very few Soviet or foreign academics considered the possibility that proposed exchange programs could contribute to a panic migration of young adults which would neither benefit them, their universities, or Soviet society. In May 1990, the International Research and Exchanges Board opened a kiosk in Moscow to provide information about U.S. student exchange programs. The response by Soviet students was so large that they decided to close the kiosk the same day.

The issue of the potential "brain drain" in the Soviet Union deserved careful attention because the migration of well educated Soviet citizens could have important intellectual, social, and political implications for their society and for general world conditions. If international programs were to have a positive impact on Soviet universities, departments, and programs, then their needs had to be taken into consideration when planning future international programs. For the most part, this was not the case. Most scholarship and fellowship programs emphasized the provision of financial resources to individual students with little or no concern for the possible negative consequences for Soviet universities (see Altbach 1990). In the spring and summer of 1990 entrepreneurial United States and European universities were making aggressive efforts to solicit the brightest and most talented Soviet students. These ventures simply involved the provision of financial resources in the form of scholarships and fellowships for Soviet students who wished to study in the United States, Canada, or Germany. Little consideration was given to the possibility that these students were not very well informed regarding international study options, or the potential difficulties that they might encounter in other countries. Clearly, Soviet students were unable to turn to knowledgeable faculty to help keep them in planning their international education programs because Soviet faculty felt that they did not have an institutional mandate to provide such advice, and many of them felt that they also lacked the knowledge and experiences to provide advice about international education.

Entrepreneurship and Suspicion Among Soviet Faculty and Staff

Most of the faculty members had not given much thought to the long-term consequences of student exchange programs for their departments and their universities. This was not entirely surprising, because at the time the Soviet Union appeared to be gripped with pervasive anxieties regarding its economic and social conditions. Their immediate concerns were about the ruble, the transition to the market economy, and the lack of goods in their stores. Other issues, such as possible student exchange programs, seemed to have little immediate relevance to them.

The potential changes in the social and political structure of the U.S.S.R. and in its universities had created considerable uncertainty and confusion in Soviet society, and among the faculty whom I interviewed. They reported that these "confusing" conditions made it very difficult to discuss potential international exchange programs. At the time, Soviet society seemed to be shifting toward more local forms of autonomy and I speculated that there was likely to be "more" not "less" uncertainty and "more" not "less" confusion ahead. The cultural view of the Soviet faculty reflected confusion and uncertainty that they attributed to the perestroika and glasnost programs. They were not sure about the responsibilities of Soviet faculty if the bureaucratic structures of the government and the party lost their powers. They often seemed frustrated by my questions and replied that they were not responsible for international education. They believed that "someone will take care of solving any future problems," even though they were not sure who that "someone" was.

Some faculty thought international student exchange programs were just a matter of letting Soviet students travel to North American and West European universities. In one instance, a somewhat cynical faculty member observed that student exchange programs were a luxury, because "we have much more serious problems in our society." He then observed that "wasting of human resources has been a national tradition in our society," and recounted a number of grizzly instances of Stalinist abuses against the intelligentsia, the schools, and the professional community that had had permanent effects on the "Russian gene pool."

Very few of the faculty had professional experiences in Western European, British, or Japanese universities. Still, most of them thought future student exchanges would primarily involve United States universities. In a few instances, academic departments had initiated contacts with universities in West Germany, Japan, and Canada.

When asked about the potential value of different types of student exchange programs for students in their academic fields, most faculty were obviously puzzled by the question. I described various models of international exchange programs, and many were surprised by the number of options available. They felt ill equipped to discuss the values of different models for their departments. They had not considered the possibility that exchange programs could involve a high degree of curricular integration between the departments of Soviet universities and the departments of foreign universities. Most were unclear about who should develop criteria for selection of students, and who would be responsible for advisement, orientation, or evaluation of student foreign exchange courses. They were also not sure, but they thought the central administration of their universities would deal with the administrative issues regarding student exchange programs.

The faculty were asked to discuss their priorities regarding future Soviet student exchange programs for their departments. Even though most alluded to universities in the Untied States as being highest priority for students in their departments, they were unable to answer more specific questions about these universities and their programs. Most thought Harvard had some good programs. Their replies to similar questions about Western European and British universities that might have relevant academic programs for student exchanges with their departments were even less specific.

On more than one occasion, I was told the following story about the administrator of an office of international education in a Soviet university. When a group of U.S. exchange students arrived on campus, they found no locks on their rooms. If they wished to have locks, they should get them from the U.S. When the locks arrived, he confiscated them and gave them Russian locks. This tale "twice told" by faculty and students may not be completely accurate from the administrator's viewpoint. However, it was in this man's office that I was told by an English speaking colleague of his that the administrator did not plan to "baby me," and if I wanted to interview Soviet faculty members, it was my problem to set up the appointments. I was instructed not to expect assistance from him in arranging interviews with faculty. And, he was not able to meet with me directly, or discuss anything with me about exchange programs. He was very, very busy!!! His secretary ultimately made an appointment with a Soviet faculty member who was told that I was a "pushy American!"

On another campus, the international education office staff member greeted me with the statement, "I can't see you! I have a report to do! If you want to interview faculty, go to the English Department and see if you can find a faculty member who might agree to talk with you!" He knew I was coming for an appointment, but he and his staff had other pressing duties.

In spite of these troublesome encounters with international education office staff on both campuses, they can't be painted with one brush. Indeed, their supervisors were actually very cordial and interested in this study. No one could have expected any more cooperative and positive collegial support. They arranged time in their busy schedules to meet, and valuable interviews were arranged with knowledgeable faculty members.

Subsequently, I made an effort to ask several faculty and students to tell me about the staff of the international education offices. Who are they? What are their responsibilities? "Well," said one faculty member, "they are an interesting lot." The party considered these offices to be very sensitive places regarding ideology. No one was allowed to go abroad who was not considered an excellent party member. "International education offices," said another Soviet faculty member, "have been important to the party because they were a 'source of rewards' that could be used in their efforts to influence faculty and students at the universities."

Another Soviet faculty member pointed out to me that the international education offices have been staffed by individuals who were to function as bureaucrats. They were not to set policies, but to enforce them. As a consequence, it is not surprising that many, if not most, of them spent considerable time on protocol issues: the negotiation of contracts for hard currency, and writing reports. The staff in these offices were mostly concerned about "self-accounting," a concept bantered about by Soviet civil servants and administrators. Simply stated, all government offices receiving Soviet funds are to "break even" or "make a profit" but not incur losses. At the end of a fiscal year the administrator is held responsible for dealing with any financial losses!

A story freely told by a staff member in an international education office reveals something about the management of these offices. On this campus, they had an exchange program with a Christian fellowship group from one of the large Midwestern states in the United States. On the day of my visit, the director of the office was to welcome them. I asked, upon recognizing the name of the group, whether they knew much about the goals of this group (i.e., Christian evangelical). "Oh yes," he said, "I know it is a pretense! They say that they're coming to study the Russian foreign language. But we know differently! We maintain an exchange program in Russia for them and then they are allowed to approach students and others with their 'evangelical' messages. Last summer the same group was here at the university, but their attempts to convert (U.S.S.R.) students were not very successful." With that he explained that he saw no problems with this exchange program, because they pay in hard currency, and the "president of the group is my friend!"

The entrepreneurial spirit was alive and well on this Soviet campus. Both students and faculty perceived opportunities in the expansion of foreign student exchange programs. Student groups were making contacts with student groups in the United States to develop new foreign exchange programs. An official exchange program with a prominent eastern United States university had lapsed, but students in a sports club were now negotiating a new contract with a sports club at that university. Not to be outdone, a Soviet administrator on the same campus had hopes to arrange an "Erasmus" or "Tempus" exchange program with a West German university and a British university as partners. He just needed to figure out how he could accomplish his goal without interference from Moscow.

In general, the Soviet faculty viewed potential student exchanges with the United States and Western European universities as very beneficial for students and for their universities (see Gullahorn & Gullahorn 1966; Schnitzer, Schaeper, Gutmann & Breustedt 1985). Most thought that the cross-cultural contacts would yield positive outcomes for individuals, Soviet universities, and Soviet society as a whole. However, they were unclear, or uncertain, about the specific types of benefits to be yielded by such programs and only one of them referred to any potential losses that might be associated with student exchanges. Many of the faculty had very limited international experiences and did not foresee the possibility that Soviet students might have difficulties coping with cross-cultural experiences, or that these difficulties could provide real obstacles to achieving their goals. In many cases, the Soviet faculty and administrators thought that the personal benefits of cross-cultural contacts outweighed any possible vocational or academic benefits.

Cross-Cultural Issues with Exchange Programs

In spite of faculty optimism, there were significant cross-cultural differences between Soviet and Western universities that could possibly impact both the organization and administration of future Soviet exchange programs and their levels of effectiveness in achieving their goals. The assumption underlying many Soviet faculty members' comments was that cross-cultural contacts between students of the Soviet Union and those in Western Europe and North America would be beneficial because this would result in better understanding between individuals from different countries. Furthermore, these contacts would provide satisfying personal experiences for students and increase their cultural awareness and promote their personal development. Although such cross-cultural contacts may lead to such beneficial effects, there is a great deal of evidence that such contacts could also lead to negative personal consequences such as role ambiguity, cultural shock, anxiety, and even depression (Furnham & Bochner 1986).

One factor that could have contributed to stress and dysfunctional behaviors among Soviet students who went abroad was that they were not prepared to deal with subtle "real" and "subjective" cross-cultural differences between the Soviet Union and Western universities. The Soviet culture differed fundamentally from many Western European and North American cultures in their worldviews about the importance of individualism, personal independence, and personal initiative. If they were going to be competent in their intercultural communication, the participants in Soviet student exchange programs would need to understand these cross-cultural differences in worldviews. They would also need to be sensitive to cultural differences between the Soviet Union and the host countries and try to understand these differences from a contextual rather than judgmental perspective. Otherwise, their interpersonal relationships in universities in Europe and the United States could deteriorate and possibly become dysfunctional for one or both parties (see Bennett 1986 for a discussion of intercultural sensitivity).

A major obstacle to developing effective international exchange was a pervasive tendency on the part of Soviet faculty and students to underestimate the nature of the cultural distance between the contemporary Soviet society and the various host countries in Western Europe and North America. An important factor that contributed to increased cultural distance between the Soviet Union and Western countries was not only the Soviet history of Marxist-Leninist ideology and its characteristic approach to social, political, and economic organizations, but also the cultural disjunction in Soviet social/political worldviews caused by the initiation of Gorbachev's programs of reconstruction. For instance, one impact of perestroika and glasnost was that Soviet faculty and students no longer seemed to regard themselves as a homogeneous communist society. The comments from students suggested that they were becoming increasingly aware of the ethnic/cultural differences in Soviet society. Soviet newspapers reported instances of ethnic/cultural unrest and "independent" political initiatives almost daily, creating a heightened sense of the pluralistic nature of Soviet society. The effects of this increased "sense of Soviet ethnic diversity" on Soviet students was difficult to document, but it appears from contacts with students that it was becoming an increasingly salient aspect of their worldviews, their goals, and their values. Western European and North American universities and institutions of higher education should not be surprised when students insist that their different cultural and ethnic backgrounds be recognized and appreciated in their inter-cultural communications with Western students and faculty. Surprisingly, not one of the Soviet faculty members and administrators who were interviewed as part of this study mentioned anything about the importance of cultural diversity in the Soviet student population. For the most part, Soviet students were alluded to as a homogeneous lot.

The cultural distance between Soviet society and North American and

Western European societies was also influenced by the dynamic change in Soviet culture and their "stereotypical" knowledge about life outside the Soviet Union. Gorbachev's programs of reconstruction had created disjunctions in the traditional Marxist-Leninist socio-cultural patterns that made it very difficult to clearly discriminate how Soviet society differed externally from Western societies. At the time, conditions in Soviet society, compared to the conditions in the past when cultural differences were more clear-cut and obvious, had made it even more troublesome for Soviet students to achieve any clear sense of cultural differences with Western societies.

Still, Soviet society was historically highly centralized and individuals were expected to accept without question institutional/authority decisions about their lives. As a consequence of their cultural experiences, coupled with the Soviet students' "communist upbringing" (*Kommunisticheskoe vospitanie*) which is a distinguishing feature of their education, it should not be unexpected if Western faculty and students view Soviet students as "dependent," "passive," "immature," and lacking in expected levels of personal responsibility and individual assertiveness. For instance, Avis (1987) reported that Leningrad sociologists found that 73 percent of the students in their survey reported that they sometimes or often used cribs in their examinations. Avis (1987) also talked about the fact that Soviet faculty use a term "student parasitism" in their discussions of student dependency and lack of commitment to high levels of academic achievement. Students who participate in exchange programs from Russia and the former Soviet Union may find their expectations regarding personal initiative and independence to be in conflict with those of faculty in their host countries.

I asked about how Soviet students might construe any cultural differences that they encountered in North America, Japan, or Western Europe. How might they interpret them and react to them? Would they deny these cultural differences? Would they find such differences to be threatening? The faculty and students who were interviewed as part of the present study described their perceptions of cultural differences between Soviet and Western societies with rather vague concepts about "free-market" and/or "East/West." Indeed, most thought that Soviet exchange students might encounter some cross-cultural differences but that these differences would not be stressful or troublesome to them. The faculty expressed a fairly parochial view about the cultural differences between Soviet and Western societies. Even though they recognized potential differences between their society and Western societies, they thought these were just due to external differences in "ways of doing things." They did not recognize the possibility that these cultural differences reflected different worldviews (see Bennett 1986).

Soviet faculty and students made assumptions about the stress that they were experiencing in their daily lives and speculated that it was associated with changes in their environment such as life events (i.e., perestroika) and/or the hassles or repeated chronic strains in their daily lives (i.e., long lines). These environmental events were seen as the causes of their stress or tension (see Biggs & Chapman 1989 for a discussion of various models of stress and their potential application to cross-cultural situations). They did not identify any individual causes for stress in either their beliefs or their perceptions about stress and how to cope effectively with it. Moreover, many of them assumed that the causes of their "environmental stress" were so ambiguous and/or unknown that they could do very little to cope effectively with these "stressful" realities in their lives. Consequently, many of the faculty and students coped with their highly stressful environments by trying to control the impact of these stressor situations on themselves. Some of them adopted passive and helpless attitudes about conditions in their environment such as learned helplessness, while others did not allow themselves to become emotional or to express negative feelings about the stressful environmental conditions. Given their interpretation and response to stress, I was not too surprised that so many of them were accepting of alcohol abuse.

The movement toward intellectual/ethical pluralism in their society may have influenced the level of perceived stress in the subjective culture of Soviet faculty and students involved. Soviet society before glasnost could be described using Perry's (1979) concept of intellectual/ethical dualism, as based on the assumption that the authorities knew what was right and wrong, and if citizens worked hard, read every word, and learned the right answers from the Marxist-Leninist authorities, all would be well.

At the time, the Soviet culture seemed to be in transition from this stage of intellectual dualism to intellectual relativism. They were being confronted with uncertainties and with authorities who disagreed and gave the citizens problems to deal with instead of answers. As a consequence, they were experiencing stressful levels of "uncertainty" and "confusion" in their worldviews and many didn't feel capable of making decisions in a "relativistic" Soviet world. As the Soviet programs of reconstruction were creating a pluralistic society, their citizens were reformulating their commonsense with high levels of intellectual uncertainty and tentativeness in their choice of worldviews and actions. The Party and the political bureaucracy had controlled Soviet life and worldviews since 1917. Suddenly as they say, times were changing! So when told about conditions in the country they would ask, "Who says so?" Gorbachev and the Party tell them that their country has erred, that Stalin erred, that the system erred! So they found themselves with conflicted feelings, "this should make Soviet faculty and students feel good! It does and it doesn't!"

Many had accepted communism and the Russian "Cold War" version of the world, and suddenly they were told to stop. They were left without "obvious meanings" and rules for understanding and judging their behaviors and those of others. Tolstoy, in the *Death of Ivan Ilyich* (1987) described a painful existential crisis that followed when he found that his bureaucratic structures for meaning were lost:

> Ivan asks, "What does it all mean? Why has it happened? It is inconceivable that life was so senseless and disgusting. And if it really was so disgusting and senseless, why should I have to die and die in agony? Something must be wrong. Perhaps I did not live as I should have," it suddenly occurred to him. "But how could that be when I did everything one is supposed to do?" he replied and immediately dismissed the one solution to the whole enigma of life and death, considering it utterly impossible.

The situation for Soviet citizens at the time resembled the death of certain ways of thinking and living that had given their lives meaning. This situation was very stressful for them because their former personal cosmologies no longer provided a sense of meaning and direction for their lives. Many of the faculty were members of the party who accepted its principles and rules, and worked dutifully for its goals. Now the party and the government seemed to be saying that the Marxist-Leninist worldview was wrong and mistaken, but they offered no other clear alternative worldview for Soviets to adopt in their daily lives. Consequently, these anxious feelings were a major source of stress that related to a loss of cultural identity, which had defined both who they were and their view of the world. Even if it was a negative identity for some of them, it still provided a way of "making sense" out of their experiences.

The Soviet culture presented an unknown factor that could either facilitate or impede the planning of effective student exchange programs. Clearly, Western faculty who sought to develop exchange programs needed to increase their own awareness of subtle but important cultural differences that could impact their cross-cultural communications with Soviet students and faculty. With increasing intercultural sensitivity that recognizes contextual relativism, Western faculty could recognize more clearly how the Soviet "worldview" and culture would influence their own interpersonal relations with Soviet students and faculty. For instance, the concept of personal planning in the Soviet culture was much more troublesome and difficult for many faculty and students than Westerners might imagine it to be.

But what of the culture of Soviet higher education and the institutional willingness to develop new or revised structures for the administration of student exchange programs? Here again, there is a need to be cautious in making generalizations. In spite of the liberalism in the air at the time, the faculty and students told me that university structures and organizations reflected two voices. The first voice was about change and the need for both increased student and faculty freedom; while the other voice was about compulsion, control, and the need to form students according to certain pre-ordained patterns that in the past were found in the works of both Marx and Lenin. This concept of education as formation according to set patterns has a long history in Russia. The Russian word for "culture" is *obrazovanie,* meaning formation, and is derived from the word meaning image or form. Tolstoy, in the 1860s, railed against this dominant concept of education as formation according to certain pre-ordained principles and said that most education at that time involved "no more than compulsory forcible actions of one person upon another for the purpose of forming a man such as will appear to us to be good, or more likely to create others just like ourselves" (Weiner 1967).

Tolstoy's pedagogical essays (Weiner 1967) are critiques of education in Russia, Europe, and the United States. They also provide insight regarding the problems he encountered in trying to make changes in how people at this time thought about education and schooling. He described those people who resisted any changes in their educational thinking and approaches as the kind of individuals who did not reflect but merely submitted to the ideas of their age and imagined it was possible to serve two masters at once. Tolstoy warned that such people in a society who appeared to reflect personal freedom were in truth the most serious enemies of personal freedom and "social change" because they had no real commitments: "They say what they say because they are afraid not to bow before the idol of their age! They praise the governor to his face only as long as he has power in his hands!"

During my visits, the Soviet university, like elsewhere in Soviet society, included persons who supported Gorbachev's programs out of fear. Since international student exchange programs were so strongly associated with his programs of perestroika and glasnost, some were afraid not to support these activities even if they didn't understand them. But many of these same faculty also maintained allegiances with "anti-perestroika" forces, and as a consequence their actions or behaviors regarding proposed exchange programs reflected their ambivalence and their passive/aggressive attitudes. Those faculty and administrators in Soviet universities who were trying to serve both "perestroika" and "anti-perestroika" forces contributed to a climate in these universities in which "deception" and "impression management" were acceptable behaviors. In such a culture, Western faculty and students may find it very difficult to engage in mutual planning activities. Given these cultural conditions, it was also difficult to be very optimistic about the ability of Soviet universities to restructure their present approaches to international education.

In the past, the culture of the Soviet university was defined by communist ideology and party structures. The university was to serve the needs of society as defined by the party. With perestroika, the cultural influences on the Soviet university were unclear. If the party abdicates, then who and what shall fill the cultural vacuum? Will those who received benefits from the "old ways" of managing universities willingly hand over power to yet undefined forces in society and in the university? How will Soviet universities develop approaches to international education that have some bases outside of arbitrary dicta determined by the party and the government?

In this context, Tolstoy's observations about Russian university faculty were timely, and may still be today: "All men are human, even professors. Not one laborer will say that we must destroy the factory where he earns a piece of bread and he will say so not from conviction but unconsciously. Those gentlemen who are concerned about a greater freedom of the universities resemble a man who, having brought up some young nightingales and concluded they need freedom lets them out of the cage and gives them freedom but at the end of cords attached to their feet and then wonders why the nightingales are not doing any better on the cords, but only break their legs and die" (Weiner 1967, p. 130).

До свидания—*Do Svidaniya*

Let me close with a story of my last trip to Kursk, Russia, in April 1996. We arrived at the Moscow Airport on April 5, again from Helsinki. I was traveling with two colleagues from the United States. My two colleagues and I were tired and excited as we proceeded through customs. My first colleague successfully answered the questions and was cleared. I was standing in front of a customs officer who looked at my visa very suspiciously and then called her boss to the table. She informed us that the visa was dated April 6 and it was now 4:30 p.m. on April 5. Finally, we were told to pay an additional $200 for each person or go back to Helsinki. What a plight! We asked to see the Boss. The Boss said, "Pay up" or "Go back to Helsinki!" I became irate and said, "You just don't understand. The visa consultants and the Russian embassy issued this visa." The representative explained to me, "In Moscow things go wrong, and no one knows who's responsible—so you have to pay. That's just the way it is! You just don't understand."

In reflecting on this experience, I was reminded of the wisdom in George Kelly's "Social Corollary" in which he argues that you can only develop satisfactory relationships with others when you understand the constructs that they use to explain and define realities. In other words, if you want to communicate with foreigners, you don't have to agree with them, but you must understand how they make sense of their worlds!

References

Altbach, P.G. (1990). Impact and adjustment: Foreign students in comparative perspective. OECD Seminar on Higher Education and the Flow of Foreign Students, April 26–28. Hannover, Germany: Hochschul Information System.

Avis, G. (1987). Soviet students: Life styles and attitudes. In J. Dunstan (Ed.), Soviet education under scrutiny (pp. 88–120). Glasgow: Jordanhill College.

Bennett, M.J. (1986). A developmental approach to training for intercultural sensitivity. The International Journal of Intercultural Relations, 10 (2), 179–196.

Biggs, D., and D. Chapman (1989, July). Toward a cognitive model for cross-cultural stress. Paper presented at the Institute Piaget, Lisbon, Portugal, Congress on Piaget and the New Challenges in Sciences and Education.

Bruner, J. (1987). Life as narrative. Social Research, 54, 11–32.

Bruner, J. (1990). Culture and human development: A new look. Human Development, 33, 344–355.

Dunstan, J. (1987). Soviet education under scrutiny. Glasgow: Jordanhill College.

Furnham, A., and S. Bochner (1986). Culture shock: Psychological reactions to unfamiliar environments. London: Metheun.

Goble, P. (1989). Restive republics. In P. Glynn (Ed.), Unrest in the Soviet Union (pp. 11–18). Washington, D.C.: American Enterprise Institute for Public Policy Research.

Gullahorn, J.E., and J.T. Gullahorn (1966). American students abroad: Professional versus personal development, The Annals of the American Academy of Political and Social Science, 368, 43–59.

Glynn, P. (1989). Unrest in the Soviet Union. Washington, D.C.: American Enterprise Institute for Public Policy Research.

Perry, W.C. (1979). Forms of intellectual and ethical development in the college years: A scheme. New York: Holt, Rinehart and Winston.

Schnitzer, K., H. Schaeper, J. Gutmann, and C. Breustedt (1985). Problems of foreign students in the Federal Republic of Germany. Hannover: Hochschul Information System.

Teichler, U., and W. Steube (1990). The Ionic of study programmes and their impacts. OECD Seminar on Higher Education and the Flow of Foreign Students, April 26–28, 1990. Hannover: Hochschul Information System.

Tolstoy, L. (1987). The death of Ivan Ilych. Toronto: Banta Books.

Traver, N. (1989). Kife: The lives and dreams of Soviet youth. New York: St. Martin's.

Weiner, L. (1967). Tolstoy on education (Phoenix Book). Chicago: University of Chicago Press.

Perestroika in Philosophy: Report from Moscow State University

DOROTHY S. MCCLELLAN *and*
JAMES E. MCCLELLAN, JR.

Gorbachev's policies of glasnost and perestroika dramatically affected many aspects of Soviet society and life. In this essay, Dorothy S. McClellan and James E. McClellan, Jr., share their 1990 interview with the dean of the Faculty of Philosophy at Moscow State University on the changes implemented in the teaching of philosophy at the largest faculty of philosophy in the world with 130 full-time philosophers. Dean Alexander Panin eloquently and candidly discusses his concrete efforts to democratize the curriculum and administration of the Faculty of Philosophy. He lays out his belief that the mission of the Faculty is to educate students to enable them to choose a worldview that helps them to lead ethical lives, "to live rightly in accordance with truth." Moscow State University is where many of the contributors to this collection of essays lectured and carried out research as part of the State University of New York—Moscow State University Scholar Exchange Program, established in 1976. This longstanding program of faculty exchanges nurtured trusting relationships between U.S. and Russian scholars.

Except as it appears in a speech by Mikhail Gorbachev, the word "perestroika" is heard no longer in Moscow. But restructuring still goes on, with consequences nowhere more pronounced, perhaps in the long run nowhere more lasting, than in the Philosophical Faculty (hereinafter "Faculty") at Moscow State University (MSU). The Faculty is the largest aggregation of philosophers in the world; even now, having shorn itself of sociology and "scientific communism," it still numbers over 130 full-time teachers. That size reflects the special place philosophy formerly held in the political life of the U.S.S.R.: the Communist Party of the Soviet Union (CPSU) was, until 1989, constitutionally assigned the "leading role" in Soviet political life. That departure from majoritarian democracy was justified by the special relation of the CPSU to Marxist-Leninist philosophy. The Party was the exclusive heir and guardian of that philosophy, both roadmap and goal for the Bolshevik Revolution of 1917. The political theory of Marxism-Leninism, in turn, upheld the need for a vanguard party, the CPSU, to retain power until all danger of successful counter-revolution had been eliminated. That degree of connectedness between philosophy and political power is a unique phenomenon in the history of Western civilization, at least since the downfall of Pythagorean city-states early in the 5th century BC.

This brief report treats of the adjustments presently underway in the Faculty at MGU, changes made both possible and necessary by the recent disruption of that close connection between orthodox Marxist-Leninist philosophy and political power. We begin with a Brezhnevian baseline, then present excerpts from an interview with the Dean of Philosophy, who describes changes now being made in the content, methods, and goal of philosophy teaching at MSU.

Philosophy During "Stagnation"

"Stagnation" is now the standard label for the period in Soviet history between the dismissal of Khrushchev in 1964 and the death of Brezhnev in 1985. Applied to philosophy, the label aptly characterizes the surface, under which there was ferment enough to satisfy the most ardent dissenter: "dialectical stagnation" would be more accurate for the whole.

Before Gorbachev, the total enterprise of philosophy in the U.S.S.R. was divided, like Gaul, tripartedly. School philosophy was taught to every student every semester at every institution of higher learning in the country, including, of course, institutions for the preparation of teachers in primary and secondary schools. Academic philosophy was practiced in institutes of philosophy (Moscow, Leningrad) sponsored by the all-Union Academy of Science, and in other institutes sponsored by national academies (Kiev, Tbilisi, Tallinn, Minsk and elsewhere). University philosophy stood somewhere between those two; it was found exclusively in the major universities giving advanced degrees in philosophy, mostly to prospective teachers of school philosophy.

The rationale underlying this system is clear enough. Suppose that in the U.S.A. we decided to establish a national curriculum in, say, physics (not a bad idea in itself), required to be taught to every freshman and sophomore in every community college and university in the U.S.A. The theories and findings to be communicated in such a course would originate in a relatively small number of establishments devoted to physical research. The large number of physics teachers required for such a program would be prepared with Ph.D. degrees granted by our major universities. There would be many and obvious problems of articulation in the resulting tripartite system, but we can easily imagine ways of dealing with those problems which would make the system workable if not perfect.

In the U.S.S.R. things were not that simple. Most importantly, textbooks in the required courses in Marxism-Leninism (dialectical materialism, historical materialism, political economy, history of the CPSU, and scientific communism) were modified periodically to meet Party policy, not necessarily reflecting research in academic institutes of philosophy. There is a story to be told, but not here, of changes in that curriculum mandated over the years since its beginnings in the early days of the revolution, of its Stalinization and de-Stalinization, of the ritualization of "dialectic," the emergence of "developed socialism" as a distinct stage of history, etc. Overall, changes in course content effected specifically to conform to current Party directives were minor and peripheral. The major thrust of the courses remained constant; updates in textbooks in general reflected sound historical and scientific scholarship. Emotional responses by students and faculty, however, were determined not by the overall content, but by the politically significant details of these courses. The result, as described by an especially astute observer, was that "teachers were forced to teach doctrines they knew to be false to students who knew they were lying."

Furthermore, institutional needs and the laws of chance rather than individual desire and effort decided teacher placement, and the Soviet system made little or not provision for internal mobility. In one case we knew, the recipient of the degree of Candidate in Philosophical Science from MSU, reflecting a level of training and an individual research effort only a shade, if anything, less than our better Ph.D.'s, found herself being shipped out to teach school philosophy at an advanced technical institute in Moldavia. This fine scholar, whose dissertation was a probabilistic model designed to satisfy Quine's objections to modal logic, could foresee no chance of advancement to university or research institute. One can imagine the enthusiasm with which she approached a life of teaching prescribed courses in dialectical and historical materialism to students of forest technology.

At the other end of the spectrum stand the institutes of philosophy within the Academy of Science. Various factors explain how it happened that the eighteenth century "Academy" retained and renewed as the dominant research establishment in the Soviet Union, having been replaced in that role by the graduate schools of the major universities in Western societies. At its inception, 1724, the Imperial Academy was a much broader institution than its French or Prussian counterparts. "It had to be. At one stroke Peter created an academy and a whole educational and support infrastructure to accompany it ... a gymnasium and university were part of its organization" (McClellan 1985, p. 74).

Furthermore, the tradition of scientific independence achieved by the university in the nineteenth century ("Lehrfreiheit") had not endeared that institution to the Tsarist government. Nor did the bourgeois class identification of both professor and student of the university add to its favor in the eyes of the early Bolsheviks. Lunacharsky, Krupskaya, and other authorities charged with the development of Soviet education and culture saw their task as twofold: to produce and disseminate immediately useful technical knowledge for agriculture and industry, and to promote a revolutionary culture incorporating ("dialectically") the highest levels of development in bourgeois culture. The Russian Academy of Science made its peace quite early with the Revolutionary government; many outstanding scholars within that institution undertook to lend their talents to the immense task of building a new world on the ashes of the old (Kim et al. 1982, pp. 56–94, 286–300).

Members of the Academy constitute a self-perpetuating elite, elected for life on the basis of scholarly accomplishment. (Brezhnev asked the Academy to expel Andrei Sakharov as a traitor. When that question arose in a plenary session of the Academy, one member took the floor to inquire whether there was any precedent for such a move. The presiding officer assured them that there was: the German Academy of Science had honored the request of Adolf Hitler to expel Albert Einstein. The Soviet Academy then defeated the motion to expel Sakharov.) Academicians are relieved of the duties of instruction, though many do teach at the university, as we shall see. They are free to pursue research without constraint of disciplinary boundaries. The Academy is supported by direct grants from the State budget, responsible to civil authorities for fiscal propriety only.

Internally, of course, competition for support of particular scientific projects in the Academy is fierce. Until quite recently, philosophy has fared rather well in this struggle. In the last election, however, three candidates from philosophy, all with outstanding credentials, were rejected by the Academy, an ominous sign. For academic philosophy in the U.S.S.R. has been, on the whole, a stunningly successful episode in the long and tortuous history of our discipline. Over the course of many decades, often in the face of intense political pressure to follow a prescribed line, research in philosophy has maintained an organic connection with developments in natural science, has investigated in a critical, often confrontational, fashion the social and political implications of those developments, has provided its initiates opportunities to exercise creative imagination in constructing worldviews consonant with the latest advances in our understanding of nature and the place of our species in it (Wetter 1957, *passim*).

Having said which, it must be added that for the vast majority of the Soviet intelligentsia (technically speaking, those employed in positions requiring the five-year diploma or higher degree) the expression "Marxist-Leninist philosophy" denotes not the work of the Academy of Science but rather the school philosophy they studied so unwillingly; it connotes boring truths blended with blatant falsehoods in a bath of incomprehensible jargon. Only the professional philosopher or the advanced scientist would appreciate the truth in Loren Graham's appraisal:

> Contemporary Soviet dialectical materialism is an impressive intellectual achievement.... In terms of universality and degree of development, the dialectical materialist explanation of nature has no competitors among modern systems of thought. Indeed, one would have to jump centuries, to the Aristotelian scheme of a natural order or to Cartesian mechanical philosophy, to find a system based on nature that could rival dialectical materialism in the refinement of its development and the wholeness of its fabric [Graham 1987, p. 429].

Such was the achievement of Soviet academic philosophy.

Standing between those two extremes was university philosophy, specifically the work of the Faculty at MSU. Of the five courses in Marxism-Leninism prescribed for university instruction, three remained in the province of the Faculty when our story begins, history of the CPSU and political economy having long since moved, respectively, to the Faculty of History and the Faculty of Economics. Long before the coming of glasnost and perestroika to MSU, the Faculty had ceased teaching dialectical materialism, historical materialism, and scientific communism to students in the natural sciences. (A very interesting story for another occasion: the growth and present prospects of the independent Chair of Philosophy for the Natural Sciences at MSU!) Successive episodes of mitosis had seen the chairs (read "departments") of scientific communism and sociology become divisions quite separated from the rest of the Faculty. In short, the Faculty had distanced itself as much as possible from teaching school philosophy, but the major duty devolving upon the chairs of dialectical materialism and historical materialism was still teaching those required courses for students in the "humanistic" faculties, including law, history, philology (a broad category), journalism, economics, and psychology.

A large portion of the work of the Faculty is carried on in specialized chairs. Those in the division of "philosophy," as distinguished from "scientific communism," included (1984) history of foreign philosophy, history of Russian philosophy, history and theory of scientific atheism (actually an excellent department of comparative religion), ethics, aesthetics, methods of concrete social inquiry (later to become an independent Faculty of Sociology), and logic.

In philosophy as in all other disciplines taught at MSU, a regular program of undergraduate education requires five years of full-time study. Prior to perestroika, students receiving university diplomas through any chair in the Faculty were guaranteed either employment or admission to graduate study as an *aspirant* (accent on the last syllable). They might do Party work in an industrial establishment; they might join the staff of a youth organization, a government ministry, a publishing house; they might teach philosophy at two-year technical institutes or even receive employment at a prestigious institute of science or philosophy as librarian or research assistant. Those performing best in undergraduate studies could proceed directly to their *aspirantura* and hope, with achieving the degree of *Kandidat,* to gain employment at a major university or research institute. Those so favored, but not those sent to Moldavia, would have the lighter duties and library resources which make possible pursuit of the doctorate of science degree and eventual rise to the rank of full professor.

Then Came Perestroika

Anatoli Danilovich Kosichev headed the chair of the history of M-L philosophy when appointed Dean of Philosophy, 1977. His appointment was effected by the rectorate of the university after the faculty had split over three major candidates. Kosichev was the highest-ranking member of the Party in the Faculty, reasonably respected and trusted as a person despite his lack of academic credentials. In 1983 he appointed Alexander Panin from the chair of dialectical materialism as associate dean. When Kosichev was asked to resign the deanship in 1987, the Faculty held an election, as fair, honest, and democratic as any ever conducted, to choose his successor. Twenty-six names were placed in nomination; in the third run-off, Panin received an overwhelming majority. He does not hold the doctor of science degree nor the rank of professor; with his present duties he has no chance of gaining either. But he is a philosopher's philosopher, as thoroughly grounded in the history of science as in the history of philosophy, widely and deeply read in the dramatic turns of contemporary Anglophone philosophy of science. It was for his character as a person and the integrity of his scholarship that his colleagues chose Panin to be their leader during the critical transition they must now seek to accomplish.

We made Panin's acquaintance in 1982. From the first of February to the last of June of that year we were guests of MSU, participants in the unique exchange program between that university and the State University of New York system. A central focus of our research on that visit was the teaching of philosophy at MSU. We interviewed either the chief or deputy chief of every chair in the Faculty, asking about the goals, content, and methods of instruction in that chair, significant instances of both success and failure to achieve goals. We also sat in on classes, interviewed students and junior faculty. (The results of our research were sufficiently disturbing that we chose, correctly we now believe, not to publish them at that time.) Panin spoke for the chair of dialectical materialism; we were immediately impressed by both his scholarship and his candor.

We became close friends during the following year when Panin spent six months on our campus at Albany, New York. On our subsequent visits to Moscow, '84–85, '90, '91, both before and after Panin's election as dean, we have had occasion to discuss at length the changing character and complexion of philosophy teaching at MGU. Several of these conversations were recorded as either stenographic notes or audiotapes. We present here some selections from the more recent of those conversations.

D&J: Could you tell us about the basic changes you expect to bring about as dean?

P: I spoke publicly about all of this in my campaign to become dean, so I can speak freely to you. We face two kinds of crisis in social science in general, philosophy in particular. On our side, we have a crisis of ideas and a crisis of specialists. On the public side, we have a crisis of confidence. We have no good new ideas to solve our immediate problems of living. We have no good specialists who can formulate and test new ideas. The people have no confidence in what we say; they don't believe us. We have no plan that people will follow to solve the problems that face us. How to solve these crises? From our point of view, the key is good specialists. People can recognize and will trust good specialists; good specialists will give good ideas. With good specialists we can solve the problems of ideas and confidence.

What were the main shortcomings of our philosophy in the past? First of all, pseudo-ideologization and politicization of philosophy. When ideological and political ideas were pressed on us from above, from Suslov and so on, we had no choice but to validate them [Mikhail Andreivich Suslov, chief of ideological section in Politburo until his death in 1982]. We ceased being philosophers; we became mere apologists for the official ideology. Now we must change all of that. In the current situation, there is no external ideology, no external politics. There is just philosophy; our job is to produce more and better philosophy.

Notice that I don't say that there is no connection between philosophy and politics. I agree with Kant that philosophy is the servant of politics.

But there are two kinds of servants. One follows behind the master and holds the edge of his mantle. The other goes ahead with a lighted lantern to lead the way. Our philosophy has usually followed behind, holding the mantle. When we did take the lead, we had no light in our lantern.

A second main shortcoming in our philosophy was provincialization. We had cut off the study of Marxist philosophy from developments in world philosophy. Further, we even cut off Soviet philosophy from world Marxist philosophy. This is a terrible thing. And its result has been a stagnation in our philosophy. You can teach philosophy in the Soviet Union, but when you go abroad you cannot teach, because you don't know the problems, you don't know what others are discussing. We had a dual complex, superiority and inferiority. Inside the country we felt superior, we knew all the answers by heart. But when we go to lectures in an international congress we feel inferior, for we don't understand the main arguments.

D & J: But surely some Soviet philosophers transcend that provincialism. You, for example, have conversed on equal terms with Quine, with Popper...

P: It's not the same. My field is philosophy of science, and science speaks a universal language. But on main, eternal problems of philosophy, and problems of social and political and ethical philosophy, our specialists are not capable of giving lectures when they visit in other countries. Now we must develop our ideas and our specialists, our ideology and politics, on sound international, academic standards.

D & J: What progress has been made toward effecting needed changes in the Faculty?

P: About progress? First, we have changed the names of many chairs. Changes in names of chairs are connected with changes in the programs of study. And certainly it's not an easy process, especially to change the program. All agree with changes of name, but changing program causes resistance. For example, the chair of dialectical materialism. We divided it into two chairs. The first will be called chair of theory of philosophy or chair of fundamental problems of philosophy. We haven't decided on that name. It will study classical problems of philosophy—being, knowledge, dialectic, determinism, and so on. The second we decided to call chair of philosophy and methodology of science, a special chair.

Then the chair of historical materialism: we renamed it the chair of social philosophy. That was easy. For six months now they have been working on a special program in social philosophy, not just historical materialism under a new name. We presented the new plan for discussion about two weeks ago at the All-Union Scientific Conference which you attended. And as you saw, most people accepted it completely. [It was our impression that none of the speakers and questioners accepted it completely; everyone had objections and suggestions for improvement. But the proposed program provides that many different points of view shall be presented to students, and no one seemed to reject it completely. We did not push Sasha on this point.]

Or take the case of Western philosophy. Before the program was called Marxist-Leninist critique of Western philosophy. Now it's just modern Western philosophy. And we accepted a new program, more positive, more representative. We try to teach students all the main philosophical trends in Western philosophy. We accepted this program almost unanimously, because it's done very professionally, by Melville and others. [Speaking of Yuri K. Melville a venerable, internationally known scholar specializing in contemporary continental thought, plus his junior colleagues, especially A. G. Gryaznov, specialist in contemporary British philosophy.]

Or the chair called history and theory of atheism; we renamed it chair of religious studies. There is a special new program which gives weight to freethinking as well as to other kinds of belief.

D & J: We know that you had a special interest in philosophy of culture. What has happened there?

P: It's a special question because for the past six months we have been organizing this. In the summer [1990] we officially established the chair of the history and theory of culture. As the leading lecturer in this chair we invited the best scientist in the Soviet Union. We did not try to fill this chair with our own people; we invite people from the institutes of the Academy of Science, like Averentsov, who is a specialist in Byzantine culture, Christian culture, and so on. [Sergei Sergeivich Averentsov, corresponding member of Academy of Science, very popular lecturer, considered a "sage."] And Vyechislav Ivanov, a very famous man who received the Lenin Prize for his book on Aryan languages and the Aryan movement into Europe. He is a specialist in ancient cultures, Babylonian, Egyptian, etc.

D & J: So that's now part of the philosophical faculty?

P: I'll put it this way. Hegel says that philosophy is the essence of culture. And Marx says that philosophy is spirit or soul of culture. That's why we try to effect some injection of culturology into the education of philosophers. And students listen very attentively to those lectures, without any problems. [It is not easy to capture and hold the attention of Soviet students in lectures. They are, it might surprise some to know, much less tolerant of boredom than American students.] Audiences for these lectures are always crowded. Some professors from departments of history and philology attend these lectures, for they are given by a famous academician, a corresponding member of the Academy of Science. We are using this chair of history and theory of culture to set a standard for the faculty of philosophy in general.

D & J: What has happened to the division of scientific communism?

P: You see, the specialty of scientific communism is closed. The division is closed, not for repair, just closed completely, finished. And in its place we established the division of politology, which consists of four chairs: chair of politology, which you would translate as theory and philosophy of politics; second is the chair of regional politology, actually world and regional, what I call applied politology. In the Western world, this is the most popular form of political science, comparative politics, political life and organization in the U.S.S.R., the U.S.A., and so on. The third chair is the history of political thought. The fourth chair is what remains of scientific communism. We call it the chair of theory and practice of socialism. Really, they study the political process in the Soviet Union and other socialist countries. Maybe. If any still remain socialist.

D & J: Have you hired new people for this division, or are the same people now teaching the new disciplines?

P: Some of the same people stay on, mainly in the chair of theory and practice of socialism. All the other chairs are with different people. For example, in the chair of theory and philosophy of politics, I could not collect the right people for permanent employment. So I just invite people from different research institutes to give lectures to our students. Because, I tell you very frankly, a qualified specialist in politology in the Soviet Union, there is no such person. Many people will say, "Yes, I am a politologist," but don't believe them, including Burlatsky and all the rest. [Fyodor Mikhailovich Burlatsky, editorial chief of *Literaturnaya Gazeta,* very popular political commentator.] Whatever they may say, they are not politologists.

We need time to prepare qualified specialists in this science. The principal qualification I seek for this chair is knowledge of foreign languages and then a sound basic education, in history or law. In theory of politics, I want to invite only a specialist in law to be its head. In regional politology, we found the right man and I invited him, a specialist in history. For history of political thought, I want to invite some people from history of philosophy who specialize in political thought, political philosophy. We are looking for those people right now.

[We inquired elsewhere about the large number of teachers formerly employed in the four chairs of that division. Many, we were told, found jobs with Party organizations in various regions of Moscow.]

D & J: So what is happening to Marxist-Leninist philosophy?

P: This is a very complicated question. Before perestroika, we had a chair of history of M-L philosophy, located in the division of scientific communism. We have changed the name to history of Marxist philosophy, and we study all varieties of Marxism—German, British, Chinese, your kind, analytic, and so on. Before, if you were not with Lenin, you were not with Marx. We either ignored or just criticized everyone who was not Leninist. Now Leninism is only one kind of Marxism, and that is good.

But there are other problems. I asked the chair of history of Russian philosophy to prepare a new program to be called history of Russian philosophy from the beginning of the 19th century. Very well. They worked for six months on the program and presented it to me. I opened it, I looked it over. It's completely Russian religious philosophy: Berdyayev, Bulgakov, Loskin, and so on. And I was terrorized with this program. I asked, "What about Lenin and Marxist philosophy?" And Kuvakin [V. A. Kuvakin, chief of that chair] answered, "It's a funny thing. They gave all of Marxist philosophy to another chair." The same thing happened in the history of Western philosophy. They give lectures in classical German philosophers, then they take up positivism. No Marxism.

D & J: We saw those programs. But isn't there a danger that Marxism will be lost altogether if it appears that you can study Russian thought, or Western thought, or modern Eastern thought, for that matter, without...?

P: This is a problem, and I will try to change this situation. We must study and develop Marxism only in the context of world philosophy, not in another way. That is the proper way to do modern Marxism. I want to repeat to you some principles underlying our organization of new chairs and new programs. Before restructuring, we tried to teach all philosophy according to some standard of Marxist philosophy, but now we try to use the problem approach. There is world philosophy, certainly, some eternal philosophical problems, problem of being, of knowledge, etc. And there are different answers to those problems. Take the new program in social philosophy. Before restructuring, we set out to teach this program so as to come to the conclusions of Marxist historical materialism. Now we organize it to bring out the eternal problems in social philosophy, for example, the problem of a sense or direction of history. It's an eternal problem. And we want the students to know how different thinkers have worked on this problem—some religious philosophy, also Hegel, Marx, Weber, Toynbee.... This is now the basis for organizing the program.

There is another part of the answer to your question. In the past, before restructuring, we tried to make people become Marxists, to take the worldview of Marxism. Now our task is different. We must educate young people, help them to make their own decisions about choice of worldview. I mean, literally, choice of worldview, an educated, not a blind choice. This is our main task now. As in politology, the individual is not obliged, or forced, or pressured to take any particular political stand. We must educate students so that they will be in a position to make educated decisions for themselves, knowing the various positions they must compare for choosing. Not by blind belief. This is the main task for our education now. It is a universal principle, and we must seek to restore that principle in the work of our faculty.

D & J: That is the noble and correct view. Do you encounter resistance in trying to put it into effect?

P: I have no external resistance for my Faculty. The higher education authorities support, help us, no problems as a rule. We do have some resistance within the Faculty, certainly from the people with a different ideology, the conservative people, who try to keep alive the ideological style of education. But it's not the majority. It's a minority, as a rule, some elderly people. I don't agree with them, but I respect them because all their lives they have lived in the old system. It's quite understandable. They say we must prepare Marxist-Leninist philosophers. I say, our business is to prepare philosophers, good philosophers, universal academicians who can hold their own anywhere in the world. It's their own business what they want to be.

D & J: Do you believe that the fundamental truths of Marxism-Leninism will emerge from the good teaching of philosophy as such? It would appear that you have more confidence in that philosophy than do the ideologists. A true Marxist believes that in a free market of ideas, if people study philosophy of nature, philosophy of history, political philosophy, principles of social authority, and so on, they will find that the Marxist hypotheses are the most rationally supported....

P: Just prove by rational argument that Marx was a good philosopher, that will solve your problem. If you can't manage to do it, keep silent. Before we considered Marx as a prophet, but not as a scientist. That is why we now have such a negative reaction. That is why some Western scientists, like yourselves, come here and listen to our people and don't understand the depth and bitterness of their criticisms. Our critics show in their analysis that they are strongly influenced by Marx, but they criticize him very strongly as well. Of course, they are treating Marx as a prophet, not a scientist, and that is the problem.

D & J: What has been the role of the Party in all these changes?

P: The supreme legislative authority in the Faculty is the scientific council, which you have visited. What the scientific council agrees should be done is what I try to do. Now the Party has no right to intervene in the work of the council.

D & J: Before perestroika, they could intervene...?

P: The Party committee of the Faculty could decide the right way to solve a certain problem, and the Party secretary would communicate their decision to the Dean, and he was obliged to accept it and carry it out. Now they have no right to intrude on the work of the Dean and the scientific council.

D & J: How was all that changed? Did it come down as an order from above?

P: You see, it depends on relations between people. Before election, I said that I would listen only to scientific council. Whatever the problem is, we can vote on it in the scientific council and I will carry it out. For example, changes in names and programs of chairs, and so on, as we discussed.

Without any problems.

D & J: The Party as a whole then...

P: Officially, they could not intervene in any decisions of Panin. But you must take into consideration other things. Our structure is now very democratized. Student representatives account for twenty-five percent of the members of the council, and certainly not all those students are members of the Party. [From our experience as visitors to sessions of the council (which are open to any faculty member or *aspirant* who wishes to observe) it appears that student members are strongly encouraged to participate actively in the deliberations of the council, even when their voices are heard in opposition to the views of the Dean.] Several faculty members who serve on the scientific council, for example, Kuvakin and Vishnikov [mentioning friends of D & J] have recently resigned from the Party. But certainly many people on the faculty are members of the Party, including me. So the Party committee is unofficially represented in the work of the scientific council.

D & J: [Pushing on this point] Does the Party committee make decisions on the work of the philosophical faculty which are then communicated unofficially to the scientific council?

P: No. I just give them some information, tell them what we are going to discuss. But till now, we have no conflict with Party committee on any of these problems.

D & J: [Still pushing] Not even personnel problems?

P: No. At the meeting of the council just before the one at which you gave your lecture, we re-elected [granted tenure to] a member of the Faculty who is not a member of the Communist Party; he is a member of another party, the Social Democratic Party. But we renewed his contract without any problem. And we have changed the heads of 75 percent of the chairs in the Faculty. The Party committee does not take part in these decisions.

D & J: Do you still have a professors' trade union?

P: Yes, and in the new situation it will grow in importance. It does not take part in scientific decisions but assists in economic matters. The trade union movement is growing in the country as a whole, not as strong yet in the university as it is with the miners and in the plants and shops. But it does necessary work. For example, just before the holidays, it did secure food and vodka that faculty could purchase without having to stand in line. That is not serious, but it is a service. And the union does help me secure furniture for our offices and arranges for faculty to purchase automobiles at standard prices. I press them all the time for more. I maintain my policy in all of this, but there are things I could not do without the help of the union.

D & J: Just a few more questions. We were quite excited about the announcement of university autonomy that you read at the scientific council. What is it going to mean for philosophy?

P: About autonomy... The Soviet Ministry of Higher Education made a decision about the autonomy of the university on 8 January 1991. So now Moscow State University has received complete autonomy from the Ministry of Higher Education. We get our money and our budget directly from the Soviet Ministry, like the Academy of Sciences. We live by our own rules, we make all our own decisions. How to teach, who we teach, how many specialists to educate every year, and so on ... that's only the business of the university now. Before, the Ministry of Higher Education gave us a quota that told us how many people to teach and so on. And how much money we pay to teachers is now our business too.

D & J: But all of that could have very severe implications for philosophy. Before, there was a state requirement that everyone should study philosophy. Now that all of that is gone, won't here be a problem in "selling" philosophy to other faculties in the university?

P: I will tell you frankly, I do not believe that the market relation is necessarily good for a university, especially for the faculties in the humanistic sciences. Now some faculties will do very well, the economics faculty, for example, and probably the law faculty. They will be able to take in much money and pay their members high salaries. We have made some efforts to seek foreign exchange programs which will bring in hard currency, but it is difficult. The Council of Ministers of the U.S.S.R. gave the university a large sum of hard currency, but probably it will all have to go for new equipment.

We are trying to solve this problem. You know the chair of philosophy for the natural sciences on the fourth floor. They work closely with the natural science faculties to organize special courses for their students, taking up problems in philosophy of physics, mathematics, ecology, and so on. We are the only faculty teaching logic, and many other faculties send their students to study it. But I tell you frankly, it is difficult to organize this interchange as a market relation. Our students need law, we need history, and natural science, and so on. Their students need history of philosophy, logic, philosophy of science, and so on. Certainly, we are working to organize programs for which we can ask money from external organizations. But within the university, it's a sensitive matter.

D & J: Is there any other problem we should discuss before we close?

P: We haven't mentioned what I call the first, main shortcoming of Soviet philosophy—the de-existentialization of philosophy. According to Marx, we must put stress on social philosophy, on political philosophy, and so on, all of which is necessary and important. But we completely ignored personal philosophy, existential philosophy, and I don't mean existentialist doctrines of the French and German schools. But we simplified personal ethical problems, and those problems have accumulated and have not been solved. And now we must restore an existential element to Marxist, to Soviet philosophy.

I want to say that the ethical problem is the main problem, the final problem in any philosophy. You can begin from philosophy of history, philosophy of cosmos, philosophy of ecology, but all such problems in the final analysis reduce to problem of existence, of human existence. And it was always so in philosophy. Ancient philosophers asked, "What is philosophy?" "It is wisdom," they said, "sageness." But what is wisdom? Some people say it is love of truth. That is not true. If you read ancient philosophy, you see that they said two things: it is love of truth and knowing how to live rightly in accordance with truth. It's an ethical problem. And that is why Spinoza says that ethics is the crown of any philosophy. You can begin with philosophy of physics like Descartes or Spinoza, but you must finish it with some kind of ethics. What is good? What is bad? How is one to live? What is your relation to the whole?

But in Soviet philosophy it so happens that ethics turns out not to be the crown but the bad pocket of trousers. How do you explain this? Worldview is some general view of the world, of the human being within this world. And the main component in any worldview is the relation between human being and world as a whole. And it is the task of the philosopher to develop this relationship theoretically. And not only critically, as Western scientists do, but in some kind of positive, even some dogmatic way.

You know that for two thousand years scientists have criticized philosophy, but philosophy is still alive, because people have need for some stable worldview. They criticize philosophy, but in the end they accept it. This is somewhat my personal mission for philosophy....

Postscript, August 30, 1991

Effects of the recent failed coup and its aftermath are likely to be minimal on the Faculty, according to Dean Panin and other senior philosophers at MSU. Telephone conversations on this date (one *can* get through by persistence) indicate optimism. Panin says, "In our Faculty we were already moving in the new direction." One notable change, "Partkom is closed." Since the influence of the party committee on faculty policy and program had already been eliminated, the "closing" (one can imagine the door taped shut) of its activities is of little practical consequence.

References

Graham, Loren R. 1987. *Science, Philosophy, and Human Behavior in the Soviet Union*. Cambridge: Harvard University Press.

Kim, M. P., et al. 1982. *History of the USSR: The Era of Socialism*. Moscow: Progress.

McClellan, James E., III. 1985. *Science Reorganized: Scientific Societies in the Eighteenth Century*. New York: Columbia University Press.

Wetter, Fr. Gustav A. 1957. *Dialectical Materialism: A Historical and Systematic Survey of Philosophy in the Soviet Union*. Peter Heath, translator. New York: Praeger.

Why, When and How We Lost Russia

James E. McClellan, Jr.

This essay represents the deeply honest attempt of a committed progressive philosopher to understand the reasons for the collapse of the U.S.S.R., to explain to himself and the reader its transition from a society experimenting in a new, idealistic form of collective endeavor that held out promise to progressives around the world to a social experiment destined to fail under the weight of its numerous burdens, most significantly, the Cold War.

The essay captures the hope and optimism felt by U.S. academics visiting Russia in the period of "The Thaw" after the death of Stalin. In personal and philosophical terms it turns to describing the transition, first to skepticism then to cynicism, and eventually the sense of loss and need for a clear understanding of exactly what led to the demise of the U.S.S.R.

Some Definitions and Presuppositions

Who are we, we who lost Russia? As a first cut, let us say that we include everyone who still considers herself or himself a participant in the struggle to transcend the capitalist mode of social production and move forward to the socialist stage of human history. Do we, then, include only those who have Rhett Butler's fondness for lost causes? Not on my understanding of just what point in history the present moment is: that first cut should include everyone whose sense of self worth requires a personal commitment to posterity. Not only is the elimination of capitalism necessary if humanity is to achieve the level of perfection, the full creation of personal autonomy, we perceive so dimly today. An end to capitalist relations of production is believed by some to be a necessary condition for the very survival of that unique experiment in natural history called human being. As Dr. Oliver S. Loud, professor of physical science at Antioch University, expressed it:

> On this, our planet, there have been about 1000 human generations since Homo sapiens, alone among several hominid species, survived to become the culture-creating animal. Only the last 200 generations have been born into hierarchical, class structured social systems. We know enough ... to calculate that posterity—if we win—could comprise 200 million human generations, while our sun continues to radiate stably into our cherished biosphere. Five generations, three of them already here, will either win or lose forever that immense human future.

We include, that is to say, individuals who think in large-scale historical terms, who hold certain beliefs and accept certain commitments and obligations because we hold those beliefs. Our political commitments touch the deepest level of our emotions; our beliefs about human history are rooted in a scientific view of the natural world.

A central belief among those who lost Russia is that history is not merely continuous, though it certainly is that; history is also, dialectically, discontinuous, coming in great, long-lasting waves or eras when one mode of production dominates the way human labor is expended in securing the material goods that make life possible. Every mode of production in the 200 generations of recorded history is built upon a system of social classes, a system which allocates the labor of social production and the goods produced unequally among those classes.

And yes, these eras not only succeed one another, but in that succession can be seen an upward direction to which we give the name progress. To invoke the concept of progress, of course, is to presuppose a moral criterion applicable to history. We, speaking still of those who lost Russia, do not hesitate to invoke our moral standard: human institutions are to be judged by the degree to which they make possible the full realization of human capacities, the perfection of human being, if you like.

Human perfection is multidimensional—physical, intellectual, social, moral, spiritual. And yes, the capitalist mode of production has made possible the full and free development of all those capacities for a larger proportion of the society than had any previous economic system. Science and democracy, the twin (but far from identical) institutions in which we ground our beliefs and commitments, throve on a capitalist economic base more strongly than in any previous era. But from that very development arises its own contradiction. A scientific worldview holds relatively certain the truth of these two statements: on the economic base of capitalism, we can never achieve peace among the various segments of our human species. Nor can we achieve peace between our species and our organic co-habitants of this planet, the natural environment that is our home, our only possible home. Thus, under capitalism we can never achieve the material conditions for further progress, the unlimited possible progress of 200 million generations, in the pursuit of our moral vision.

So that's who we are, we who lost Russia. We call ourselves Marxists for obvious reasons. If we read history as I do, we should also call ourselves Leninists, for we believe that a worldwide political movement aimed at revolutionary struggle against the class structure of capitalism is the only effective agent of historical progress. Those whose courage and dedication to this struggle led them to join a disciplined Marxist-Leninist party may identify themselves as Communists; the rest of us must be content with the label of socialist or, as in my case, fellow traveler.

One more presupposition before turning to our questions. To lose something, one must first have it. Did we, as defined, ever *have* Russia? The academic consensus these days is clearly negative. But since I am speaking from a personal perspective, I can answer with an unequivocal yes: for at least one bright, shining moment—perhaps an ephemeral, evanescent moment—Russia was *ours*. I'm speaking of my first visit to the U.S.S.R. The only time in my life when I've been thrilled in the full somatic sense of the term, other than riding roller-coasters or flying small planes, was when Zoya Mal'kova, our Intourist guide, greeted us in Moscow, Metropol Hotel, June 1958. "Welcome," she said, "to the U.S.S.R. You are no longer in the U.S.A. You are in a free country. You may go wherever you like at any time you like. You may speak of anything you like to anyone with whom you share a common language. You will not be robbed or raped, insulted or assaulted. We are still a poor country, but we are rich in art, literature, and music. You may buy whatever you fancy in our shops, confident that you will not be cheated in any encounter. So enjoy your supper, sleep well, and be prepared for a full day's work tomorrow."

During the two weeks that our group of upper-echelon American educators spent in Moscow and Leningrad, nothing in my personal experience gave me cause to call Zoya's speech untrue. We did encounter Soviet citizens who would have preferred to be citizens of the U.S.A.; given the radical disparity in the economic conditions of the two countries, who could blame them? We spoke with those who could be called "dissidents," those who believed that the shameful shadow of Stalin and state terror forever blackened Khrushchev's rhetoric of socialist reconstruction. We were quite aware that, even five years after Stalin's death, many wrongfully accused people still languished in prison and exile. We were vaguely aware that repressive forces in the state and Party, those complicit in Stalinist crimes against humanity, were still alive and functional in Soviet life. (How strong those forces were became apparent only with Khrushchev's dismissal.) But we were also aware of the serious moral failures in our own society. So, taking one thing with another, and after meeting with their Soviet counterparts and visiting educational institutions at every level, even our college presidents and deans and public school officials would have been hard-pressed to claim U.S. superiority in aught save wealth.

The point to be emphasized from this experience is that, by the ordinary meaning of the term, the Soviet Union of the time was a civil society, one where streets are safe, schools educate, shops are honest, even strangers treated cordially, welcomed into homes and into serious political conversation. After 1987 one began to hear much talk about the need to reestablish what proponents of capitalism call "civil society" in Russia and the countries formerly allied with the U.S.S.R. But at its best, the U.S.S.R. proved that a society does not require class exploitation in order to be civil.

Zoya's speech may leave some among you unpersuaded that even during the Eisenhower-Khrushchev thaw, Russia was really ours. Let me offer another bit of anecdotal evidence. In the evenings of our summer tours in the late fifties, I sought the company of young Russians from the universities and academic institutes, those interested in serious talk and in drinking good vodka, then readily available at reasonable prices at any *magazin* or *pectopah*. Those young scholars, artists, scientists, teachers, men and women in about equal proportions, were—as were their descendants until almost yesterday—a superb tribute to the capacity of the U.S.S.R. to develop human potential. When the vodka had done its beneficent work, I would ask around: "How many of you are members of the Party?" At that time, the answers from many of the participants were either a proud but modest "Yes, I became a member this year," or an earnest and eager "No, but my application is submitted, I hope that I will be found to have the courage, dedication, and intellect required for Party membership." From others, of course, ... one would hear, "Never. I'll never give up the evenings and weekends I might devote to x [where x = that person's favorite pastime—painting, fishing, drinking...] just to go to meetings or talk to factory workers." Such responses drew laughter and "Don't worry, the Party's too smart to take *you*."

The next question, of course, was "Why would you want to join the Party?" holding in reserve good reasons for not wanting Party membership. And here the answer from a number was surprisingly sincere: "So that I can help our leaders to reach the goals that Soviet society has set out to achieve." As you may well imagine, I couldn't resist needling: "So, you want to help crush a workers' revolution in Hungary, for example?" "On the contrary, we want to help build socialist societies here and around the world where workers will not be misled by the CIA and other forms of capitalist propaganda." Well, that's one way to look at the matter. And to be quite candid about it, that has been my perspective on the historical role of the U.S.S.R. from that day till this.

Fast-forward nearly a quarter-century to January of 1982 when my wife and I set up our Spartan living quarters in the dormitory at Moscow State University, complete with a beautiful Lenin poster on the wall. Our doors were usually open, our little room filled with graduate students from all over the U.S.S.R., indeed, from all over the world. Our guests were the same caliber of young people I had known in 1958 and 1959. And I always, eventually, asked the same questions. And from no one in that setting did we get a positive response on the matter of Party membership. "Oh, I may have to join if I'm appointed to a position where membership is required." Or "The only people who want to join the Party are careerists looking to get the perquisites that go with it."

The best and brightest even in 1982 were blessed with hope, energy, dreams. They saw ahead a time when the U.S.S.R. would be a social democracy like, say, Scandinavia or West Germany. It would combine the socialist ideals of equal opportunity, full employment, gender equality and social programs with American freedom and material wealth. With few exceptions, these young men and women had turned their backs on politics and directed their plans for the future to their individual careers. (How different from the 1950s when the question, "Where do you intend to go when you leave the university?" was usually answered, "Wherever it is thought my work will be of most use.")

In the 1980s few of our young friends regarded Marxist-Leninist political theory as a serious branch of scholarship, few regarded the socialist vision of human life as actually directing the course of their own history. By 1982 for many, by 1992 for nearly all university students, that language and that vision had become a mask, repulsive or farcical as mood varied, for an exploitative, repressive, inefficient, and cynical political hierarchy. For them, the spark that energized the previous generation had been extinguished. Let come what may they seemed to say, it must be better *for me* than what we have now. Even while the Party still held state power, Russia was no longer ours.

We must, of course, acknowledge a small group of still devoted socialists among our Russian friends of both generations. No illusions, no apologies for Stalin's crimes or Brezhnev's stagnation, no vainglorious parade of slogans. What guides their thinking is knowledge that the world system of capitalism promises nothing but disaster for all humankind, most immediately for Russia and other republics of the U.S.S.R. They are still out there, as active in the political struggle as the fight for daily survival will allow them to be, striving to create a political movement uniting intelligentsia, industrial workers and farm workers, one aimed at freeing Russia (and Belarus and Ukraine and...) from domination by the IMF, World Bank, and the great transnational corporations. In my view, they are heroes: some, I fear, are destined to become martyrs.

My perspective on the U.S.S.R., you now realize, is, like the one from our windows at Moscow State University, fairly long but quite narrow. Our experience with our Soviet friends and acquaintances was and still is intense, unimpeded by political constraints, based on total trust and openness, but except for quite casual contacts, limited to our intellectual, academic colleagues. What we know of the lives of the *rabochyi klass* we learned from books or conversation. We do know certain individuals who had quite impressive Party positions, but we knew nothing of their work except as it affected university activities. Our friends, we might add, are intellectuals of great talent, intently concerned that we understand their life without illusions, just as we, when they visit us here, insist that they understand the U.S.A. without illusions.

The Search for Explanation

As we turn to the question of *why* we lost Russia, please allow me a moment of philosophy. A why question can be answered in two ways. The first way is by appeal to general principle, either a scientific or moral principle. Optimally, in science we answer a why principle by appeal to a grounded theory. Why is the sky blue? We invoke our theory of optical refraction, specify the conditions of the atmosphere as a refracting medium, and a blue sky comes out as a logical inference: Q.E.D. In ethics, optimally, by appeal to fundamental moral value. Why should I rush into the street to retrieve a stranger's baby carriage? Because you are a human being; every human being is obligated to help a neighbor in distress, therefore you are so obliged. In both science and ethics the why question is answered by claiming that the particular case falls under what we call a covering law.

A second way of answering a why question is to show that an action follows from practical reasoning. In general, we explain why an agent did X by showing that that agent wants or desires Y, and believes that doing X is the only or at least best way to get Y, and so does X. Why did the butler administer a slow-acting poison? Because he wanted revenge for shameful treatment and believed that, by using a slow poison, he could both kill his master and make his deed known before the victim died. That's why he did it that way. I bring up the why question to eliminate some of it. Many commentators you can find will answer the why question by invoking a covering law in the form of a simple syllogism. Premise 1: Some systems of fundamental political ideas or, as they are usually called, some "ideologies" are morally evil. Premise 2: Any state system or, as it is usually called, any "regime" which bases its legitimacy on a morally evil ideology is nothing but a criminal conspiracy. All such regimes are doomed to fail. Marxism-Leninism is a morally evil ideology. The CPSU was a criminal conspiracy. Thus it falls under the covering law, was doomed, and eventually fell: Q.E.D. to the why question.

If you want to see such argument in detail and if you have the stomach to do so, read Richard Pipes, Robert Conquest, Martin Malia, or David Remnick, just to mention certain more respectable names among the odious. Their works, as far as I can tell, are relatively accurate on basic facts; they provide enlightening details on the how and when questions. But my gag reflex is hair-triggered; it causes problems for my dentist and restricts my reading of such literature to eyedropper quantities at a time.

Our loss of Russia, then, from my perspective is not to be explained by reference to violation of moral law. Was the Soviet experiment doomed to failure because it violated some empirical, historical law of social development? We should think very carefully on that questions, but let me first eliminate one other possible, often-heard explanation. It is said that we lost Russia because Mikhail Sergeyevich Gorbachev *wanted* to restore capitalism and *believed* it necessary to destroy the Soviet economy and political structure in order to achieve that end. Thus, when Gorbachev acted (or, more often, failed to act) in ways that seemed either cowardly or incompetent, upholders of this theory will point out that before becoming General Secretary of the Party, Gorbachev's record indicated great reserves of courage and cleverness. Those seemingly stupid moves were in fact, this theory holds, shrewd steps toward the domination he wanted to reach.

Enough said: I don't believe a single word of it. When Mikhail Sergeyevich spoke to a plenary session of the Party's Central Committee in June 1986, he portrayed in realistic terms the economic problems the country faced, argued with irrefutable logic that these problems could not be solved within the political and legal framework they inherited from the 1930s, he begged them to implement the goals of the 27th Party Congress, and asked as he had on other occasions, "If not we, comrades, then who will do it? If not now, when?" In every phrase he was but expressing what all devoted Communists knew in their heart to be true.

I find no reason to suppose that Gorbachev was a conscious traitor to socialism. His belief that socialism would be strengthened rather than threatened by democracy was shared by every astute Marxist I knew. Then why did Gorbachev adopt policies that virtually guaranteed socialism's downfall? Why did he not take those steps that, even at that late date, might conceivably have restored Russia to its revolutionary stature? Historians and biographers will puzzle over those questions for generations, but no sober scholar will conclude, I'm convinced, that Gorby killed socialism because he wanted to.

Does that mean that no explanation of that form, one referring to desires and beliefs, will help us understand this major historical phenomenon? On the contrary. Consider, if you will, the desires and beliefs of the most strategically significant stratum of the Soviet leadership, those responsible for managing industrial and financial establishments central to the Soviet economy. Let us consider them first as Martin Malia, David Remnick, et al., regard them. In their view, those managers were merely mafia legmen, keeping their share of the loot and passing on the share that must go to those above them in the hierarchy. Their support of the Soviet state system was guaranteed as long as, and only as long as, that system supported them, i.e., only as long as the mafia and "socialist" state system were one and the same thing. When perestroika became a reality, that unity was broken; the managerial class shed, predictably, the facade of socialist rhetoric and became what they are today, openly capitalist crooks.

That there is some truth in that view is supported by all the evidence, including our personal experience. That disastrous consequences flowed from that truth is also undeniable. But it is not the whole truth, nor the one I am most concerned with here. Let us recognize both that the individuals who came to occupy those positions were also members of a technically trained intelligentsia with an ideology geared to efficiency and technological progress, and that the mafia identification was not spread equally to all parts of the Soviet productive system. So let us take for a moment the other view and consider the truly socialist factory manager, the sort displayed by *Soviet Life* in the early days of perestroika. Operating under *Gosplan* and Party control, employing workers who enjoyed both formal and informal means for resisting his demands for hard work and technical efficiency, denied access to equipment and information up to world standards, holding his position ultimately on the sufferance of those above him in the hierarchy, even the most dedicated manager in those days would have had difficulty in seeing the benefits to be derived from "actually existing socialism."

Oh, the perks and privileges of Soviet managers were quite nice when compared with the lifestyles of front line workers in their plants and offices. But the differential was inconsequential compared to that enjoyed by their counterparts in the U.S.A. Furthermore, what advantages they enjoyed, they were supposed to hide. They were subject to (though seldom prosecuted for violating) strict laws against the use of office to pass on their hard-won advantages to offspring. Now if *Gosplan* is working well, if Party control guarantees freedom from corruption and sloppiness all around, if one's children are guaranteed a productive place in the society commensurate with their actual talents, why, yes, the truly dedicated industrial or financial manager will do the best he can to fulfill his quota, promote efficiency, help perestroika succeed. But when those ifs are *all* answered in the negative, would it not be quite natural for him to say, in effect? "Well, if we introduce a little capitalism here, so that I can become the owner, or maybe part owner, rather than just the manager of this place, it will surely be rough and risky, but it's a gamble well worth taking. In the meantime, I'll keep my nose clean, my contacts active, and my eye on the main chance."

Which is just what they did, as a rule. Which explains, as much as anything else, why perestroika proved such a failure. Perestroika would work only if that particular stratum of individuals exercised energy, creativity, and technical expertise of the highest order, if they formed among themselves efficient, flexible links tying production of raw material to distribution of product to final consumer. But where was the incentive for those individuals to take risks, invest all that extra work, in an untried experiment? Remember, for the most part, these individuals had risen to their positions under Brezhnev. And they are to lead a revolution in production?

I concentrate on that point to emphasize a more general one: perestroika could not work as a revolution from above. Nor did the Soviet educational and political systems, for all their magnificent achievements, generate either the institutional mechanism or the psychological orientation required for the U.S.S.R. to effect the needed changes in its economic and social structure *without* a political revolution.

The brute facts are clear enough. Well before the coups of August 1991 and September to October 1993, we had not only lost Russia, we had lost all chance of regaining it.

What's to Be Learned from the Loss of Russia?

Asserted above was the belief that Russia was ours in 1958, that it embodied, in the persons of its best and brightest youth, the promise of creating a socialist society and eventually a socialist world. Let me now assert an equally controversial and apparently contradictory claim: that we lost Russia in 1948! By this thesis, then, we lost Russia before we had it, and we had it ten years after we had lost it! I'm not concerned with the paradox but with certain lessons that may be gained from the downfall of the U.S.S.R., the greatest experiment so far in our species' never-ending struggle to gain control of our own destiny.

Marx himself might argue that the entire experiment was doomed from the beginning, for Russia was not an advanced industrial society at the time of the October Revolution, and only such are ready for socialism. The bourgeoisie, Marx and Engels insisted on more than one occasion, will not be replaced before they have completed their progressive role in history, that is to say, until under their direction and control, the productive forces in society have advanced to the point that they can supply all the material requirements for the full development of human personality. Well, the success of the U.S.S.R. proves exactly the contrary: you don't need a bourgeoisie to build an industrial economy, or a post-industrial economy, that can fulfill human needs even beyond our present imagination.

Orthodox economists dispute that conclusion. They claim that the command system of economic decision-making, that system employed from beginning to end by *Gosplan* is manageably effective in the early stages of industrial development; but such a system, they say, cannot accommodate the so-called scientific-technical revolution, without which productive forces come quickly to stalemate. The orthodox case is correct, I believe, but it does not contradict the capacity of socialist development to reach any desired level of technical and scientific complexity.

This point was drilled into my head by several young Soviet economists, specialists in planning. Most non-specialist but "good" Soviet citizens during the Brezhnevian stagnation would insist that *Gosplan* was fine, only the individuals responsible for carrying it out were rotten. But *Gosplan*, however sophisticated in detail, still carried the fatal flaws of any command system of decision-making. A socialist economy is a planned economy, true, but a command system is not the only way an economy can be planned. Planning can be flexible, utilize market mechanisms where appropriate, provide rational material as well as psychic incentives for socially productive efforts, be responsive to new developments in science and technique, etc., all this while remaining an organized system that does *not* empower a class of capitalist owners.

But *Gosplan*—just visualize the immense, block-sized structure that housed its central office in the middle of Moscow—*Gosplan* was not merely a neutral planning bureau, it was an enormous structure of immense political power. Was it to be scrapped, abandoned, replaced by a thoroughly different form of economic decision-making? As things turned out, yes indeed it was. But as these young economists realized so sadly and so early on, the system that replaced it was *not* going to be a technically possible *socialist* system, such as they could design. The only *politically* possible alternative to *Gosplan* was a profit-oriented system imposed by the international capitalist class. Both Daniel Singer and Stephen Cohen have expressed admiration for such Russian economists. Russian advice, of course, was ignored by Yeltsin, who employed Jeffrey Sachs but, according to the latter, seldom followed the advice he had paid for. How unkind can history be?

Another lesson from the downfall of the U.S.S.R. is nothing new, nothing that Aristotle did not demonstrate from his studies of the constitutions of

Hellenic city-states: You leave any self-selecting, one-party government in power for more than two generations, and you get corruption, inefficiency cronyism at best, repression and brutality if that party is headed by a tyrant. What has to be explained is how the Soviet people, well educated, well organized, intensely conscious of their unique revolutionary role in history, possessed of a brilliant and, at times, thoroughly socialist intelligentsia, allowed themselves to be held captive to a clearly failing political and economic system? How did it happen?

Let me close with this thought. It happened, among other reasons, because we came in a poor fourth in a field of four in the presidential elections of 1948, *we* being the supporters of the Progressive Party and the candidacy of Henry Wallace and Glen H. Taylor. Harry Truman's spectacular victory and our dismal defeat guaranteed the unquestioned dominance of bipartisan Cold War politics, both anti–Communist internally and anti–Soviet internationally. That election was the cusp: after 1948 the international peace movement, despite heroic efforts and often brilliant leadership, was faced with insuperable odds in its efforts to capture popular support in this country. The U.S.A. initiated the arms race and escalated it with new technology whenever it seemed to reach a stalemate. And nothing is more conducive to a siege mentality than running second in a nuclear arms race. When a country is operating with a siege mentality in its foreign relations, it is quite unlikely to undertake revolutionary struggle against internal oppressors. Why did the Soviet people put up with the CPSU after it had ceased to be a progressive force in history and an effectively functioning leadership cadre in running the country? Ask yourself: would the Party have been able to retain its hegemonic and misused power if the U.S.A. and NATO had offered peace and disarmament? How long did it retain power after the U.S.S.R. withdrew from the arms race?

So, one more old lesson to be relearned from this great experiment: no socialist economy can keep up with a capitalist economy under conditions of a long-continued arms race. A capitalist economy necessarily generates excess productive capacity. Large employment of unproductive labor in military units, heavy investment in useless commodities like military equipment, and, in this era, allocation of extraordinary resources to research aimed at increasing the destructive power of weapons, the accumulation of a huge internal debt—all these economic moves add a balance wheel to a capitalist economy, keep its cyclical recessions from becoming full-blown, socially explosive depressions. A socialist economy, on the other hand, will tend to restrict its capital investment and distribute its social product to current consumption. A socialist economy thus moves toward stability, whereas a capitalist economy must constantly expand or collapse. Thus, in a socialist economy, expenditures on armaments are pure drains on the living standards of workers.

To the extent, then, that the economy of the U.S.S.R. can be described as socialist—and I defer to Szymanski and Perlo, rather than to, say, Malia or Remnick & Wolf, on this point—that nation simply could not have competed in the arms race without a dictatorial political state, one that extracts surplus value from workers, allocates productive efforts to unproductive military expenditures. And our defeat in 1948 guaranteed that the U.S.S.R. must either compete in that race or accept defeat with the consequences it was, in the end, forced to suffer, *i.e.*, with calamitous deprivation imposed on its citizens and loss of its sovereignty as a political unit.

From the standpoint of economic theory, then, the question is not so much why we lost Russia as how the U.S.S.R. managed to hang tough for so long. With any people other than the Russians at its center, I believe, it would have been strangled long ago.

We all recognize that the speed and completeness with which the U.S.S.R. fell apart after 1989 indicates over-determination of the outcome. If it had not been done in by factor X, it would have fallen because of factor Y.

The Universality of Liberal Capitalism and the Possibility of Renewed Socialism: Reflections on the Soviet Coup of August 1991

JAMES LAWLER

The following essay was originally written in 1993. In the first place this was a defense of the policies of perestroika by which Soviet President Mikhail Gorbachev had attempted to lead the Soviet Union on a new path between the old system of state-based socialism, and a radical turn to the neo-liberal, deregulated capitalism that was then being proposed by Western advocates as the only way to bring the Soviet Union out of "stagnation." The essay explains why Gorbachev's policies, while justifiable in general terms, failed in the face of contradictory pressures. The main reason for the failure was the fact that the market-oriented socialism that he advocated implicitly gave increased power to workers to manage their own enterprises, and thereby undermined the powers and privileges of the old management class. The only way for this class to preserve its position in society was to embrace capitalism.

Hence the paradox that the main beneficiaries of the turn to capitalism in Russia were the elites of the former Communist Party. Thus arose what Russian critics call the "kleptocracy," the government of "thieves and swindlers" who took advantage of the upheavals at the time of coup and counter-coup of 1991, and then of market deregulation in 1992, to avail themselves of the enormous wealth of the former Soviet Union. The application of "shock therapy" to the old system—i.e., the sudden turn to a free market—was indeed a great shock to the ordinary citizens whose savings were depleted overnight as the value of the Russian ruble plummeted under international market forces. It must have been a shock for the population as well to see a class of capitalists emerge directly from the class of former communists.

The sharp turn to the pro-capitalist market society was disastrous to the economy and social system of Russia, and to the other countries of the former U.S.S.R. As a consequence of the collapse of the Communist state system, and the failure of the deregulated market economy, Russia inevitably had to move forcefully back in the opposite direction. The discredited neo-liberal, pro-capitalist government of Boris Yeltsin, which gave a bad name to both capitalism and democracy, thus gave way to the neo–Tsarist orientation of Vladimir Putin, who has been ruling Russia for the past twelve years. Such oscillation between extremes implicitly vindicates the moderate, centrist orientation, with its cautious introduction of a complex system of still-socialist market reforms, pursued by Mikhail Gorbachev from 1985 to 1991.

The conclusion of the essay evokes Russia's ancient Tsarist tradition, disparagingly called "Asiatic despotism" by Hegel and, more neutrally, "the Asiatic mode of production" by Marx. The essence of this social formation was the fact that the Tsar in Russia, or the Emperor in China, was seen as a bulwark of security by a peasantry whose powerlessness, due to its social isolation, made it extremely vulnerable. Its salvation, against the more visible forces of aristocratic privilege as well as foreign incursions, lay with the strong but benevolent hand of the Good Tsar, who, if only he was not misinformed by his devious entourage, was concerned for the little people of Russia. Thus the powerless peasantry naturally adhered to a romance of government in which everything depended on the righteousness of the central power of the Tsar.

The Russian revolutionaries called Narodniki, or Populists, turned to Marx himself for advice regarding the possibilities of Russia's future development. In correspondence with Narodnik leader Vera Zasulich, Marx warned against taking the Western path of historical development as a model for Russia. While the West had passed from feudalism to capitalism, and was then moving on to socialism or communism, the same pattern of development was not inevitable for the East. Only if capitalism had become sufficiently implanted in Russia or in China, could the revolutionaries there follow the Western model of development, and seek to bring about a form of socialism stemming from capitalism, as Western socialists were then attempting. Otherwise, without a capitalist springboard to socialism, a non-capitalist path, resting on the peasant community, would be necessary. The main direction of such a path had to be for the peasants to find ways of connecting with one another horizontally, as it were, rather than vertically—with direct exchanges between peasant communes, and so obviating the otherwise inevitable plea for help on the part of isolated communities to the central state and its sovereign ruler.

It is a little-appreciated fact that Western socialists were significantly successful in overcoming the pure, unfettered capitalism of the nineteenth century by introducing limits to the capitalist free market. Regulations of market forces promoted by socialists and communists led to forms of the "mixed" economy, as seen by social democracies in Europe and the American New Deal. One of the main planks of Marx's Communist Manifesto, for example, was a public system of education for children—a reform and restriction of unregulated capitalism that Adam Smith himself advocated, but despaired of seeing realized because of the power capitalists held over the British government.[1]

Russian history of the twentieth century can be described in terms of failed attempts to follow Marx's advice to the Russian revolutionaries. The New Economic Policy initiated by Lenin in the 1920s was an attempt to develop market relations between the peasants—in order to counter the rapid drift after the Russian revolution back to a heavy emphasis on the state and its bureaucracy. Stalin's rise to power at the end of the 1920s put an end to this first experiment with market socialism. Gorbachev explicitly evoked the New Economic Policy of Lenin as providing Marxist-Leninist credentials for his own market-oriented reforms. This time, however, the reform movement would end by idolizing the market rather than the state. It was inevitable then, that this exaggeration should be countered by Vladimir Putin's reestablishment of the power of the central state, beginning in the year 2000.

End of Socialism?

Everywhere there are signs that socialism is a thing of the past. There has been a collapse of the socialist regimes in Eastern Europe and in the Soviet Union. Changes in political structure have brought about the end to one party rule and the advent of multiparty political pluralism. This by itself would not mean the end of socialism since representatives of reformed socialism, including the last Soviet president Mikhail Gorbachev, were advocates of democratic institutions similar to those in capitalist nations. But with the collapse of the old political structure has come, more or less quickly, a radical shift in the economic policies of the new ruling groups. On the economic plane, there have been radical changes, which the Polish called "shock therapy." The aim of these changes is the restoration of capitalist economies, and perhaps even the attempt to be more capitalist than the capitalists themselves. After six years of moving along the path of democratic reforms of socialism, such a change took place in the Soviet Union, beginning in August 1991, with an attempted coup by rearguard Soviet leadership in defiance of Gorbachev's reforms. The defeat of the *coup d'état*, led by the Russian President, Boris Yeltsin, created conditions for a fundamentally new turn in Russia towards the creation of a capitalist economy.

Elsewhere, in China, Vietnam, in Africa, events may have been proceeding more slowly, but the goal, declared to be the creation of "market economies," seems to many to be essentially in the same direction. Such relatively slow and cautious changes on the economic plane had been taking place in the U.S.S.R. during the six years of Gorbachev's "perestroika"—although in the U.S.S.R., unlike China, changes on the political and cultural levels proceeded rapidly from the beginning. Now, however, the former countries of the now-dissolved Soviet Union, above all the Russian Republic, have entered a post-perestroika period. One Russian commentator calls the new era "Novostroika"— implying that instead of "re-structuring," the new government is doing something radically new. As Soviet President Gorbachev's economic reforms are replaced by those of Russian President Yeltsin, the previous attempt to carefully dismantle the top of the Soviet mountain boulder by boulder threatens to turn into an avalanche.

On the level of ideas, the so-called winning of the Cold War by liberal capitalist democracies led to the proclamation of the "end of history." Neo-liberalism, which involves a return to the spirit of unfettered capitalist competition, was once consigned to the far-right lunatic fringe. Now its main program sounds like reasonable economic thinking to many if not most people. In the past, Marxism was viewed as a serious, but probably dangerous outlook, as in the media phrase, "Marxist terrorists." But now to be labeled "Marxist" is to risk smiles and jokes, not unlike those reserved for serious believers in the flatness of the Earth. But it isn't just Marxists, to say nothing of Marxist-Leninists, who are being consigned to history's dustbin. Twentieth century liberalism, with its defense of government intervention in the economy and the promotion of a welfare state, is also only a short step behind Marxism as a candidate for historical obsolescence. Reagan-Bushism in the U.S., Thatcher-Majorism in the U.K., and the perennial Mulroneyism of Canada, have made privatization and free trade the battering ram of radical and perhaps post-modern "deconstructing" of the Keynesian welfare state. Social-democratic governments, such as that of France, have been forced to follow the same trend.

Hence, it is not only in the former socialist world that radical changes are taking place. So-called "socialistic" features of capitalist economies too are being dismantled. Realistic and unsentimental adaptation to "globalization" under conditions of free trade is supposedly essential to survival in the computerized jungle of today's increasingly competitive world. We recall the arguments of General Motor's spokespersons in Michael Moore's film *Roger and Me*. When the devastation of lives of the laid-off workers in Flint, Michigan, was pointed out to them, they offered their condolences, and then evoked the natural law of the world market place. To compete in the new world economy it is necessary for companies to produce with the cheapest possible labor and materials. A capitalist corporation, they suggested, is not a welfare agency. But governments, which are welfare agencies, cannot tax corporate wealth to previous levels out of fear of rendering them uncompetitive, and because of their ability to move elsewhere.

Universality of Capitalist Liberal Democracy?

Current world trends in both the former socialist countries and in the developed capitalist ones have added weight to the argument that capitalist liberal democracy has become a universal world system to which every other country is fated sooner or later to turn—or else face some kind of collapse. In the minds of some authors, the dramatic events of recent times have taken on dimensions of Hegelian world–historical significance. In responding to such an outlook two aspects of the matter should be distinguished. On the one hand, the idea of the universality of certain basic civil and democratic rights—including freedom of speech, press and religion, together with the right of independent political organization—has become more deeply entrenched in the collective consciousness of mankind. In this sense the Hegelian claim that history moves from the "freedom of one" through the "freedom of some" to the "freedom of all" has been re-confirmed in recent years. For this achievement, the six years of perestroika in the Soviet Union must be credited with making a significant historical contribution.

But "liberal democracy" is usually also taken to include capitalist economic relationships, i.e., the system of multi-party political democracy erected on the foundations of private ownership and control of the main instruments of the production and distribution of wealth. Have the events in Eastern Europe and the Soviet Union meant the universal triumph of such capitalist democracy? Some old-time communists might have said that political rights are fine for the well-to-do, but you can't eat words. And are there not also rights of a social and material nature—such as rights to social assistance, health and education, and the right to work with decent pay? As far as democracy is concerned, is there not also a right to workplace democracy? In the former socialist countries the establishment of such rights was once declared to be the major achievement of the socialist system. In the U.S.S.R. traditional "bourgeois" civil and political rights were once held to be legitimately restricted or suppressed to guarantee the preservation of such allegedly more fundamental human rights. Reform socialists in the U.S.S.R. had attempted to preserve the old "socialist" set of rights, make them in fact more real, while adding those civic and political rights that had previously been curtailed. Democratization, Gorbachev argued, was crucial to a modern economy, for if you can't eat words, a worker with a gag in his mouth will not grow food.

Now as socialist economic systems unravel or are being dismantled, such traditional socialist rights, no doubt imperfectly realized as they were, are being forcibly jettisoned. Defenders of the new militant capitalist world order argue that only capitalist democracy "delivers the goods." Any attempt to affirm a "workers' democracy," a socialist democracy, is a utopian dream which, if put into practice, leads inevitably to poverty and statist totalitarianism.

But even the practices of "political democracy," which expanded rapidly during the "reform socialist" period, are increasingly coming under fire as they appear to present obstacles to imposition of unpopular aspects of the new capitalist order. The advent of the new order in Russia was vividly presented to the world as President Yeltsin, by his own personal decree and while the Russian parliament looked on without being consulted, outlawed the Communist Party of the Soviet Union in the very presence of Soviet president Gorbachev, who at the time was also head of the Party. The coup that was defeated created the possibility of a second surreptitious coup, as the constitutional power of the Soviet government was ignored or scorned in the name of national independence and emergency conditions. If there was no second coup in the legal sense, as Gorbachev insists in his recent book,[2] this is because, with the goal of maintaining legality under pressure of events, he forcefully persuaded the Soviet parliament to acquiesce in the new relations of power in hopes of finding acceptable compromises in the future. Nevertheless, for the time being, the period of "messy parliamentary squabbles," even within the context of the individual republics, has come to an end. Elections in Russia have been postponed. Participation by grass roots organizations is discouraged. Laws cease to have legitimacy in the face of Presidential rule. The result is the maintenance of a kind of minimal democracy, based on a continuing popular mandate given by the Russian people to President Yeltsin.

New Sufferings

If the choice of liberal capitalist democracy has suggested a kind of bourgeois universalism, the results have not yet confirmed the hypotheses upon which the choice has been made. There are many indications that all is not well at what has been termed "the end of history." The news from Eastern Europe is that people are increasingly regretting the haste with which certain major changes have been made, if not yet the main direction of the changes. In an article in a recent National Geographic magazine, William S. Ellis provides a bitter sweet summary of the pluses and the minuses of former East German socialism—with the sweet distinctly recollected in contrast with the bitterness of the present situation:

Of a work force of between eight million and nine million, close to 50 percent are idle. The figure is startling when set against the fact that for four decades, up until the very last, there were jobs for all in the GDR. The East Germans had their workers' holiday camps, low rents, and all but free medical and dental care, and other adornments that served to distract from the stifled life of a closed society. Most of all, there were the jobs. That is not to say, of course, that the work was usually of much quality or quantity, and certainly the salaries reflected that. In a way it was like the state pretending to pay, and the workers pretending to work, and in the end it all came out even. Still, the GDR became an industrial giant, and for all of the problems there was always that bedrock of security; the people would never have much but always something.

For women, especially, there have been losses of benefits, such as a year's paid maternity leave, free day care centers, and free abortion on demand. They hold protest rallies on weekends in many cities, and the speakers, filled with the spirit of sisterhood, rail against a life given over to what they call the three K's—Kirche, Kinder, and Küche, or church, children, and kitchen" ("Germany, The Morning After," *National Geographic Magazine*, September 1991, Vol. 180, No. 3, 13).

The East Germans thought that by grasping at Western capitalism when it was offered to them, together with the incentive of exchange of marks at par, their dreams for a better life, as portrayed on West German TV, would be fulfilled. But the amount of marks that could be exchanged was limited, and the amount of things that one could buy with them even more so. Where before the prices were low, but the shops uninteresting, now the shops are fabulous, those that are open, but the pockets are empty. In such circumstances, many East Germans are unwilling to blame the capitalism upon which they have staked so much. The majority wait with less and less hope for market forces to sort things out and bring the promised rewards. For the less patient, an easier target of blame are the Turks or other foreign workers, who are thought to possess unjustifiably what has become the new scarcity, jobs.

The example of East Germany is especially instructive, since there the process of restoration of capitalism has gone farthest and fastest. But East Germany is a special case, situated within Europe's richest economy, and possessing a strong claim to special aid from West Germany. East German patience under current difficulties may have greater claim to justification than elsewhere.

Problems of Perestroika

In the U.S.S.R., until the attempted coup of August 19 to 21, 1991, the examples of Eastern Europe were being slowly assimilated. Here, where the dangers of disintegration are greatest, changes were going forward slowly—as many in both West and East Germany now wish had been the case there. The reasons for the slow pace were complex. There are problems inherent in the difficulty of "restructuring" itself. There are tremendous obstacles in changing over from a "command-administrative" economy to one in which real market prices play a key role in economic decision-making. For example, a large number of Soviet enterprises enjoy near-monopoly status, and could not be free to set prices at will. When a detergent factory in Azerbaijan stopped production there was a soap shortage throughout the Soviet Union. So for market forces to play a role, these monopolies would have to be broken up and new smaller and competitive enterprises created.

But the purely technical difficulties of reform were not the only ones. There was the matter of the old, potentially explosive institutions of power and privilege that Gorbachev was cautiously defusing. These included opponents of market reforms to the extent that such reforms decentralized economic power and decision making. It seemed, however, that such opposition was steadily losing ground as the argument for allowing market forces to play a significant role became increasingly persuasive. The restructuring of the old system of rule went considerably far in connection with the Communist Party. Under Gorbachev's leadership the Communist Party had given up its constitutional right to rule, and was in the process of adapting to multi-party democracy. A Party congress scheduled for October 1991 would have taken another major step in this process of democratization. However, Gorbachev thought, the mobilization of a reformed unified party would be essential to carry through difficult changes in a vast, multi-ethnic society.

Crucial to the crisis of August was also the unleashing of nationalist sentiment brought about by the loosening of central control and freedom of political activity. While market reforms threatened to render a large percentage of the central bureaucracy redundant, nationalist movements posed the same challenge for the main Soviet institutions of power, especially the central state police and the army. The very reason for the existence of these institutions was menaced by independence for the republics. Until August 19, however, it seemed that an agreement had been reached for a renewed union with decreased but still substantial central powers. It is difficult to say how much the pace of reform until August had been determined by intrinsic "technical" difficulties, and how much had been due to obstacles of a political nature. Gorbachev now claims that he overestimated the political obstacles and could have moved forward more decisively with economic reform by mobilizing liberal democrats.[3] With the failure of the attempted coup, conditions had clearly been created for eliminating the political opposition to reform, and for engaging in a more concerted attack on the basic economic problems. But instead the new political conditions gave rise to a fundamental change in the main goals of reform. To understand the new situation, it is necessary to have a clear idea of the specific nature of the reform process itself, prior to the August events.

Market Socialism

A Canadian evening news report in July of 1991 announced a feature study of "capitalism in the USSR." After billing what was to come as an outbreak of private property in the heartland of communism, the actual account of the "new" U.S.S.R. was something less than what one might have expected. Instead of a portrait of a Soviet entrepreneur making millions through ownership of something more substantive than a sausage stand, what the CBC presented were several interviews with workers who had bought out their plant from the state. They had borrowed capital for this purpose from their industrial customers, for whom they promised, in return, timely delivery of products at a fixed price for a certain period of time. The result reportedly was positive. Workers worked harder and better, and earned more money, and the customers were satisfied with what they received. If this is capitalism, it is not what is typically regarded as such. Rather than private ownership, with decision-making power in the hands of a few owners and their representatives, in this case ownership had shifted from the state to the direct producers as a whole.

A major motive force for worker ownership is the abandonment of unprofitable enterprises by owners seeking greater profits elsewhere. But for cooperative market socialism to be viable it is not enough to show that worker ownership of industries may be a necessity for enterprises that are uninteresting to capitalist owners, uncompetitive in the world market—as is true of the vast majority of enterprises in the former socialist world—or have been abandoned by their capitalist owners because the technology is outmoded and labor expensive relative to alternative possibilities in other parts of the world. While the buyout of lagging economic enterprises may save the jobs of workers in the short run, in the long run they still face the harsh realities of an increasingly competitive world.

What is needed is a future-oriented perspective, which shows that private ownership and the profit motive, as the dominant form of economic organization, increasingly impede the economic advancement of society. It is necessary to argue that worker ownership can incorporate the main features of the emerging economic revolution more fully, as well as more humanely, than the capitalist method.

If the central feature of the new technology is the primary role of knowledge, rather than physical effort, the production of knowledge is something intrinsically interesting. It is not necessary to threaten creative minds with unemployment in order to get them to work. What they need is freedom. The level of performance required by advanced technology requires greater independence on the part of the workers, and the capacity to determine the course of production themselves. Hence, cooperative ownership is not only a way of preserving "second-rate" enterprises; it is also the key to creating first-rate ones.

No doubt the highly educated scientists and professionals of the socialist world felt that the centrally planned form of socialism was an obstacle to creative work. It is understandable that the idea of reforming socialism as a way of "saving the system" was treated with suspicion. They therefore have tended to embrace capitalism as a system that allows the individual to exercise initiative. Clearly, there is a great increase in creative potential when decision making power passes from a small number of central planners who try to come to an agreement on a single approach to a complex society to a much wider number of individuals, capitalist owners of enterprises, who have room to experiment with different approaches. But the famous initiative promoted by capitalism is still confined to a tiny fraction of society. Giant industries stifle smaller ones, and management decisions channel scientific and technical energies in paths where short term profits often dictate the suppression of advanced technologies. Cooperative socialism opens up the possibility of liberating the initiatives of the majority of workers.

The Essence of Perestroika

To understand the essence of the struggle between Gorbachev's reform and the reforms demanded by supporters of Yeltsin, it is necessary to be clear that Gorbachev never claimed to be creating a capitalist economy (and still does not recommend this).[4] What he convinced even most old-time Soviet conservatives of was the need for replacing a fully centralized regulation of the economy with a more decentralized economy, in which market forces would play a major role in determining the success or failure of enterprises. Cost accounting in individual enterprises was to replace many (not all) of the decisions of central planners by decisions of the immediate producers and managers, and the consumers. Under these conditions, ownership of industries could pass increasingly into the hands of the direct producers.

This objective helps to explain an important motivating factor behind recent changes in the U.S.S.R. In addition to the threat that perestroika posed to central state economic institutions, there was also a threat to local industrial and agricultural management as a result of the fact that the market reforms proposed by Gorbachev were *socialist* market reforms. The main form of property was to remain social, not private. Decentralization meant that the scope of state property was to be diminished, while that of cooperative property was to be increased. In many cases the formation of small-scale "cooperatives" were in fact thinly-disguised forms of private property, since the equality of participants was largely fictitious. However in large-scale enterprises, cooperative management, with significant worker involvement including the election of managers, was a more likely outcome, at least in the long run.

Previously the authority and privileges of management were backed by a powerful central state. A breakdown of central economic planning in its strictest form, as once existed in the time of Stalin, took place over the years as the economy became more complex, and second-generation managers replaced first generation revolutionaries. This transition to a kind of feudalistic socialism meant increased power for industrial and agricultural managers. Primitive capitalism began to develop alongside official socialism, as barter relations between enterprises and black market production grew increasingly important. Perestroika was a response to the "stagnation" caused by such developments. Market relations that had appeared in a complex "parallel economy" should be brought into the official economy.

As long as the reformed economy adhered to the principle of social ownership, the situation of the traditional management was increasingly vulnerable. The reforms left managers without the backing of the central state, and potentially without the private economy that had been infiltrating the public one and in which the bureaucracy, simultaneously functioning in the official state-socialist system and the emerging primitive-capitalist one often played a key role. The manager was left face-to-face with workers who, thanks to the market reforms, would have a more direct stake in successful economic activity. The alternative was either the growing power of workers or the legal protections that would come with private ownership. To preserve previous economic privileges, therefore, the Soviet managerial class had an interest in blocking reforms until they could become full fledged capitalist reforms, with a government willing to facilitate the transfer of ownership to former managers and their partners in the underground economy.

Hence, the paradox that among the leaders of the coup of August 19 were admirers of Augusto Pinochet, the Chilean general who destroyed the socialist government of Salvadore Allende after a U.S. backed military coup. The Soviet coup of August 19 was not simply an attempt to roll back the clock and reestablish the old command-administrative socialism of the past. It apparently brought together supporters of quite different trends who were united in opposition to the socialist market reforms of Gorbachev.

Hence, Gorbachev's reforms were "moderate" for three different reasons: (1) because of the inherent difficulties of introducing market prices in the context of the centralized Soviet economy; (2) because of the need to appease a traditional power structure—in the central state bureaucracy, in the institutions of power, in management of individual enterprises—that was being gradually undermined by the changes; (3) and because this was a reform process within the context of socialism—of social ownership of the main means of production, but social ownership increasingly in the form of cooperative worker ownership, rather than state ownership.

Critics of Gorbachev "from the left" (in the classic sense of this term) have argued that Gorbachev had failed to appeal sufficiently to workers to take advantage of possibilities opened up by reform for self-managed enterprises. In fact, in some cases the Soviet government positively opposed workers when they did attempt this, as when coal workers went on strike for control over a large share of their product—following in fact the stated ideas of perestroika. However, in the days before the August coup, Gorbachev had to appease "conservatives" interested in preserving as much as possible of the old power structure. While there was general agreement about the need for price reform, the question of effective ownership and control was in dispute. The term "market economy" was used by proponents of fundamentally different long range perspectives. Until August, the outcome of the struggle between contending forces seemed to favor the Gorbachev "centrist" position.

Soviet "liberals" point out that the leaders of the coup were all appointees of Gorbachev, who, in some cases, had to twist the arm of parliament to get its support. Hence, they argue, Gorbachev himself was partly responsible for the coup of August 19. But this position assumes that Gorbachev ought to have followed the pro-capitalist line that was increasingly favored by prominent liberal reformers. The liberals, on whom Gorbachev had originally relied, had become convinced that only a full turn to private ownership would solve the country's economic problems. Since Gorbachev maintained his commitment to social ownership, with a combination of state and worker cooperative forms of ownership remaining dominant over private ownership, the pro-capitalist liberals turned away from his government. Complicating matters was the slow pace of introducing the limited market reforms envisaged in the program of perestroika. Gorbachev now regrets having not engaged more forcefully in these reforms, mobilizing liberals in this effort, while preserving the general socialist outlook.[5] Such a policy might have prevented the defections of the liberals. Hence, Gorbachev was increasingly dependent on the "conservatives," members of the old "apparat" whom he mistakenly believed would at least follow his leadership. So liberals themselves should take a share of the blame for having attempted to force an increasingly radical, pro-capitalist policy instead of bolstering Gorbachev's reformed-socialist one.

Implications of the Coup for Soviet Development

The anti-bureaucratic economics of Gorbachev pointed to the desirability of transferring ownership of large-scale productive property from complete control by the state to significant control by worker cooperatives. This direction was not only the result of ideological motives, but seemed to be dictated by obvious economic necessity. Just as no capitalist wants the outmoded steel plant in Sault Sainte Marie, so no international capitalist wants those of the former U.S.S.R. There may be a few exceptions such as the giant Togliatti auto plant where 30 per cent of ownership was acquired by Fiat. Of course there are also the great natural resources of the countries of the former Soviet Union.

On the other hand, the Soviet liberals have pushed for pro-capitalist shock therapy. Proponents of drastic action argue that it is better to make the transition to a market economy, meaning a capitalist one, quickly. It's not a good idea, they say, to pull teeth out slowly, because the patient might have the chance to knock out a few of the dentist's before the operation is over.

Gorbachev has recognized that what might be possible to do to fifteen million people in a Germany that has some considerable wealth to cushion the blow and absorb some of the chaos, cannot be done in a country of nearly 300 million. Still if Gorbachev has proceeded cautiously, price rises and shortages, as well as incipient unemployment, made him most unpopular. The worst, famine, seemed always to be around the corner. Economic reforms and democracy did not bring a better way of life to the Soviet people. Such discontent appeared to some to create a popular basis for an anti-reform *coup d'etat*.

There were other reasons for a profound sense of alienation that gripped Soviet society. Thanks to the new press freedom of *glasnost*, an intrinsic part of Gorbachev's perestroika, seventy-four years of history, in which people believed they were working and sacrificing for a better future, were painted in much of the popular media as a gigantic fraud. Communist ideology, which had given a sense of purpose to life, had been widely dismissed as an unnatural illusion. A sense of Soviet greatness in world affairs had been lost thanks to changes in Eastern Europe and elsewhere. In reply, the coup leaders believed it was better to be respected if disapproved of than to be laughed at or pitied by the peoples of the West.

Clearly, the extent of popular discontent was overestimated by the coup plotters. But one wonders what would have been the result had Gorbachev employed the shock therapy recommended by some economists. The economic dislocation would have been much further advanced. The discontent, much greater.

The failure of the coup is a testimonial to six years of radical democratic reforms. While Yeltsin's role in defeating the assault on democracy was crucial, one should not forget that his actions—and those of the people in Moscow and Leningrad who went to the barricades—were made possible only because of the changes patiently brought about by Gorbachev. Moreover, by refusing at gunpoint to sign a statement handing over power, he personally played an indispensable role in frustrating the coup.

The democratic changes that have taken place in Soviet life were accomplished because Gorbachev did not rush into the abyss, because he continually calmed the dominant conservatives while undermining their ability to act in the old way. When they finally realized that it was do or die for the old system of power, it turned out to have been too late. They pulled the old strings of power whose top ends remained on their desks, but there was nobody at the bottom ends to respond. This was especially true of the army. On the one hand, thousands of people went into the street to defend their new lives. On the other hand, the army refused to fire on them when they were given the command. So deeply have the democratic and legal reforms penetrated the Soviet psyche, that the counterrevolutionary junta had to pretend that they were acting legally, that power had been legitimately transferred to them by the illness of the President.

Out of this crisis, which was the trial by fire of the Gorbachev reforms, the esteem of the Soviet President in the eyes of the Soviet peoples may have somewhat recovered. It takes the threat of disaster to make people appreciate what they may have begun to take for granted. Free speech and elections had been regarded by many Russians and members of alienated republics as so much wind and so many windbags. Now they are better appreciated as great achievements of social renewal in a society that was beginning to sink in a quagmire.

But if the coup failed in part because of the success of the democratic political reforms, it also failed because of Gorbachev's reformed socialist economic policy. The failure of the conspirators to pull the old bureaucratic strings is the result of the political and civil libertarian reforms of perestroika. The failure of the coup leaders to find popular support is due to the fact that Gorbachev did not follow the simplistic economic panaceas of Soviet neo-liberals, who have found a welcome mat in the Russian government.

And yet the economic problems that had previously undermined Gorbachev's prestige still remain. Elation after the victory over the conservatives, together with popular attention focused on nationalist issues, has led Yeltsin, with powers yielded by the central government, to employ the shock therapy previously recommended by his advisors. To accomplish this task, it seems that the Russian leadership has decided to focus public attention on national pride to distract it from unemployment and skyrocketing prices.

The dynamics of nationalism has found a new stimulus in the emergence of Russia as a central power intent on achieving its own national interests. Nationalism often takes the form of finding scapegoats in "the others" as an explanation for difficult times. Instead of stressing the democratic reforms that were the main achievement of perestroika, the Russian government now waves the national Russian flag, and recalls the grand days of Tsarist glory. The strong hand, which the coup leaders had attempted to impose on the disintegrating Soviet Union, has been raised now by Russia. The other Republics, including the minorities of Russia itself who occupy fifty percent of Russian territory, defend themselves by asserting their own independence. Gorbachev remains the only individual who can still speak to the hundred nationalities whom history has tied together but who are now arming themselves against one another.

The End of "Nihilistic Socialism"

It remains to be seen whether the project of reformed, market, or cooperative socialism will be revived. The question of whether liberal capitalism has become a universal social system cannot be answered in the affirmative as long as the alternatives have not been given a chance. One form of socialism, described as "Stalinism," has been discredited. I call this "nihilistic socialism" because it had a completely negative attitude to capitalism and any form of market economy. Nihilistic socialism was established in the late twenties in the Soviet Union as a result of Stalin's rise to power. The preceding period of Soviet history, governed by Lenin's "New Economic Policy," was not nihilistic but "dialectical," attempting to combine aspects of capitalism with those of the emerging communist tendencies.[6]

Gorbachev's policy of perestroika was an attempt to revive the spirit of this early period of Soviet history. After the devastation of World War I and the subsequent Civil War, Soviet Russia recovered, thanks to a policy which combined commodity-producing family farms and voluntary cooperatives in the countryside, small private enterprises and state-owned but self-managed large enterprises in the cities. This "market socialist" policy was economically successful, but was destroyed for ideological and political reasons.

The collapse of nihilistic socialism today can only be understood in the context of world history of the twentieth century. Although conditions for its establishment in particular countries were complex, there are certain general causes. While we are today witnessing the final collapse of what was once the Russian Empire of the Tsars, the prolongation of that empire to the present was the result of imperial struggles of the late nineteenth and early twentieth centuries. The vast "feudal" empires of the East, which Marx described as "the Asiatic mode of production"—Russia, China, and those of Islam—were under attack from the imperial capitalist states of the West. The Great Wall of China was rendered porous by the combined battering rams of advanced Western military technology and cheaper goods. Moghul India fell to England, while the Ottoman Empire was subordinated to the Western powers. Russia was jolted out of complacency by defeat in the Crimean War and later by rising capitalist Japan. The Russian state, in large part belonging to Asia, had been attempting to appropriate the scientific and military achievements of Europe since the reign of Peter the Great, at the beginning of the eighteenth century. However, the giant power of Eastern Europe shared many features of great non–European states, above all the relative weakness of its private economy and its authoritarian state centralization.

The old style of life of ancient and proud aristocratic empires was disintegrating under the new high tech weaponry of capitalism. The lives of artisans and peasants too were dislocated by capitalism from without and within. Nihilistic socialism, which is a form of socialism that rejects capitalism rather than (as in the Marxist perspective) builds on it, stems from social classes and national cultures that were threatened with ruin by the advanced world capitalist order. The development of a dependent form of capitalism increasingly made the great Eastern empires hostages to foreign Western capitalism. Nihilistically interpreted socialism appeared to offer an alternative.

History is not a straight path. Nihilistic socialism in Russia and China, and other forms of socialism such as that of the Islamic states, were an historic attempt to bypass the unequal conditions of development imposed by already developed capitalist nations. In the colonial world, the inequality of opportunity provided by the world capitalist order was exponentially magnified. The establishment of nihilistic socialism in the rest of Eastern Europe was essentially the result of external Soviet pressure on socialist regimes that were prevented from following independent policies.

An historic path of development has therefore been undertaken which has attempted to avoid the global capitalist environment, rather than to transform it. This path has reached a dead end, but that does not mean that it went nowhere. Despite great costs imposed on its peoples, it succeeded in many respects. In the U.S.S.R., success in raising the cultural level of the population used to centuries of autocratic rule has created peoples who seek a more democratic and creative form of society.

One form of socialism has therefore been exhausted and discredited. But this is not proof of the eternal triumph of capitalism. The socialism that was defeated was the product of backward nations seeking a simple solution to disruptions produced by the dominant capitalist world environment. The alternative, "dialectical" form of socialism, as a mixture of elements of private, state, and cooperative ownership, was economically successful in Russia in the nineteen twenties, but was destroyed by the turn to nihilistic socialism under Stalin. The attempt to return to this conception of socialism has for now been stopped in the countries of the former Soviet Union. Perestroika was at first blocked by "conservative" opponents of change. Now that these forces have been discredited for the time being, pro-capitalist liberal democrats have hijacked the reforms. The Soviet Union had gone too far down the wrong lane and too few believed in the possibility of finding their way to another one—especially when nearby there are the blaring lights and roaring sounds of the ten lane capitalist highway.

Notes

1. See James Lawler, *Matter and Spirit: The Battle of Metaphysics in Modern Western Philosophy before Kant* (Rochester: University of Rochester Press, 2006); chapters 8 and 9 on Adam Smith.
2. Mikhail Gorbachev, *The August Coup* (London: HarperCollins, 1991).
3. Ibid.
4. Ibid.
5. Ibid.
6. See James Lawler, "Marx as Market Socialist," in Bertell Ollman, ed., *Market Socialism: The Debate Among Socialists* (New York: Routledge, 1998), 23–52.

About the Contributors

Donald A. **Biggs**, a visiting scholar at Siena College, is a professor emeritus of educational psychology and the former director of urban education programs at the University at Albany. Prior to his work at Albany, he was a professor of educational psychology at the University of Minnesota where he served as the director of Student Life Studies and Planning and assistant to the vice president for student affairs. He has served as a consultant to many national and international organizations. His research interests include moral development, citizenship education and urban education. He is the author of several books including *Foundations of Ethical Counseling* and *The Dictionary of Counseling*. His academic work in Russia spanned a ten-year period, beginning in the spring of 1990.

Aaron **Bindman** is a professor emeritus of sociology and former chair of the Sociology Department at the State University of New York at New Paltz. He taught at the University of Saskatchewan after completing a Ph.D. in sociology of labor and industrial relations at the University of Illinois. He was a labor organizer before and after serving in the U.S. Army in World War II, until his retirement in 1987. He received two Fulbright awards and conducted research and lectured on worker self-management in Australia, New Zealand, Sweden, Yugoslavia and the U.S.S.R. He spent the winter of 1986 in Moscow as a State University of New York–Moscow State University Faculty Exchange scholar, coinciding with the 27th Party Congress of the Communist Party of the Soviet Union, the first presided over by Mikhail Gorbachev.

William J. **Byrne** III is a professor emeritus of sociology at Orange County Community College of the State University of New York. He earned a Ph.D. in sociology of education from the University of Denver. His teaching, counseling and coaching career spans 46 years from 1956 to 2002. He was the recipient of the SUNY Chancellor's Award for Excellence in Teaching. He is in the Dutchess County Baseball Hall of Fame, and as he approaches the eighth decade of his life, he still plays in a competitive softball league. His selection as a State University of New York–Moscow State University exchange scholar in 1990 provided him the opportunity to forge a link between his earlier career in baseball and his subsequent career as a sociologist.

Freda **Casner** (1914–2013) taught U.S.-U.S.S.R. comparative social structures and human services in the Sociology Department at the State University of New York at New Paltz from 1979 to 1995. She was a State University of New York Faculty Exchange Scholar in 1983 and 1988 in the Sociology Department of Moscow State University, where she lectured and carried out research on Soviet education and the changing status of women in Soviet society. Earlier in her career she taught Russian and French language and civilization, and organized exchange programs with Russia at Dutchess Community College. She earned an M.A. in Russian studies from Vassar College. Her scholarly work was supported through National Defense Education Fellowships.

Robert **Colesante** is a professor of education at Siena College. He received his Ph.D. from the University at Albany in the Department of Educational Psychology and Statistics where he developed his interests in moral development, urban youth development, and the use of narratives in teaching. Recent articles have appeared in the *School Community Journal* and the *Journal of Moral Education*. He is co-director of the Saturday Scholars Program at Siena College, an enrichment program for urban middle school youth.

James **Lawler** is an associate professor of philosophy at the State University of New York at Buffalo. He was a State University of New York Faculty Exchange Scholar at Moscow State University for extended periods in 1978, 1984–1985, and 1992. Gorbachev's reinvigoration of Soviet life with glasnost and perestroika inspired his participation in debate in Bertell Ollman, ed., *Market Socialism: The Debate Among Socialists*. His publications include *The Existentialist Marxism of Jean-Paul Sartre; The God Tube: Uncovering the Hidden Spiritual Message in Pop Culture;* and *Matter and Spirit: The Battle of Metaphysics in Modern Western Philosophy before Kant*. His book *The Intelligible World: Metaphysical Revolution in the Genesis of Kant's Theory of Morality* is forthcoming.

Carla **Lipsig-Mummé** is a professor of work and labour studies at York University, Canada. She has taught at Queen's University and Université Laval in Canada. In the last decade, she was research professor of political and social inquiry at Monash University. She has been a union organizer of garment workers and has organized with Cesar Chavez' United Farmworkers. She has also been an educator and negotiator for unions in Québec. In the early 1990s she worked with trade unions in Russia. Founding director of the Centre for Research on Work and Society, she directs the Work in a Warming World research program at York University. She is the author of more than 200 works that have been translated into a dozen languages and a frequent commentator in international media.

Dorothy S. **McClellan** is a professor of criminal justice and Regents Professor at Texas A&M University–Corpus Christi. She earned a Ph.D. from the Rockefeller College of the State University of New York. She was an exchange scholar at Moscow State University in 1982 and 1984–1985. She returned to Russia for extended academic visits in 1989, 1990, 1993, 2004, 2005, and 2008. She has published widely on international justice issues, women and criminal justice, juvenile delinquency, and American prisons. She is the recipient of three Fulbright awards and is a Piper Outstanding Professor for the State of Texas. *American Prisons, Foreign & Domestic*, a documentary she produced with Nikola Knez, received the WorldFest International Film Festival 2012 Special Jury Award for film production and a platinum award for its screenplay.

James E. **McClellan**, Jr. (1922–2001) was a professor emeritus of philosophy of education at the State University of New York at Albany. Over the course of his career he held professorships at Columbia University, Temple University and Texas A&M University–Corpus Christi. He served as chief educational consultant to the U.S. Office of Economic Opportunity. His major works include *Education and the New America, Toward an Effective Critique of American Education, Philosophy of Education*, hundreds of scholarly articles, and a novel. At Columbia University he led college presidents and correspondents on tours of the Soviet Union in 1958 and 1959. He participated in the SUNY–Moscow State University Faculty Exchange Program in 1982 and returned for extended study trips in 1985, 1989, 1990, and 1993.

John J. **Neumaier** was president of the State University of New Paltz and of Moorhead State University. He is a professor emeritus at Empire State College (SUNY) and visiting professor of philosophy at Goethe Universität. A native of Frankfurt am Main, he came to the United States in 1940 and served in the U.S. Army during World War II. He earned a Ph.D. in philosophy from the University of Minnesota. He was an exchange scholar at Moscow State University for three semesters: 1979–1980, 1984–1985, and 1990–1991. His publications include numerous journal articles and books on higher education and Soviet thought. He was co-editor with Sara F. Luther and Howard L. Parsons of *Diverse Perspectives on Marxist Philosophy: East and West*. In addition, he was a columnist for the *Daily Freeman* in Kingston, New York, for twenty-four years.

Howard L. **Parsons** (1918–2000) was a professor emeritus of philosophy at the University of Bridgeport where he served as chairman of the Philosophy Department. He received a B.A. and Ph.D. from the University of Chicago. In 1980 and 1990 he was a visiting professor at Moscow State University. He was a prolific writer who authored and edited several books and contributed over two hundred articles and seven monographs to philosophical, religious, and educational journals. His major works include *Humanism and Marx's Thought*; *Man, East and West*; *Self, Global Issues, and Ethics*; *Marx and Engels on Ecology*; *Marxism, Christianity, and Human Values*; and *Christianity in the USSR*. He was a founding member of the Society for the Philosophical Study of Marxism, and served as its president and editor of its proceedings.

Herman **Schwendinger** and Julia **Schwendinger** (1926–2013) have published collaborative articles and books on American sociology, human rights, crimes against women and delinquency for more than sixty years. Their seminal writings have received the Distinguished Scholar Award from the Crime, Law and Deviance Section of the American Sociological Association, the Outstanding Scholar Award from the Society for the Study of Social Problems, the Tappan Award from the Western Society of Criminology, the Major Achievement Award from the Critical Criminology Division of the American Society of Criminology, and the Special Recognition Award for Scholarship and Research on Women and Crime from the Women's Division of the American Society of Criminology. The Schwendingers are counted among the *Fifty Key Thinkers in Criminology* from the 19th century to modern times. Julia co-founded the first anti-rape crisis group in the United States. Herman is a professor emeritus of sociology at the State University of New York at New Paltz. He is the recipient of the State University of New York Excellence Award. He and Julia participated in the State University of New York Faculty Exchange Scholar Program at Moscow State University for the 1988 fall semester.

Index

academic exchange programs: American educators, group of upper-echelon 205; brain-drain and 174–175; Christian fellowship group from Midwestern U.S. state 178; cross-cultural issues with exchange programs 179–185; exchange programs in sociology 169; first university-to-university exchange program between Russia and the U.S. (1976–1977) 127; with former Eastern Bloc countries 169; Gorbachev encouraged 7; "international education offices" in Moscow 178; International Research and Exchanges Board and 175; pessimism of Soviet university students and faculty about the future 7; Soviet faculty's thoughts about 176–179; State University of New York and Moscow State University (SUNY-MSU) 98–99, 126, 137, 155; United States and European universities solicited the brightest and most talented Soviet students 175; universities, culture of the 171–172; *see also* Moscow State University
Academy of Science 27, 127, 132, 190, 195, 200; institutes of philosophy within 189
Acts 2:44 59
Alexei (scholar's scholar) 18–19
All-Russian Conference of Orthodox-Patriotic Forces 43
All-Union Council of Trade Unions 122, 135
All-Union Scientific Conference 194
al-Saud, Bin Salman (astronaut Sultan) 9
American embassy (Moscow) 85, 101, 111, 159
anarchy 23, 40
Andreev, Leonid (author) 44
anti–Communism 111
anti–Perestroika forces 168
anti–Semitism 112–114, 120
anti–Yeltsin, post–Party forces 119
anti–Zionists 101
apparatchiks (Communist party member) 97, 138, 145, 150
aristocracy in Ukraine 17
armaments expenditures 213
Armand, Inessa (Women's Section head) 156
Armenia 65, 113–114, 172–173

arms race 8, 26, 102, 213–214
Asiatic despotism 153, 216
Asiatic mode of production 216, 230
assets, state-owned 148
Association of Librarians 165
Athenians, fifth century BC 19
Athletes in Action 86
authoritarian state centralization 230
authoritarianism 8, 40, 45, 61
autocracy 51
Averentsov, Sergei Sergeyevich 195
Azerbaijan 57, 65, 113, 172, 222

barter 56, 122, 225
baseball, American: 62–63, 66, 69, 72, 77–78, 86–88, 90, 94
baseball cards 78, 88
baseball coaches: American 76, 87; Bryne, William J., III 65–68, 71–72, 75–77, 80, 83, 87–88, 92, 94, 233; Chihriadze, Gela 72; Clark, Dave 85; Cuban 62, 76; Halid 71–73, 74–77, 79, 90–91; Japanese 76, 91; MGU 66; Nicaraguan 62, 76; Russian 69; South Korean 91; Soviet 75–76; Tashkent 80; Varinsky, Valeri 63, 71, 74, 76, 86, 91
baseball, Russian 5, 62–63, 65–68, 70–72, 75–77, 80, 83, 87–92, 94
Beauvoir, Simone de 159
Belarus 2, 207
Belchuk, Alexander (Institute of the International Labor Movement) 127, 132–133
Bell, Daniel (sociologist) 116–117
Biggs, Donald A. 7, 170
Bindman, Aaron 126, 131, 133, 138, 233
black economy (*nomenklatura* capitalism) 120
black markets 13, 20, 147, 150, 225
Bobrova, Maria (Ph.D. candidate) 131, 135
Bolshevik revolution (1917) 49, 104, 107, 188
Bolsheviks 36, 50–51, 53–54, 60–61, 111, 149, 152, 162, 190
bourgeois universalism 220
Boyer, Ernest (State University of New York chancellor) 126
Brezhnev, Leonid (General Secretary): Andrei Sakharov and the Academy of Science 27,

237

190; Bolshevism and 111; bureaucracy's grip on society 150; crisis of legitimacy, "kitchen politics" 143; death 188; and Dnepropetrovsk province party secretary 139; doctrine and paternalism towards East European allies 102; *Gosplan* and 212; income gap 150; last three years 159; neo-Stalinist regime 139; nickname "ballerina" 139; party propaganda rejected 143; and social services 142; war in Afghanistan 64; and "woman question" 160
bribes *(blat)* 56, 147, 150
Bronski, Sergei (astrologer) 35
Brooklyn Dodgers 66, 69, 72, 94
Bruner, Jerome 167
Bulgakov, Sergei 45
"bureaucratic hacks" 153
bureaucracy 41, 47, 56, 138–139, 142, 147–148, 150, 153; centralization 130; international education offices 178; party-state 146, 149; policy-making 138; Soviet 89, 129, 144
Buzgalin, Alexander 118
Byelorussian Federation of Unions 123
Byelorussian republic 57
Byrne, William J., III 65–68, 71–72, 75–77, 80, 83, 87–88, 92, 94, 233

campaign of repression 32
camps, forced-labor 139
Canadian Broadcasting Corporation (CBC) 223
Capital 55
capitalism: of Adam Smith 217; barter and black market 225; black economy (*nomenklatura* capitalism) 120; CBC news report on 223; Christian church's approval 60; civil society and 206; class structure of 205; class system and 144; class war and 52; collapse prophesied 144; Communist Party elites 8, 215; "democratic capitalism" and private enterprise 97; deregulated 215; East Germans and 221–222; economic base of 3, 204; free market 41, 216; and Gorbachev 209; greed and 2, 16; idealization of American 146; ideology of 116; individual initiative vs. central planning 224; industrial democracy and 119; Lenin's "New Economic Policy" 107, 109, 119, 148, 217, 229; market-oriented economy 105; Marxist 40, 51, 54; and material conditions for progress 205; mode of production 203–204; necessity to eliminate 203; neo-liberal, deregulated 215; peace vs. 204–205; promises disaster 207; robbery 52; romanticized notion 173; Russian culture and 89; Russian transition to 216; socialism vs. 39, 107–108, 143, 153, 230–231; state 148; state-monopoly 153; struggle against class structure 205; universal social system and liberal capitalism 229; war and imperialism 3; West transition 216; Western materialist viewpoint 54–55; Western Protestantism and individualism 43; Western socialism evolution from 216; worker-directed, 119; Yeltsin's shock therapy 7, 96, 164, 216
Carnegie, Dale 48
carpetbaggers 124
Casner, Freda 7, 155, 157, 159–160, 234
Catherine the Great 15
Caucasus 2
Caucasus Mountains 69
CBC *see* Canadian Broadcasting Corporation (CBC)
CCCP National Team 62, 90
censorship in libraries 96
Center for Public Opinion and Market Research 163
Center for Research on Work and Society (CRWS) 123–124, 124*n*1
Central Committee of the CPSU 32, 38, 48, 139, 143, 154*n*5; Mikhail Sergeyevich and 208–209; *Zhenotdel* (Women's Section) of 156, 162
centralized control 6, 40
Chekhov, Anton (author) 18
Chernenko, Konstantin (General Secretary, Communist Party) 3
Cheskov, M.A. 147–148
Chihriadze, Gela (Georgian baseball coach) 72
Chinese Cultural Revolution 50
Christianity 23, 35, 59–60, 86, 172, 178, 195
Christianity in the USSR 235
Christmas 17, 23, 66
civil bureaucrats 138
civil society 40–41, 144–145, 165, 206
Civil War 38, 46, 65, 146, 148–149, 156, 229
Clark, Dave 85
class: and ethnic division 117; exploitation 206; *nomenklatura* (class-like group) 32, 36, 52, 146–147, 151–153; structure of capitalism 205; struggle 36, 38, 40, 104, 108; system and capitalism 144; war and capitalism 52
cockroaches 66, 81–82, 158
Cohen, Stephen (Russian scholar) 212
Cold War 49, 203, 218; deprivations and stresses of 46; political origins of 93–94; politics 8, 213; Russian version 182–183; U.S. Progressive Party's defeat and 8; Vietnam War and 94
command economy, centralized 2, 46–47, 148–149
Commonwealth of Independent States 1
communal apartments 142
Communist Manifesto 217
Communist Party Congress, 28th 5
Communist Party of the Russian Federation 44, 52
Communist Party of the Soviet Union (CPSU): anti-Semitism of leaders 113; apparatchiks

97; authority of leaders 129; baseball and 72; centrists around Gorbachev 41; clichés 23; conservative and reactionary forces 102; constitutional right to rule 222; elections 52; elites as beneficiaries of capitalism 8, 215; extreme right-wing authoritarians and, 52; and Gorbachev 5, 92, 128; government payment of bills for 64; hegemonic power in U.S.S.R. 8; hostility of citizens toward 27; ideological hegemony of 97; and industrial workers 26; membership in 199; national liberation struggles 26; nationalists in the Soviet Republics 146; orthodox *partinost* praise 95–96; policies 154*n*5; postwar children joined 14; Russian parliament outlawed 220; Shevardnadze's foreign policy 102; Social Democratic Party vs. 199; Social-Democratic Platform and the first congress of 44; socialist orientation of 103; Yeltsin's career within 111; Zoya Pukhova and 152, 161; *see also* Brezhnev, Leonid; Central Committee of the CPSU; glasnost and perestroika; Gorbachev, Mikhail; Khrushchev, Nikita
Communist state system 216
concentration camp society 39
Confederation of Anarchisto-Syndicalists 43, 45
Congress of Peoples' Deputies 19, 32
Conquest, Robert (historian) 209
conservative cultural movement 37
consumer shortages 145
consumerism 37, 48, 84, 89, 145
cooperatives, voluntary 229
corruption 4, 27, 32, 36, 97, 105, 138, 150–152, 164, 210, 213
Cosmos Hotel (Moscow) 81
Council of Ministers 32, 135, 171, 200
countercultural revolution 37
counterrevolutionary junta 228
CPSU *see* Communist Party of the Soviet Union (CPSU)
Crimean War 230
cronyism 213
CRWS *see* Center for Research on Work and Society (CRWS)
Cyrillic alphabet 13, 83, 159

Dadamyan, G.G. (sociology) 141
DeMaio, Ernie (U.S. trade union representative) 127
democracy 121
democratic movements 31, 146
Deng Xiaoping 32
dialectical materialism 18, 189, 191, 193–194
"dialectical stagnation" 188
dictatorship *(diktatura)* 30–32, 130
divorce rate 160
Dolan, Edward (economist) 110

Dostoyevsky, Fyodor (novelist) 18
Driachlov, Nikolai Ivanovich (sociology professor) 127–128, 131–133, 135, 157–159

East Germany 119, 221–222
economic privileges 151, 225
Einstein, Albert (theoretical physicist) 27, 190
Eisenhower-Khrushchev thaw 206
employment discrimination against women 164
Engels, Friedrich (German social scientist) 46, 49, 56, 211; *Origin of the Family, Private Property and the State* 155, 157
Erhard, Werner 48
Evangelical-Christian Baptists 35
existentialism 35, 44
extreme nationalists 52

family farms 229
family subsidies 160
far-right lunatic fringe 218
fascist ideology 116
Federation of Russian Unions 122
feminism, 42, 57, 155–156, 159, 162–163
First International Conference of Trade Unionism and Self-Management 6
free market 37, 40–41, 44, 52, 64–65, 111, 145, 150, 181, 198, 215–216
Friedman, Milton (economist) 40
Fusfeld, Ira (*Daily Freeman* editor) 97

Gaidar, Yegor (Yeltsin's deputy prime minister) 96
Garvey, Steve (baseball player) 86
gender equality 3, 207
gender roles 42, 59
General Confederation of Trade Unions 122
Georgia 2, 68, 70–73, 75, 77, 89–90, 150
German Academy of Science 27, 190
glasnost and perestroika: academic exchange programs 7; background arguments 25–26; central authority 146; Chase Manhattan Bank and 109; free speech and elections 228; future 30–33; Gorbachev's policies 8, 96, 132, 160–162, 187, 218, 224–227, 229, 234; at Moscow State University 3, 191; National Westminster Bank and 109; openness and reconstruction 167; optimism in universities 19; philosophy and ideology changes 99; political and civil libertarian reforms 228; press freedom 227; problems 222–223; Russian academics and 3–4; Russian culture and 89; Russian feminist thinkers and 155; socialist restructuring 26; Western business investments and 78; women and 7; *see also* Communist Party of the Soviet Union (CPSU)
"globalization" 218
Goebbels, Joseph (Hitler's Minister for Propaganda) 98

Goodwill Games (Seattle) 90
Gorbachev, Mikhail Sergeyevich (General Secretary of the Communist Party): academic exchange programs with West 7; anti-bureaucratic economics 227; "anti-perestroika" forces 184; Armenia and Azerbaijan 65; brain drain 112; bureaucratic planning structure 128, 134; centrists 41; constructive leadership 113; cooperation among collectives 134; coups 4, 217, 227–229; democratization 8, 220; economic crisis 143; elected general secretary of Communist Party 3, 6, 126, 157; feminist responses 155; Five-Year Plan 160; free speech and elections 228; glasnost 92; higher education 168–169; juvenile delinquency 161; legal standards to judge government's actions 168; Ligachev, attempted defeat 93; marriage 160; Moscow Federation of Trade Unions general strike 121; Moscow State University 3, 27; nationalism 229; "New Thinking" 102, 107–109, 159, 162; nihilistic socialism, collapse of 229–231; openness and restructuring, called for 7; opposition from opponents of market reforms 222; perestroika policies 8, 96, 132, 160–162, 187, 218, 224–227, 229; political groupings 121; reconstruction programs 180–181; referendum (March 17) on Gorbachev's plan for the preservation of the Union 102; restructuring Soviet governance 95; Russian feminist responses 7; socialist market reforms 216–217, 225–226, 228; struggles with Yeltsin 6; 27th Congress 128, 155; 28th Congress 92–93; Zaslavskaya, Tatiana (sociologist) 163; *see also* glasnost and perestroika
Gorbachev, Raisa 3–4
Gordon, Lou (AFLCIO) 127
Gosplan (Soviet planning system) 28, 31, 144–145, 149, 210, 212
Graham, Loren 191
Great Mob Wars 5
Great Patriotic War 38, 53–54, 66, 68, 72, 74
Great War 140
Gryaznov, A.G. (British philosophy professor) 195
gulag 19
Gulf War protest 101

Halid (head coach) 71–73, 74–77, 79, 90–91
hard currency 22, 29, 78, 105, 108, 150, 164, 178, 200
Hegel, Georg Wilhelm Friedrich 5, 55, 195, 197, 216, 219
Hellenic city-states 213
higher education system 168–169
Hitler, Adolf 27, 116, 190
hockey coaches, youth 87
Homo Sovieticus 3

homosexuality 42
Hotel Cosmos (Moscow) 83
Hotel Intourist (Moscow) 83
Hotel National (Moscow) 16
Hotel Rossiya (Moscow) 92
Hotel Uzbekistan (Tashkent, Uzbekistan) 77, 80
House of China (Leninskii Prospekt, Moscow) 15
human rights 41, 51, 59, 174, 219

identity card *(Kartochky)* 101
IMF domination 207
Imperial Academy (1724) 189
income, per capita 152
income gap 150
individualism 43–45, 48, 55, 180
industrial democracy 119
industrial unions 32, 122
inflation 36, 57, 65, 110, 120, 122, 164
Institute for Applied Labor Research (IRAT) 124
Institute for Socio-Economic Studies of the Population 160
Institute of Marxism-Leninism 64
intelligentsia 25, 31–32, 103–105, 107–108, 176, 191, 207, 210, 213; *see also* Moscow State University
inter-ethnic conflicts 14, 114
International Labour Movement 132
International Olympic Committee 62
International Research and Exchanges Board 175
International Tchaikovsky Competition 89
International Trade Center (Moscow) 16
International Women's Day 104
Inter-Republican Council of Works Collectives 123
Iraqi invasion of Kuwait 101
IRAT *see* Institute for Applied Labor Research (IRAT)
Irene (journalist) 88, 94
Ivanov, Vyechislav 195
Izvestia 143

Jews 43, 58, 112–114
John XXII, Pope 60
joint ventures 17, 22, 36, 107–109, 169
juvenile delinquency 161

Kabaidze, Vladimir (general director) 153
Kagarlitsky, Boris (sociology professor) 120–121, 140–141, 143, 150, 153–154n2
Kazakhstan 2, 137, 140
Kerblay, Baslie H. 156–157
Keynesian welfare state 218
KGB 13, 29, 32, 41, 65
Khrushchev, Nikita (General Secretary) 21, 53, 139, 150; forced out of office 139, 205;

Index

free speech experiment 139; replaced by Leonid Brezhnev 139; rhetoric of socialist reconstruction 205; women's dual roles 160
Khrushchev Spring 139
Kierkegaard, Søren 35
"kleptocracy" 215
Klimenkova, Tatiana (feminist) 165
Kollontai, Alexandra (Russian feminist) 156, 161–162
Komsomol (youth and young adult organization) 129, 140
Kosichev, Anatoli (professor) 133, 135, 192
Kotz, David 130
Krugler, Dima (second baseman) 90
Krupskaya, Nadezhda (politician) 190
Kuleshov, Mihail (Timber, Paper and Woodworker Union) 127
Kulikov, Vladimir (pastor) 35
Kuvakin, V.A. 197
Kuzmich, Ivan 17

labor councils 122
Latvian People's Front Movement, 137
Lawler, James 234
Lenin, Vladimir Ilyich (Russian communist revolutionary) 156, 169, 184, 197, 217; "New Economic Policy" 107, 109, 119, 148, 217, 229; tomb 16, 96
Leningrad University 7, 170
Leningradski Train Station 66
"liberal democracy" 219, 231
Ligachev, Yegor 152–153
Lipsig-Mummé, Carla 123
Literaturnaya Gazyeta, 141, 143
Little League Championship Series (Williamsport, Pennsylvania) 63
living conditions, Soviet 95, 99, 156
living standards 95, 105, 142, 145–146, 152, 213
Loud, Oliver S. (professor) 204
Lozansky, Edward 110
Lunacharsky, Anatoly Vasilyevich (Marxist revolutionary) 190
Luther, Sara (Sally) 6, 98–99, 101, 112
Luther, Sara F. 6
Lysenko, Trofim Denisovich (Soviet biologist and agronomist) 27, 33*n*1

mafia 4, 29, 36, 40–41, 52, 60, 210
Maharaja (guru) 35
Malia, Martin (historian) 209, 214
Mal'kova, Zoya (Intourist guide) 205–206
Mamonova, Tatiana (feminist) 162
managerial elite, 32
market deregulation (1992), 215
market economy 48, 61, 64, 84, 106–108, 119, 145, 149, 157, 162, 164, 169, 176, 216, 226–227, 229
market socialism 223–224
market society, pro-capitalist 215

Marx, Karl (German philosopher) 43, 44, 55, 184, 194–195, 197–198, 201, 211, 216; Asiatic mode of production 216, 230; *Capital* 55; class struggle 40; *Communist Manifesto* 217; critique of Western European capitalism 51; historical doctrines of 46; historical evolution and socialism vs. capitalism 5, 54; revolutionary traditions of 26; secular faith in 40; social inequality, economic explanation of 56; social power, purpose of 31; surplus value 56; thesis on Feuerbach 97; "utopian socialists" 49; Western path of historical development 216
Marxism 35–36, 40, 44, 45–53, 55, 57, 197, 218
Marxism-Leninism 41, 115, 218; courses in 99, 173, 189, 191; erosion of belief in socialism and Marxism 45; free market principles vs. 111; fundamental truths 198; ideology 41–42, 115, 209; perestroika and glasnost vs. 35; political theory 188; rejection 116; "renewed socialism" vs. 121; repression under 116; trickle-down theory 38; utopian concept of socialism 49
Marxist Platform Group 118
maternity leave 160
May Day 66–67
McClellan, Dorothy S. 7, 11–12, 19, 22, 30, 33, 187, 200, 207–208, 234
McClellan, James E., Jr. 7, 11–12, 19, 22, 30, 33, 187, 200, 207–208, 235
McDonald's (restaurant) 32, 67, 81–82, 86
Medvedev, Roy 121
Medvedev, Vadim 27
Melville, Yuri K. 195
memorial to the Unknown Soldier 68
Mendeleyev Chemical Institute of Moscow team 89–90
Mensheviks 54
Menshikov, Stanislav 149
Metropol Hotel (Moscow) 205
militarists 52
military 4, 9, 26, 32, 40–41, 49, 64–65, 69, 73, 90, 96, 103, 120, 150, 213, 214
Ministry of Higher Education 31, 200
Moghul India 230
Moldavia 2, 172, 192
monarchy 41, 52, 138
Moscow Academy of Labor and Social Relations 112
Moscow Aviation TEAM 71
Moscow Centre for Gender Studies 165
Moscow Conservatory 89
Moscow Federation of Trade Unions 121–123
Moscow legal collective 137
Moscow *limitchiki* 142
Moscow Musical Theater 89
Moscow News 41, 50, 102–103, 105, 134, 153
Moscow State University 2–3, 7, 12–13, 19–24, 30–31, 35, 43, 45, 47, 53–54, 56, 58, 60–61,

68, 82–84, 97–100, 103–104, 108, 111, 112, 126–127, 131–133, 138, 140, 157–158, 171–174, 176–179, 187–202, 207; "academic hierarchy" 173–174; Averentsov, Sergei Sergeyevich 195; Biggs, Donald A. 7, 170; Bindman, Aaron 126, 131, 133, 138, 233; Bobrova, Maria (Ph.D. candidate) 131, 135; Byrne III, William J. 66, 94, 233; Casner, Freda 7, 155, 157, 159–160, 234; Dadamyan, G.G. (sociology) 141; Dasha and Dimitri 20; Department of Sociology 127; Department of the Theory and History of Religion and Scientific Atheism 34–35; Driachlov, Nikolai Ivanovich (sociology professor) 127–128, 131–133, 135, 157–159; exchange scholars 2; friendliness toward Americans 59; glasnost and perestroika 3, 191; Gorbachev law degree 3; Gryaznov, A.G. (British philosophy professor) 195; Ivanov, Vyechislav 195; Kagarlitsky, Boris (sociology professor), 140–141, 143, 150, 153–154n2; Kosichev, Anatoli (professor) 133, 135, 192; Kuvakin, V.A. 197; Lawler, James 234; Leonid (senior international scholar) 19–20, 22–23; Lipsig-Mummé, Carla 123; Luther, Sara F. 6; Marina 23; Marxism 30, 34–35, 173, 195, 197; McClellan, Dorothy S. 7, 11–12, 19, 22, 30, 33, 187, 200, 207–208, 234; McClellan, James E., Jr. 7, 11–12, 19, 22, 30, 33, 187, 200, 207–208, 235; Melville, Yuri K. 195; Ministry of Higher Education 31, 200; Neumaier, John J. 6, 95, 97–99, 109, 235; Panin, Alexander (dean of philosophy) 187, 192, 193–202; Parsons, Howard L. 34–35, 55, 58, 235; private enterprise at 109–110; professors' trade union 200; religious philosophy 197; Schwendinger, Herman 236; Schwendinger, Julia 236; scientific council 198–200; Semyon and Lara 21; shopping, off-campus 100–101; Slava (Platonov) 24–25; slave labor 19; Suvorin, Elena 12–14; Suvorin, Misha 12–14; Tsipko, Aleksandr (professor) 17; *see also* academic exchange programs; intelligentsia
Moscow Synagogue 111–112
Mothers of Soldiers 165

Narodniki (Russian social movement) 216
Natasha (interpreter) 18
national academies 188
nationalists 41, 52, 138, 145–146
Nazi invasion, 46, 48
neo-liberals, Soviet 215–216, 228
neo-Slavophiles 41
neo-Stalinists 41, 52, 139, 146
neo-Tsarist orientation 216
Neumaier, John J. 6, 95, 97–99, 109, 235
"New Economic Policy" 107, 109, 119, 148, 217, 229

"New Thinking" 102, 107–109, 159, 162
New York Post 62
Nietzsche, Friedrich 35
nihilistic socialism 229–231
Niul'chenko, V. (seamstress) 143
nomenklatura (class-like group) 32, 36, 52, 120, 146–147, 151–153
Nove, Alec 147
nuclear arms race 213
nuclear holocaust danger 58

Obshchina (Community) journal 44
October Revolution 16–17, 54, 163, 211
Odessa Dockers 89
oligarchy 96–97, 138
Origin of the Family, Private Property and the State 155, 157
Ottoman Empire 230

Pamyat (extreme nationalists) 52, 113
Panin, Alexander (dean of philosophy) 187, 192, 193–202
"parallel economy" 225
parliamentary democracy 28, 41, 51, 96
Parsons, Howard L. 34–35, 55, 58, 235
Party of Labor 121–122
peasant mentality 51
perestroika *see* glasnost and perestroika
pessimism, pervasive 105–106
Peter the Great 230
"petty bourgeois socialism" 36
Pinochet, Augusto (Chilean general) 225
Pipes, Richard (Polish-American academic) 209
Plekhanov Institute of Economics 131
pluralism 38, 41, 111, 116, 182, 217
Poland 118–119
Populists 145, 216
pornography 43, 164
Posadskaya-Vanderbeck, Anastasia (feminist) 162, 165
Posle Kommunisma (After Communism) (Slava Platonov) 25–33
Posner, Vladimir (U.S. television personality) 93
Postfactum Information Service 41
Poughkeepsie Journal 62
poverty 32, 41, 49, 60, 106, 108, 138, 142, 144, 149, 164, 220
Pravda 135, 147
private markets 101
private ownership 3, 60, 155, 219, 223, 225–226
private property 39–41, 51, 60, 148, 155, 223, 225
privatization 60, 138
pro-capitalism 130, 215, 227, 231
proletarian culture 50
propaganda 96, 98, 116–117, 143, 206
prostitution 164
Protestant Reformation 60

provincial party conservatives 139
Pukhova, Zoya (Soviet Women's Committee) 161
Pushkin, Aleksandr (author) 18
Putin, Vladimir (prime minister) 5, 8, 216–217

"Queen Bee" 80

Radio Liberty (Radio Free Europe) 120
Radio Moscow 74, 92, 105, 111
Rather, Dan (journalist, television news anchor) 93
ration coupon 15
Reagan, Ronald (president) 100
Rechnoi Vokzal (Grand River Station, Moscow) 18
Red Guards 50
Red Square 15–16, 66–67, 88, 92–93, 96
reform socialism 219–220
Remnick, David (American journalist) 209, 214
repressive forces 205
Revolution from Above: The Demise of the Soviet System (Kotz and Weir) 130
right-wing groups 40–41
Rimashevskaya, Natalia 160
Roger and Me. 218
Roman Catholic authoritarianism 45
ruling elite, Soviet 130
Russia *see* Russian Federation (Russia)
Russian-American University 110
Russian Empire of the Tsars 230
Russian Federation National baseball team 63
Russian Federation (Russia) 41, 63, 96; *see also* Union of Soviet Socialist Republics (U.S.S.R.); Yeltsin, Boris
Russian imperialism, 57
Russian little league team 63
Russian Orthodox Church 35, 41–43, 45, 51, 53, 57
Russian Revolution (1917) 3, 156, 216–217
Russian Sociological Association 163
Ryzhkov, N.I. (premier) 29, 111, 145

Sachs, Jeffrey (U.S. economist) 96, 212
Saint Basil's Cathedral (Moscow) 16
Sakharov, Andrei (Russian nuclear physicist) 27, 190
Salyut-7 (Soviet orbiter) 99
samizdat (underground) publications 144
Sasha 63–65
sausage lines 104
Sausage Platform 44
Scandinavian Airlines Office 85
Schneerson, Menachim Mendl (rabbi) 113
Schwendinger, Herman 236
Schwendinger, Julia 236
scientific Communism 64, 115, 143, 187, 189, 191, 196

scientific-technological revolution 28, 212
Second Annual International Baseball Tournament 90
Second Watch Factory 132
secret police 24, 139
self-actualization 39, 143
self-management 118–120, 123, 126, 133
self-realization 37
shadow economy 40, 52, 57
Sheremetyevo Airport (Moscow) 157
Shevardnadze, Eduard (foreign minister) 102
shortages 15
Siberia 2, 21, 142, 145
Singer, Daniel 212
Slavophiles 41, 44–45, 53–54
slogans 207
social consumption funds 152
social control 97–98
Social Democratic Party of Russia 41, 138, 162, 164, 199
social egalitarianism 105
social inequality 56
socialism 8, 21, 26, 36, 39–40, 45, 51, 135, 143, 203, 207215, 220–221, 223–224, 231
Socialist Party of Workers 121
Soviet All Union Team 87
Soviet Army Sports Club 89
Soviet Constitution 28
Soviet Georgia 68, 75, 89–90
Soviet Ministry of External Affairs 118
Soviet Sociological Association 112, 147
Soviet Union Council of Ministers 135
Soviet Women's Committee 111
Soviet youth culture 171–172
stagnation (1964–1985) 24, 28, 36, 49, 51, 92, 188–192, 194, 207, 212, 215, 225
Stalin period,
Stalinism 2, 4, 16, 43, 52, 138–139, 147, 174, 176, 205
Stanislav (Russian economist) 130
state capitalism 148
state centralization 230
state socialism 36, 38, 40–42, 148
state system 210
statocracy 147–148
steel mills 151
stereotyping, sex-role 163
Supreme Soviets of the U.S.S.R. 41
Suslov, Mikhail Andreivich (Politburo) 193
Suvorin, Elena 12–14
Suvorin, Misha 12–14

Tajikistan 142
Tashkent Opera House 79
Tchaikovsky Concert Hall 104
Textile and Light Industry Workers of the U.S.S.R. 122–123
Thatcher, Margaret (prime minister) 41, 218
Times Herald Record 62, 77–78

Tolstoy, Leo (author) 18, 184–185
Trans-Siberian Railway 2, 18, 38
Tsipko, Aleksandr (professor) 17
Turgenev, Ivan (Russian novelist) 18

Ukraine 2, 17, 89, 207
unemployment 31, 41, 64–65, 138, 144, 164, 224, 227, 229
Union Academy of Science of the U.S.S.R. 188
Union of Soviet Socialist Republics (U.S.S.R.): academic philosophy 190; authority structure 134; collapse 1, 8, 34, 96, 203; Communist Party's hegemonic power 8; "decline of perestroika" 103; female roles 156; Jews in 113; labor-relations in 127; long range political outlook 30; Marxism and socialism 51; social and political structure 176; study of corruption 150; Supreme Soviets 41; *see also* baseball, Russian; Russian Federation
United States (U.S.): air-to-surface nuclear missiles 73; anti–Vietnam War demonstrations 67; arms race 213; bombing of Hanoi 66; capitalist propaganda 205; civil liberties 138; crimes against women 137; Cuban policy 66; debt 213; Employee Stock Option Plans (ESOPs) 119; equal pay for equal work 160; evangelical religion 46, 48; freedom and material wealth 207; Jews, prejudice and discrimination against 114; Michael Moore 218; military and diplomatic policies in Gulf region 101; military coup in Chile 225; National Guard 67; nationalism 96; permissive morality 43; "Philosophical Systems of Analysis in American Sociology" 131; right to suffrage 156; "robber barons" 108; Rosie the Riveter 156; Salvadore Allende (Chile) 225; social problems 84; Sun Myung Moon's Unification Church 35; superiority 206; trade barriers 108; women's movement 155, 159; *see also* baseball, American
universal human values 36, 39
University of Kazakhstan 140
University of Kiev (Ukraine) 7, 170
utopian socialism, 36, 49, 148
Uzbekistan 2, 58, 74, 78, 142

Varinsky, Valeri (assistant coach) 63, 71, 74, 76, 86, 91
Victory Day 66
Vladivostok Forest Tigers 89
vodka, price of 111
Volvets, Sergei (writer) 41
Voronina, Olga (feminist) 165

wages and salaries, 152
war in Afghanistan, 64, 78
We Can't Live Like This Anymore 93

Weir, Fred 130
Weltanschauung (worldview) 103
Western capitalism 41, 143, 221, 230
Whitehead, Alfred North 35–36
"woman question" 160–161
Women, Environment and Civil Society 165
women in Soviet society, status of 155–165
Wonder Bread 85
work collectives 134, 145
worker self-management in Yugoslavia 6, 126, 133
workers' democracy 220
workers' revolution in Hungary 206
working conditions 142
working-class 40–41, 50, 52, 87, 130–131, 134, 142, 145
World Bank domination 207
Writers Union 151

xenophobia 120

Yakovlev, Aleksander, 140
Yatsutovsko, Grigorii (mysticism), 35
Yeltsin, Boris (first president of the Russian Federation): anti-communism and free market position 111; capitalist economy 217; Communist apparatchik, former 96; Communist Party 111, 220; corporate schemes 4; country's wealth 4; defied the constitution 4–5, 65; and deputy prime minister Yegor Gaidar 96; economic measures 4; elected first President of Russia 111; failed coup d'état 4, 220, 228; impeachment by the parliament 5; industrial Federation of Russian Unions and 122; marketization 6, 118, 121; and Moscow, Leningrad, and Volgograd labor councils 122; national pride 229; neoliberal, pro-capitalist government 216; Perestroika and restructuring of Soviet governance 95; privatized property 40, 52; privileges afforded party functionaries 152–153; resignation 5; Russian Federation replaced the U.S.S.R. 96; shock therapy 7, 96, 164, 216, 229; struggles between Gorbachev and Yeltsin 6, 224; *see also* Russian Federation
Youth Initiatives Program 92
youth, malaise of spirit among 47

Zabotkina, Vera (linguist) 88–89
Zakharov, Alexander (second secretary of Leningrad Communist Party) 93
Zaslavskaya, Tatiana (sociologist) 147, 149, 153, 163–164
Zaslavsky, Victor (sociologist) 150
Zasulich, Vera 216
Zhenotdel (Women's Section) of the Central Committee 156, 162